HOUSEHOLD Almanac

TIPS FOR EVERYDAY LIVING FROM COSTCO

It is only possible to live happily
ever after on a day-to-day basis.
Margaret Bonnano

HOUSEHOLD
Almanac

TIPS FOR EVERYDAY LIVING FROM COSTCO

Tim Talevich and Anita Thompson

Editors

With a foreword by

Peter Walsh

Issaquah, Washington

**Senior Vice President
E-commerce and Publishing**
Ginnie Roeglin

Publisher
David W. Fuller

Editors
Tim Talevich, Anita Thompson

Art Director
Doris Winters

Graphic Designers
Brenda Tradii

Ken Broman, Bill Carlson, Chris Rusnak,
David Schneider, Dawna Tessier

Staff Writers
Will Fifield, Steve Fisher, T. Foster Jones,
Stephanie E. Ponder, David Wight

Business Manager
Jane Klein-Shucklin

Advertising Manager
Kathi Tipper-Holgersen

Advertising Assistants
Melanie Woods, Steve Trump

Production Manager
Pam Sather

Assistant Production Manager
Antolin Matsuda

Color Specialist
MaryAnne Robbers

Print Management
James Letzel, William Ting, GSSI

Proofreader
Miriam Bulmer

Indexer
Nan Badgett

Distribution
Rossie Cruz

Costco Household Almanac 2008.
Copyright © 2008 by Costco Wholesale
Corporation. All rights reserved.

For information, contact Publishing
Department, Costco Wholesale Corporation,
999 Lake Drive, Issaquah, Washington 98027.

Printed by Daehan Printing Company
Seoul, South Korea
ISBN-13: 978-0-9722164-9-4
Library of Congress Control Number:
2008924538

TABLE OF **CONTENTS**

FROM THE **PUBLISHERS**

WE ARE PLEASED TO PRESENT our second Costco *Household Almanac*—a resource meant to help you with the everyday things in life. Brought to you through the support of our valued suppliers, the *Almanac* offers tips, how-to's and information on hundreds of topics related to the products you can find at Costco. Browse through the table of contents to see the wide range of subjects we have tackled in this book, then keep it handy throughout the year. You'll never know when you might need to know how to remove a tricky stain (page 128), fold a fitted sheet (page 117), safely jump-start a car (page 148), prepare for an emergency (page 104) or set up your new HDTV (page 41).

We are especially excited this year to feature informative articles from leading experts in the *Almanac*. These include Dr. Michael Roizen and Dr. Mehmet Oz on health topics, Borghese's Georgette Mosbacher with skin beauty-care tips, Rick Steves on international travel and even legendary workout guru Jack La Lanne with 10 tips for fitness. And you'll find sprinkled throughout the book tidbits of wisdom from Costco members. All in all, we hope you find it useful in your everyday living!

Ginnie Roegle

Ginnie Roeglin is Senior Vice President E-commerce and Publishing.

HOW CAN THIS SECOND Costco *Household Almanac* be of use to you? Let me count the ways:
1. It can tell you that if you can't pass your clenched fist between the back of your calf and the front of your office chair that the chair seat is too deep. Solutions? There are several on page 57.
2. It can help you reduce landfill waste by telling you about a kind of carpet fiber known as Type 6 nylon (N6) that is recyclable. Learn more on page 80.
3. It can help convince you to keep an old-fashioned corded phone around the house, which could be a lifesaver in an emergency. Really! Check page 105.
4. It can help put power in your golf swing, thanks to some swift advice from Long Drivers of America Hall of Famer Art Sellinger; pages 136 through 138.
5. It tells you how to obtain a government report detailing what's in your local water supply—and how to filter out the bad stuff. Page 206.

Just five ways this book can be of use? Hardly. I stopped counting somewhere beyond 2,000. How did I choose this list of five? I simply opened the book at random five times. Each time I had to choose from many pieces of useful information. (I call it "fun with reference books.")

That's the what of the *Almanac*, but what is the why of the *Almanac*? It is two-fold:
  • To assist you in judging the quality of a product or service
  • To help you get the most out of their purchases
If we can do that, we will have succeeded in our task.

David M. Fuller

David W. Fuller is Publisher of the Costco *Household Almanac*.

FOREWORD

WELCOME TO THE 2008 version of the Costco *Household Almanac*. You're about to delve into a resource of tips, advice, information, how-to's and occasional trivia—all intended to help you in your everyday living. In true almanac fashion, I'd like to start off the book right away with a tip on this topic: managing clutter!

Dealing with clutter is my job. To the amazement of many, I love it! Helping people dig out from under the overwhelming mess that fills their homes is part of my daily routine. Hundreds of families have invited me into their homes and hundreds of thousands have seen on TV how I tackle clutter or have cleared their own spaces using the same techniques that have worked so well for me.

Everyone deals with clutter to some degree, whether it's clothes bursting out of our closets, boxes that stop us friom parking in the garage, bills and paperwork that are spread over the dining room table or kids' toys that seem to cover every square foot of the home. When the stuff we own starts to own us, the message is clear: What we own is stopping us from living the life that should be ours.

All clutter is not the same. Many homes are filled with "memory" clutter—reminders of an important person, event or achievement in the past. Other homes are filled with "I might need that one day" clutter. You know what I'm talking about. The amount of stuff seems to increase daily, and we have no idea how to get it under control.

I'll share a secret with you: If you focus on the stuff as you attempt to get organized you will never succeed. Never!

I learned long ago that the very first step in successfully decluttering your home and getting organized is to ask yourself what kind of a life you want to be living. What do you want from your life or your home or each room in your home? Only when you have a clear answer to those questions can you then look at what you own and ask, "Does this item move me closer to the life I want or farther away from it?" "Does this item help me achieve the life I want or not?"

If it does, hold on to it. If not, what's it doing in your home?

Your home should be a haven for you and your family—a place of peace and calm that welcomes you and makes you feel safe and nurtured. Everything that you bring into your home should help you achieve that goal. It's as simple as that.

I have a belief that Costco seems to share with me: We each have one life to live. Live it as well as you can!

Peter Walsh is a noted international organization expert, a regular guest on The Oprah Winfrey Show *and the author of the* New York Times *bestsellers* It's All Too Much: An Easy Plan for Living a Richer Life with Less Stuff *(Simon & Schuster, 2007) and* Does This Clutter Make My Butt Look Fat?: An Easy Plan for Losing Weight and Living More *(Free Press, 2008). More details may be found at* www.peterwalshdesign.com.

An insider's guide to Costco's resources

IF YOUR TYPICAL warehouse shopping trip is to ogle the big-screen TVs, then pick up steaks and head for the register, you may be missing some of the best values Costco has to offer. Besides great products at great prices, Costco offers a wide range of services and resources that enhance your membership. We've compiled the following reference, which, while not comprehensive, will alert you to some of these hidden values you may not have known about. Consider it your own Costco insider's guide.

In the warehouses

High-quality items at great prices are just part of the bargain in Costco warehouses. Here are some of the other things you'll find.

Cash-card reader. If you have a Costco Cash card but are not sure how much cash is left on it, look for the cash-card readers to see your balance. The red kiosks are located near the front door or between the candy shelves and the big TVs in all warehouses. (Your balance is also printed on your receipt.)

Cell-phone kiosk. Wireless phones and service plans are available from companies such as T-Mobile, Verizon and AT&T (depending on location). Knowledgeable personnel can answer your questions regarding handsets and carrier plans. And because they don't work for the wireless companies, they can help you choose the product that's best for you. As a bonus for Costco members, accessory packs with an ear bud, vehicle charger and a case or belt clip are included with any phone purchase. (Note: Cell-phone packages are also available on costco.com)

Health screenings and flu shots. Screening events are available in many warehouse pharmacies to give you a heads-up on potential health problems. Screenings cover osteoporosis, cardiovascular health, diabetes and allergies, among others. Flu shots are also available in October and November. Check your local Costco pharmacy for scheduled screenings.

Hearing Aid Centers. Hearing Aid Centers are located at more than 237 Costco warehouses, offering free hearing tests to determine if your hearing loss could be helped by hearing aids. The centers offer numerous state-of-the-art products, such as the Kirkland Signature™ Premium Hearing Aids & Accessory Kit, for much less than you'd pay elsewhere. A full list of Costco Hearing Aid Centers is available on costco.com. Click on "In the Warehouse," then on "Hearing Aids."

Membership desk. It's the place to go for returns, membership renewals or upgrades, new membership cards, credit-card applications and questions, including product availability.

Optical department. More than 380 Costco warehouses have optical departments featuring designer frames and sunglasses, and many include on-site independent optometrists to provide thorough exams and prescriptions. For information on optical department locations, or frames, lenses and doctors, visit costco.com, click on "In the Warehouse," then on "Costco Optical," or search for "optical."

CALLING COSTCO •·········

BUSINESS DELIVERY
1-800-788-9968

COSTCO.COM
1-800-955-2292

COSTCO.COM PHARMACY
1-800-607-6861

COSTCO TRAVEL
1-877-849-2730

EXECUTIVE MEMBERSHIP AND COSTCO SERVICES INFORMATION
1-800-220-6000

MEMBERSHIP INFORMATION
Renewals, general membership questions, general warehouse information (excluding product availability*)
1-800-774-2678

SPECIAL ORDER DIAMOND PROGRAM
1-877-864-8695

SPECIAL ORDER KIOSKS
1-877-483-6226

SUBMITTING MEDIA REQUESTS
(books, CDs, DVDs) to Costco
(425) 313-8648

SUPPLIER INQUIRIES
Costco corporate offices
(425) 313-8100 ⊡

*Product availability differs from warehouse to warehouse.

Online at costco.com

Costco.com offers thousands of items you won't find in warehouses, at great prices, with efficient delivery and Costco's famous satisfaction-guaranteed policy. And for convenience, returns can be made to your local warehouse. The Web site can also help you find the items and information you need. Here's a look.

Business delivery. In addition to six business centers around the country, costco.com offers a full array of standard office items, ink and toner cartridges, technology products, break room and janitorial supplies, and furniture. Delivery to a business or home address is next-day in most areas. To order a free catalog go to costco.com and search "catalog."

Commercial sales program. Just when you thought Costco deals couldn't get any sweeter, along comes a new program designed for businesses that need large volumes of goods—at least $15,000 worth of an item—with even greater value than before. For more information, e-mail *volumesales@costco.com* or call toll-free 1-800-955-2292 and ask for the commercial sales program.

Home improvement, inside and out. Review the entire line of Hunter Douglas blinds, shades and shutters in the comfort of your home on your schedule; design your own dream closet online; or design and order storage for your connoisseur wine collection. Go to costco.com and click on "Decor," then "Custom Blinds, Shutters, Shades, Closets & Wine Cellars" for more information. Depending on location, a free in-home design consultation may be available for blinds, shutters and shades. And online "wizards" are available to help you design your own closet or wine cellar. For custom garage doors, tiling, screens and more, search "home improvement."

Electronic gift certificates. Costco.com provides fast, easy and convenient gift giving in the form of electronic gift certificates. Within 24 hours of the purchase of the certificate, an e-mail is sent to the recipient, inviting him or her to choose from the thousands of items online. A personalized message can be added to the gift, and the purchaser receives an e-mail verifying that the certificate has been sent. To purchase an electronic gift certificate, go to costco.com and enter "electronic gift certificate" in the search box or click on "Gifts & Tickets," then on "Tickets & Gift Certificates."

Online publications. Issues of *The Costco Connection* dating back to September 2004, the *Costco Way* series of cookbooks and the *Costco Household Almanac* are online. Also available are resource guides covering food safety, buying diamonds, digital cameras and Kirkland Signature wines; and gas station and hearing center locations. Go to costco.com and click on "Costco Connection Magazine" or search for "Connection."

Product notices. Occasionally an issue arises that may involve a safety notice, recall or update being issued by Costco or a particular product's

● SPECIAL ORDER KIOSKS

MAKING A BETTER ABODE

WHEN IT comes to home improvement, if you're not a do-it-yourselfer, how do you choose the right person for the job? Costco eliminates that worry by seeking the most reliable companies in any given area to provide quality products with professional installation. Products include custom counter-tops featuring DuPont surfaces and specialty granite; California Closets; Amarr garage doors; Schrock cabinetry; Lennox heating, air-conditioning and air-quality systems; Leaf-Guard gutter protection; Pella windows and doors; Graber "do-it-yourself" blinds; Sealy mattress delivery; and Shaw and Mohawk carpets and Hunter Douglas window fashions serviced by Custom Decorators.

One important note: These services and products are not available in all warehouses. Visit your local warehouse to see the Special Order kiosks available in your area or call toll-free 1-877-483-6226. ▲

DIAMONDPROGRAM •······

FINDING THAT SPECIAL DIAMOND

THE QUALITY AND VALUE of Costco's diamond selections are unquestionable. Costco diamonds come with appraisals—jewelry containing a diamond of any size includes a Costco-generated appraisal, written by a graduate gemologist; items containing a 1-carat diamond include an International Gemological Institute (IGI) appraisal; those containing a 1.25-carat or larger diamond include a Gemological Institute of America (GIA) Diamond Grading Report in addition to the IGI appraisal. The only thing left to do is make your choice. Costco provides four ways to unearth the gem you have in mind.

1. Go to your local warehouse and choose from the selection of diamond jewelry in display cases.

2. E-mail *specialorderdiamond@costco.com* or call Costco's Special Order Diamond Program at 1-877-864-8695 to select from our inventory.

3. Go to costco.com and choose from online selections, or use the "Build a Unique Diamond Solitaire" tool in the "Jewelry" menu.

4. In addition, the costco.com collection of loose diamonds showcases a selection of diamonds that possess amazing quality and value. Your loose diamond arrives secured in an elegant protective box, along with the appraisal certificate and a jeweler's loupe.

For more information on selecting a diamond, go to costco.com, click on "Jewelry," then on "Diamond Education & FAQs" or search "diamond education." ◼

manufacturer. To see all notices, go to costco.com and click on "Help," then on "Product Notices."

Pharmacy. Not only can you order new prescriptions or refill your existing prescription online, to be shipped directly to your home, but you can find a plethora of information on individual drugs, Medicare Part D, warehouse Hearing Aid Centers and more. Go to costco.com and click on "Pharmacy."

Rebates. If you have purchased products offering rebates in the warehouse or online, and the rebate comes from Costco, not the manufacturer, you can easily submit the rebate online or learn if one exists. Once you have submitted the rebate, it's even possible to check on its status. Go to costco.com and click on "Rebates," or enter "rebates" in the search box.

Special-order printing. When you need to send out invitations or announcements with maximum impact but reasonable expense, costco.com provides customized printing for every need. Go to costco.com and enter "invitations" in the search box.

Wedding floral program. If you're planning a wedding, you can avoid one element of angst by turning to costco.com for wedding flowers. The site's wedding collections provide affordable and elegant bouquets along with items for the wedding party and reception at incredible savings. Go to costco.com and click on "Floral."

Combo offerings

Some services can be found online as well as in the warehouse or even by phone.

Costco Services. Costco offers a wide variety of services for small businesses and/or personal use to help members save money on insurance, real estate sales and loans, check printing, auto buying, small-business Web sites, 401(k) plans, merchant credit-card processing and more. Executive members receive additional benefits. Look for brochures in warehouses, or go to costco.com and click on "Services." Many service pages include interactive calculators or applications to help you determine your needs and see how much you'll save.

Costco Travel. As a Costco member you can save on a variety of exciting vacation choices. The value is in the bundle! Look for Buyer's Choice and Your Way packages, which assure you of great vacation value. The Costco Travel buying team has bundled together some of the most popular accommodations with various travel options to ensure the best Costco member savings. The program includes something for nearly everyone, including family vacations, tropical island escapes, spectacular cruises, exotic destinations and more.

Member benefits include Kirkland Signature vacations, additional values for Executive Members and 2% cash back when you use your TrueEarnings® card from American Express.®

To begin planning your ideal vacation, visit costco.com and click on "Travel" or pick up a Costco Travel brochure at any U.S. warehouse. Contact Costco Travel toll-free at 1-877-849-2730, 7 a.m. to 7 p.m., Monday through Friday; 8 a.m. to 5:30 p.m. on Saturday and Sunday, Pacific Time.

Gas station and warehouse locater. When you are in an unfamiliar location or unsure of options beyond your nearest Costco, you can find a complete list of Costco warehouses and the ancillary services they offer online. Go to costco.com and click on "Locations" for warehouses; for gas stations, click on "In the Warehouse," then "Gas Stations" or "Costco Connection Magazine" and look under "Resource Guides," or search for "gas stations."

1-Hour Photo. Warehouse 1-Hour Photo labs provide high-quality one-hour photo printing for photos from digital and film cameras, passport photos and personalized holiday greeting cards. Photos can be delivered on archive-quality gold CR-Rs for long-term preservation. Home movies, VHS and camcorder videotapes and 35 mm slides can also be transferred to archive-quality gold DVD-Rs.

The online Photo Center at costco.com has easy-to-use tools for uploading, editing and ordering prints of your photos for pickup at your local warehouse or delivery by mail. You can also buy photo-related gifts, such as calendars, photo mugs, personalized photo books, posters and more, and set up online photo albums with unlimited storage to share with friends and family.

Visit the 1-Hour Photo lab at the warehouse or go to costco.com and click on "Photo Center."

Tire Centers. The Tire Centers are in the warehouses, but you can order tires online and have them waiting at your local warehouse for installation. In addition, costco.com has special-order tires not found in warehouses. Go to costco.com, click on "Auto," then on "Tires."

Costco in the community

It's not enough for Costco to just do business in a community. We also strive to take an active role. Here are some examples.

Fresh Start Backpack Program. Since 1993 Costco has donated nearly 2.9 million backpacks to children in need in the United States, Canada, Mexico, Taiwan, Korea, Japan, Puerto Rico and the UK. For those who might not have a backpack, Costco provides a sturdy new backpack containing basic school supplies at the beginning of the school year. Warehouse managers select a local elementary school with a high rate of low-income families. To enter a school in the program, contact a local warehouse manager for more information.

Charitable causes. Costco supports charities in communities where we conduct business. Areas of focus are children, their education, and health and human services. Of particular note are Children's Miracle Network and United Way because they reach a large number of agencies that address local needs.

For more information on Costco's charitable giving, including grants and in-kind warehouse donations, visit costco.com, click on "Help," then on "Charitable Giving Guidelines" (listed under "Costco Information").

Costco National Membership Programs (NMP). Costco's NMP program offers a variety of programs for businesses. Bulk purchases of Costco Cash cards or Costco membership certificates can be used for customer/employee recognition or gifts. The NMP offers special Costco membership opportunities designed for companies with more than 5,000 employees. E-mail *NationalMembershipPrograms@costco.com* or call toll-free 1-888-668-9668 for more information.

Online employment applications. To seek employment at Costco, go to costco.com and click on "Employment Opportunities," at the bottom of the home page.—*Steve Fisher*

SPECIAL EVENTS

SEEKING A SPECIAL SURPRISE

SPECIAL EVENTS IN our warehouses showcase unique product offerings. Costco hosts around 8,500 such events each year, featuring items from hundreds of manufacturers. Event offerings vary from warehouse to warehouse and, on average, last for 10 days.

The events showcase high-end national brands and regionalized specialty vendors, with categories including, but not limited to, home furnishings, apparel, fine art, musical instruments, major electronics, automotive, jewelry, housewares, collectibles, small electrical appliances, home-improvement hardware, sporting goods, rugs, lawn and garden, and home décor.

For more information on upcoming Special Events, go to costco.com and enter "Special Events" in the search box, then click on your region, or even check out events in other regions—in case you want to add some fun to a road trip. **A**

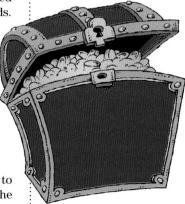

Sight and Sound

IF GEORGE EASTMAN was its founder, why is Kodak the name of the famous camera and film company?

The company, founded in 1880, was in fact initially known as the Eastman Dry Plate Company. But while getting ready to introduce the first simple roll camera, Eastman—ever aware of the power of image and advertising—wanted a name that was memorable. So he made one up.

He liked the letter K—"a strong and incisive sort of letter." He experimented with various combinations until he came up with Kodak. It was short, unlikely to be mispronounced and unique.

The plan worked. The original Kodak camera and its successors, including the Brownie, are among the most popular products in the world. Eastman, by the way, was a high school dropout.

Easy does it with the compact digital camera

THE PHOTOJOURNALIST ARTHUR FELLIG, better known as Weegee, is often credited with this bit of legendary advice for photographers: "f/16 and be there." These days the camera will take care of the exposure settings for you, but the "be there" part is, of course, still a key to getting great photos.

It's also one of the best reasons for buying a compact digital camera.

Size

Small and lightweight, compact digital cameras are great for turning moments into memories. Best of all, packed into these smart wonders is the power and performance to capture those moments in all their vivid detail.

Features

Pick up a compact camera and the possibilities seem endless, thanks to a wide range of standard features. You can expect:

- Autoexposure
- Autofocus
- Automatic face detection
- Automatic red-eye fix
- Brightening of dark scenes
- Image stabilization, minimizing the effect of camera shake
- Preset exposure choices that match the situation—portrait, landscape, beachscape, fireworks, close-up, cuisine and more
- Movie mode, complete with sound

Choosing the right compact digital camera for you

Pick one up and check it out.

- How intuitive are the controls and menus?
- How easy is it to set the functions and choose the features?
- How does it feel in your hands?
- How many megapixels do you want—or need? Any 6-, 7- or 8-megapixel compact is going to give you stunning images. If you're thinking about big prints and blowing up sections of images, the more megapixels, the better.

Once you've chosen the right model for you, how do you get the most from your new camera? Try thinking about your subject and letting the camera's auto features take care of just about everything else for you. How you creatively approach your subject is what will make your pictures really special. A

FOR TIPS ON DIGITAL SLRS, SEE STORY ON PAGE 4.

Before red-eye fix

Without image stabilization

Before brightening feature

After red-eye fix

With image stabilization

After brightening feature

Automatic face detection

Red-eye reduction is a carryover from film cameras, but in-camera red-eye fix, image stabilization, face detection and other special enhancements are digital technology developments. Never before have you had so much control over your point-and-shoot photos.

Powerful performers: digital SLR cameras

WITHOUT A DOUBT, digital single-lens reflex (SLR) cameras represent the fastest-growing segment of the digital photography market. That's because digital SLRs:

• Are powerful and versatile
• Are surprisingly easy to use
• Deliver stunning pictures
• Are available for all levels of interest and expertise, from weekender to professional
• Offer a wide range of features

If you're looking for creativity, not to mention value, a digital SLR is your camera. The big advantages: speed, power and range.

Speed: response time

Digital SLRs offer incredibly swift start-up, shutter response, autofocus and framing rate for continuous shooting. There is virtually no shooting lag—that annoying delay between the time you push the shutter button and the time the picture is actually taken. Swift response means you'll capture those perfect moments other cameras miss.

Power: resolution and metering

Then there's pixel power—and that doesn't mean just the number of megapixels. Not all resolution is created equal: A 10-megapixel digital SLR packs more power than a 10-megapixel point-and-shoot because its sensor is bigger, which means its pixels can be bigger. Bigger pixels support higher overall picture quality.

The exposure systems of today's digital SLRs are marvels of precision and speed. The better ones can actually analyze the lighting, color and contrast of a scene, instantly reference an on-board database of picture-taking information and immediately choose the correct exposure—even in the most challenging lighting situations. And the high ISO sensitivity of several cameras makes once impossible low-light pictures now commonplace.

Range: wide potential

Digital SLRs offer not just lens interchangeability, but an incredible array of lens choices, from ultra-wide angles to super telephotos. In addition, many interchangeable lenses offer specially engineered image-stabilization systems for handheld picture taking that's sharper than ever.

While they're powerful and loaded with features, many digital SLRs are also amazingly friendly. You can find digital SLRs that offer point-and-shoot ease when you select from their auto-program choices and will quickly turn full manual control over to you when you want it. And they can handle anything—sports, wildlife, landscapes, close-ups—while allowing you to employ creative, automatic and even wireless flash techniques.

Simply put, if you're looking for exceptional picture quality and enduring value, plus capabilities that will keep pace with your picture-taking interests, take a close look at today's digital SLR cameras. You'll be happy you did. ▲

HOW A DIGITAL SLR WORKS

In a digital SLR camera, light passes through the lens (1), then is reflected by the mirror (2) and projected onto the focusing screen (3). Passing through a condensing lens (4), the image is transmitted via the pentaprism (5) to the eyepiece (6) and the photographer's eye. When the photographer presses the shutter release the mirror swings up and out of the way (see arrow), and the shutter (7), which functions as a small curtain, opens, allowing light to fall onto the focal plane (8), where the image is captured by the camera's electronic imaging sensor.

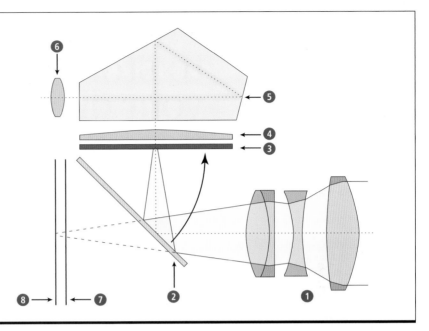

ADDITIONAL**ACCESSORIES**

Depending on your digital SLR, you might be able to use lenses you already own. There are additional flash options when you need more flash power than the built-in flash delivers.

The complete guide to storing and using your digital photos

DAD GOT A DIGITAL CAMERA for his birthday, and it came with a 2 GB memory card. He's taken hundreds of photos that he proudly exhibits on the tiny camera display—pictures of the grandkids, his new boat, the raccoon on the backyard birdfeeder and hundreds more.

His pictures are surprisingly well done, probably because his camera is so easy to use and has so many foolproof features. But so far, all those photos are still in the camera on the memory card. He doesn't have a clue about what to do with them next, and that memory card might fill up any second now.

For Dad and all the other novice digital photographers out there who haven't made the leap off the memory card, here's a comprehensive guide to what can be done with those digital photos.

Photos to computer

The camera memory card is not intended for long-term photo storage, and the space on the memory card needs to be free for acquiring new photos. Your computer, not your camera, should serve as the central repository for your digital photos. That's also where you can organize, edit, share via e-mail and print your photos.

There are some simple methods for moving digital photos off your camera and onto your computer.

• Digital cameras typically come with a dedicated cord for transferring photos from the camera to your computer via a USB connection. The only drawback with this method is the drain on the camera battery during the transfer.

• You can buy a computer peripheral device called a card reader. Simply take the memory card from the camera and insert it in the card reader. Readers are available that take several different memory card formats.

• Many computer printers have dedicated slots for memory cards. These printers allow you to print directly from the memory card, or to download the card contents to the computer as you would with a card reader.

Once the photos are on your computer, you can organize them into different folders, work with photo-management and photo-editing software programs and send photos as e-mail attachments to family and friends.

High-quality photo prints: Costco 1-Hour Photo

When photos were on film, Costco members could drop off a roll and pick up prints after shopping in the warehouse. The only difference with digital prints is that there is no roll of film to leave at the

Every print order delivered on archival-quality gold CD includes the Costco Photo Organizer—powerful software that helps you edit, print and e-mail your photos.

1-Hour Photo lab. Instead, you simply bring your digital photos on a camera memory card or a disc (CD or DVD) that you burned on your home computer.

The digital kiosks at 1-Hour Photo allow you to select which photos from your memory card or disc to print. The kiosks accommodate every type of camera memory card, and also allow easy cropping and editing. The order process is fast, and your prints will be ready in an hour—a convenient and cost-effective option for getting quality prints from your photos.

High-quality photo prints:
Photo Center on costco.com

The convenience of ordering prints online for pickup in an hour at the Costco warehouse near you is sweetened by tons of other features. The Photo Center is where you can store and share your photos free, accessible from any computer with an Internet connection. It's also where you can edit and organize your photos, or create very personal gift items that incorporate your photos—calendars, cards, mugs, posters, T-shirts and more.

Creating your account. It's easy! Just go to costco.com. You can access the Photo Center through the blue "Photo" link on the top of the page. The landing page will prompt you to either sign up for a new account or log in to an existing account. A "Get started" prompt will then help you to:

- Upload photos from your computer, organizing them into online albums. It's also possible to upload photos from a camera phone.
- Order prints for pickup in an hour at the Costco location you choose, or have prints or gift items delivered by mail. (Delivery time varies by destination and shipping options.)
- Share your albums with family and friends whom you invite via e-mail to view your photos.

Archiving and storing your photos. Your computer isn't the safest place for long-term storage of your photos. Computer hard drives can crash, losing everything. Regularly backing up photos and files to an external hard drive provides some security.

Burning a CD or DVD can provide backup security for photos and files, but typical CDs are not guaranteed for long-term storage. Some lower-end, nonbranded CDs can start to degrade after only two years.

Your digital images can be copied onto archival-quality gold CDs with proven storage longevity. The gold discs are cost-effective storage alternatives, and a good practice is to order duplicate gold CD copies, storing one copy in a safe deposit box for guaranteed backup security.—*David Wight*

THIS&THAT

PHOTO GIFTS AVAILABLE FROM THE PHOTO CENTER AT COSTCO.COM

- Mouse pads
- Photo mugs
- Calendars
- Porcelain ornaments
- Pewter ornaments
- Postcard ornaments
- Canvas prints
- T-shirts
- Notepads
- Notebooks
- Stickers
- Greeting cards
- Posters (up to 20 by 30 inches)
- Collage prints
- Scrapbook prints

Your camera and your vacation

SO THE VACATION you've slaved away for all year has arrived, and exotic locales are the destination. You and that special partner will be sailing off into two weeks of sunset after sunset.

Preserving the memories of any vacation has never been easier, thanks to the ease of use and convenience of digital cameras. But most people fail to master the full range of control that a digital camera provides.

Here are some tips with vacation photography in mind.

Advance preparation

Don't forget to pack the camera, and a few other necessities for capturing those vacation memories.

Power requirements. Plan to pack enough power to support camera use throughout your trip. Most vacation spots tend to mark up the price of batteries, so if your camera uses disposable batteries, it's most cost-effective to stock up at home and pack them in your luggage. If your camera uses a proprietary rechargeable battery, don't forget to pack the battery charger. Remember to charge the battery overnight. If you're in a location without power for a long time, a spare battery might be smart.

Memory. Memory cards are the new film. Thankfully, the cards are available in larger capacities than ever before, with some topping out at 4 GB. A 1 GB card should do nicely for most vacation picture storage, but it may be a safe bet to have a backup memory card.

Bring along the manual

The more you use your digital camera, the more you master the controls. The owner's manual is an essential reference that you probably haven't spent much time reading.

Luckily, vacations come with built-in relaxation time, and exploring the manual is a great way to fill that downtime—on the plane, on the beach or in your hotel room. Be sure to have the camera on hand as you explore the manual so you can get a sense of the key menu and control sequences.

Valuable presets: the scene modes

Most compact digital cameras offer a variety of exposure presets called "scenes," which are usually represented by icons, such as a head represent-

ing the portrait scene preset or a mountain representing the landscape scene preset. These icons will vary depending on the camera brand.

Each scene preset is designed for optimum results given specific shooting conditions. Select the scene and the camera defaults to the presets associated with the requirements for the conditions you've selected. This is a practical shortcut that allows even a novice photographer to shoot like an expert.

Some cameras offer as many as 20 or more preset scene modes. Here are some of the more common scene types. They will vary by camera brand or model.

- Portrait scene mode automatically puts the subject in focus and the background out of focus.
- Landscape scene mode achieves greater depth of field with everything in focus.
- Sunset scene mode enhances warm colors and works well for sunrises too.
- Self-portrait scene mode works well for an arm's-length shot when there's no one else to shoot you or no safe place to set the camera for a self-timer shot.
- Beach and snow scene mode compensates for exposure so snow looks white and sand doesn't look gray.
- Cuisine scene mode is perfect for shooting food. It compensates for a close distance (1 to 3 feet), reduces flash output and adds color saturation to make food look yummy.
- Fireworks and candlelight are other common scene modes.

Once you've experienced the performance of the different scene presets, start thinking outside the box. You might achieve some cool special effects by applying scene settings in creative ways. For example, try shooting a pumpkin with the sunset scene mode.

Vacation photography tends to get you comfortable with shooting interesting photos, and then, suddenly, it ends. The camera goes back in its case and is no longer an extension of your no-longer-vacationing hand. Don't let that happen. Keep using the camera expertise you've honed during those two weeks all year round.—*David Wight*

• TIPS&TRICKS

A NEW DIMENSION: UNDERWATER SHOOTING

SOME MULTIPURPOSE compact digital cameras may have underwater capability. That feature should be obvious in the way the camera is packaged and sold, and you need to be aware of the depth-limit rating for the camera—the underwater depth (in feet) at which the camera can be safely used.

With underwater capability will come additional scene presets, including motion, wide shot and close-up settings specifically for underwater use.

For anyone new to underwater photography, here are some helpful tips for best results.

- Whether in the pool, lake or ocean, air bubbles can obscure the subject and/or the camera lens, so be sure to hold your breath while snapping a picture.
- When taking a picture in a shallow lake or the ocean, avoid stomping in the sand as this will cloud the water.
- On a bright, sunny day in clear water you should not need a flash within approximately 15 feet of the surface.
- Even in visibly clear water, a lot of microscopic debris is floating freely. An underwater flash will make that debris appear as a cloud of smoke between the camera and the subject. For best results, be sure to get as close as you can to your subject when using the flash underwater.
- When shooting other people in the close-up scene mode, face them and anchor yourselves together—try locking forearms—so you don't float away from each other when the photo is taken.
- After using a camera in the ocean (salt water), make sure to rinse it off in fresh water. ◮

Preserving your photos the right way

WHEN YOU TAKE THE TIME to frame pictures in today's digital age, it is important to ensure that the frame will protect your memories for a lifetime. Whether it is a family gathering, a summer trip, fast-growing children or just everyday experiences, once you've chosen the right pictures, you can take some simple steps to keep them safe now and in the future.

Contrary to popular thought, special skills and professional assistance are not necessary to frame and preserve photos. Ready-made photo frames that satisfy certain basic requirements are good selections for safely displaying photos. It just takes a few steps to ensure that you frame them with the proper materials. Here's a primer.

Use acid-free and lignin-free face papers

Acid can cause your pictures to deteriorate at a faster rate. Lignin is a natural component of wood that can lead to yellowing. If the face paper is not acid- and lignin-free, it will shorten the display life of your photo.

Use conservation-quality mats

These mats are acid-free, lignin-free and buffered. They are made with fine-quality pigments to provide optimum colorfastness and fade resistance. Conservation-quality mats are normally twice as expensive as regular mats, but well worth the investment.

Fasten your print to the mat and face paper

Turn the face paper over and mount the unprinted side to your photo. This will protect your photo from contaminants. Then mount your picture to the back of the mat or the barrier sheet. Double-sided, nontoxic, acid-free mounting tape that has passed the Photographic Activity Test (PAT) is the best choice. (The PAT is designed to predict whether there will be harmful chemical reactions between products and photographs.)

Hang the picture out of direct sunlight

Sunlight causes photos to age at a more rapid rate. Today's picture inks can last 80 to 100 years if stored correctly, away from direct outdoor light and high temperatures.

Following these simple framing steps will help to preserve them in an enclosed environment and away from moisture and degrading materials. This greatly increases the life of your photos and keeps your memories secure for future generations to enjoy. ▲

Finding the best album to keep your photos

MANY OF US HAVE DONE IT: opened a photo album filled with precious and irreplaceable photos, only to find yellowed pages and damaged photos. This is all too common, and it may be happening to your old album as you read this.

What differentiates a high-quality photo album from those that won't adequately preserve your photos? Here's a look.

The cover of a photo album is certainly important, and conveys style, quality and personality. But it also protects the pages from bending, warping and general abuse. Look for a cover and spine that are sturdy. Some albums have special "cap" bindings that are designed specifically for durability. Don't be shy about grabbing the album and feeling for yourself.

Gone are the days of sticky paper-backed adhesive album pages. Today's high-quality albums use polypropylene or Mylar pages that protect photos from damaging chemicals—especially acid, which slowly destroys photos. Standard configurations include a 100 percent polypropylene photo sleeve and a paper page with polypropylene covers. If the pages contain paper, they should be lignin-free, as lignin breaks down over time, emitting acid in the process. Photo albums that claim to be acid-free should have pages with a pH level between 6.5 and 7.5.

The expression "archival quality" is a good place to start, but make sure to look for specific features, as they are not subjective. Finally, look for a photo album manufacturer that stands behind its products and offers a satisfaction-guaranteed warranty.

Photo albums that incorporate high-quality materials might look just like the cheaper options, but the differences are substantial. Not sure if your photos are really protected? Don't wait—go pick out a new high-quality album and protect those precious photos today! △

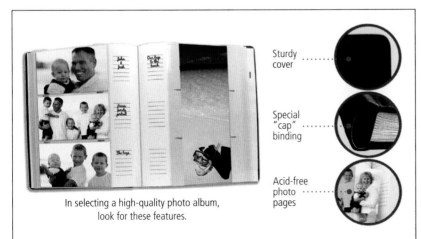

Sturdy cover

Special "cap" binding

Acid-free photo pages

In selecting a high-quality photo album, look for these features.

TIPS & TRICKS

CREATING A PHOTO DISPLAY

ONCE YOU'VE framed those photos, why not create a wall display? How and where should photos be arranged? Consider where you would like viewers' eyes to focus.

Arranging a group of photos on a wall is an excellent way to create an interesting focal point in a room. First, lay out all your framed photos on the floor to determine how you'd like to arrange them. This way, you can move them around without leaving holes in the wall. The secret to creating a pleasing arrangement is balance. Carefully measure the distances between several pictures that will hang in a row to be sure they are equal. Four small pictures on the right of a large picture can be balanced with two medium-size pictures on the left. Don't rush this planning stage. Measure and remeasure.

Some experts suggest that all frames and mats should match to create a unified look. Others suggest a more diverse approach with frames and mats that are different sizes and shapes, but that complement one another.

Pictures should hang just above eye level. However, what is "proper" eye level is debatable. Some say eye level should be considered as if viewers were standing. Others say eye level should be considered as if viewers were seated. Still others say that eye level should be determined according to the primary use of the room.

Basically, if most of the time people are standing in the space, such as a hallway, then eye level should be directed at viewers who are standing. In a room where viewers will spend the majority of the time seated, such as a living room, eye level would be from a seated position. △

Making your printer a personal photo lab

THERE'S A SIMPLE SAYING about taking photos in the digital age: If you care—you share! Unfortunately, many photo takers today are turned off by complicated steps needed to transfer photos from the camera to a printer or a software program.

A smart solution is to make your printer into your personal photo-printing lab. Here's how.

Direct printing from your camera

Top-quality printers have direct printing options, allowing you to print photos directly from your camera. Use one of the following options to transfer photos to the printer.

Through a cable. With this quick and easy method, you use the cable that came with the camera. Specify on the camera the pictures you want to print or share (for example, through a Print/Share button). You may also be able to enhance photos before printing, although any changes you make will not be saved back to the camera.

With your memory card. Take the memory card out of the camera and insert it in the proper slot on your printer (some cards may need a special adapter). Some printers will make a photo index sheet. Just choose your photos, choose a size, select simple enhancements, choose the number of copies, then print.

Wirelessly. Camera phones and other wireless devices let you transfer photos directly to the printer without wires. Your printer may require an optional Bluetooth adapter. It's a simple process: Set up your device (phone, PC or PDA) according to manufacturer's directions. Then, select the photo, select the printer and transfer ("beam") the photo.

Quick photo improvements

Some printers offer tools to make basic improvements to your photos without bringing the photo into a software program. In these cases, you can make your photos better with tools on the printer. These tools may include:

One-touch image enhancement. Uses face detection and scene analysis to evaluate an image, then applies enhancements (if needed). Canon Auto Image Fix, for example, corrects backlighting, fogging and over- or underexposure, and adjusts face tones while adjusting the background.

Red-eye reduction. Removes the effects of flash photography.

Color adjustment. Adjusts brightness or contrast, makes background colors more vivid without distorting skin tones and lets you try special effects.

Face correction. Corrects out-of-focus faces, smoothes facial lines and adjusts skin tone.

Crop and trim. Selects just the area you want to print. ▲

Ten essential tips for great digital photos

DIGITAL CAMERAS TODAY HAVE AN incredible array of features. Still, the photographer has ultimate control over the image. Follow these tips for the best results.

1. **Don't ignore the fundamentals.** The same basics that have made certain film images great over the years continue to make digital images great. Composition is one of those basics. In great pictures the main subject is rarely dead-centered in the frame.

2. **Move in close.** While wide-angle vistas certainly have a place in good photography, always consider moving as close as you reasonably and safely can to your subject. Make the primary subject the primary point of interest in your picture.

3. **Timing is everything.** Waiting that extra moment for a subject to look into the camera and smile or react to something can take a picture from nice to exceptional.

4. **Sharpness starts with steadiness.** Always be aware of holding the camera as steadily as you can. This is increasingly important as the light around you becomes progressively dimmer.

5. **Be in charge of what you focus upon.** Today's autofocus cameras are technical marvels, but for the best pictures the photographer always has to have the final say on exactly what is focused upon.

6. **Photography is all about light.** You're still capturing subjects as they're struck by light. You can't move the sun, but always be aware in daylight of how light and shadows are affecting your subject.

7. **Use your flash outdoors.** Strange as this may sound, turning your flash on when you shoot outdoors in sunlight or even on cloudy days gives an added shot of brightness to live subjects such as pets and people.

8. **Use the power of lenses.** Many users rely on telephoto settings for much of their work. It's often a mistake: Using the wide-angle setting and moving in close often results in a powerful image.

9. **Your camera is the photo lab.** Digital cameras have a variety of in-camera controls to change how color is rendered, and it's worth experimenting to see what settings enhance what sorts of scenes.

10. **Print it.** Many users do little more with their pictures than look at them on the camera's LCD monitor, and that's a shame. A good printer is one of the finest accessories a photographer can have for his or her digital camera. ▲

Professional photo printing at home

WITH A WIDE VARIETY of top-quality inkjet printers available at reasonable prices, printing photos at home is an excellent option for many photo enthusiasts. Printing at home gives the photographer creative control over the final print. Here's a primer to achieve the best results.

Use the right paper

By choosing the right paper you will maximize the quality of your prints, whether you are printing digital pictures, making photo enlargements, producing reports and presentations or scrapbooking.

Specialized inkjet photo paper features a microporous ink-receiving coating on a resin-coated base paper. This coating, coupled with today's high-resolution inkjet printers, results in exceptional image clarity and resolution. The photos dry instantly and the images are water and smudge resistant.

The special papers typically come in two popular sizes: 8.5 by 11 inches for larger prints, and 4 by 6 inches—the traditional photo-print size.

Software for the job

After you transfer your images from your camera to your computer, one of the key things that will determine how well your printed photos turn out is your ability to use your photo software. Take the time to familiarize yourself with key features of your software. With many programs, you can:

- Sharpen your photo. Use the image editor's sharpening tool to correct an out-of-focus, "soft" or grainy look.

- Increase the gamma. If your photo editor has a gamma correct tool, use this function to manipulate dark images to correct the brightness. The changes will be more apparent in the midtones of your image and less on the extremes.

- Make the subject stand out. A variety of techniques enable you to accentuate the subject of your photograph, such as cropping the image and softening the background. By softening the background of your photograph you can draw attention to the main subject. To accomplish this, select the area comprising the main subject, then reverse the selection to select the background. Use your software's softening function until you achieve the desired result.

TIPS&TRICKS

All software products are slightly different and offer a variety of features that enable you to enhance the look of your images. Other features include creating artistic touches such as adding patterns of brush or pencil strokes, blurring the edges of the photo and modifying the color.

The feeding and care of your printer

Whatever type of printer you use, it is a good idea to calibrate your printer's head every time you change your ink cartridge. This can generally be done using the printer's built-in utility program accessed through your computer.

Other items that will improve your output:

- Use the printer instruction sheet included with your paper and select "Photo" or "Best photo options" from the printer properties and settings.

- Select "Photo paper" or "Premium photo paper" from the paper-type settings.

Depending on your needs, take into account that the printer software allows you to lay out multiple-size prints on a single sheet of paper. This flexibility allows you to maximize the use of the paper so you can print several smaller prints on an 8.5-by-11-inch page or create rows of wallet-size prints to hand out to family.

- For ink, do your research to find a high-quality, inexpensive source for

DIGITAL SCRAPBOOKING

FOR MANY PEOPLE, once they print those photos of the kids in their Halloween costumes, that special vacation trip or a family holiday celebration, the next step is creating a scrapbook. Over the past several years, scrapbooking has taken off as a creative way to preserve memories. Photos are combined with colorful background papers, embellishments and captions around a theme that tells a story.

As the hobby has grown in popularity, the supplies for creating scrapbooks has grown exponentially. Entering this market is the new approach of digital scrapboooking. Instead of paper, glue and scissors, the backgrounds, embellishments and other elements are available for download from various Web sites. Combining them with the help of graphic software programs allows the digital scrapbooker to create pages, import digital photos and assemble a scrapbook that can be shared via the Internet, saved on the hard drive, burned onto a CD or printed out to be preserved in an album.

One advantage of digital scrapbooks is that they can be easily changed or revised. Say you want to crop your ex out of a photo and then reprint the page—no problem. It is easy to experiment with different looks and themes, without the investment in special papers, etc. And two photos can be combined, one as background, the other as foreground, to create a scrapbook page. The approaches are virtually limitless.

As you create a page, save often. Once the page is finished, save at 180 to 225 dpi for printing to inkjet printers; 300 dpi for professional quality.—*Anita Thompson*

your ink cartridges. Several printers now come with several densities of black, which can enhance black-and-white output of prints.

Match pixels and size

You will need to experiment with the different settings in your photo-editing program to find out what works for your personal needs. Generally, try to set your camera to a higher-resolution setting if you plan to enlarge your images and print them. Lower-resolution images are fine for e-mail or posting on an Internet site.

HELPFUL**HINTS**

SUGGESTED MEGAPIXELS FOR HIGH-QUALITY PRINTS

MAXIMUM PRINT SIZE	BUY A CAMERA WITH	RESOLUTION
4" x 6"	2 MEGAPIXELS	1600 x 1200
5" x 7"	3 MEGAPIXELS	2048 x 1536
8" x 10"	5 MEGAPIXELS	2560 x 1920
11" x 14"	6 MEGAPIXELS	2816 x 2112
16" x 20"	8 MEGAPIXELS	3264 x 2468

Getting creative

Many people are getting out of the darkroom and onto their computer to create the look they're after. One popular trend is to alter color photos and turn them into black-and-white prints for that antique look, especially for scrap-booking projects.

This can be accomplished using an off-the-shelf photo software product. By changing the color setting to black and white, your printed images can take on a whole new look and sense of time. Consider one of the latest inkjet printers that now come with different densities of black ink that offer better monochrome printing capabilities.

Preserving your photos

You can increase the longevity of your photos by reducing their exposure to air and sunlight. Just as with traditional photos, store photos in frames behind glass, in scrapbooks or in other places where light and air exposure is reduced and moisture is avoided. ▲

Making a home movie with video, photos

TODAY'S CAMCORDERS AND CAMERAS have become smaller in two ways: size and price. That means it's easier than ever to shoot both video and still photos. In fact, many camcorders enable you to do both. But what do you do with the video and the photos after you've taken them?

One fun and easy solution is to combine the video and photos in a home-made documentary. I have done this with family vacations, ski trips with friends and group events. The finished product is much more compelling and entertaining to watch than a simple slide show.

Choosing the right software

The first step is to choose the right software for your project. If you have a computer with Microsoft Windows XP (as I do) or certain versions of Vista, you may already have a good basic tool in your hands: Windows Movie Maker. Later-model Macs come with iMovie. Both are very easy to use and can do most of the work for you.

If you want a program that offers more creative tools and a larger library of transitions and special effects, you'll have to purchase one. I have tried Adobe Premiere Elements 4.0 and some similar programs. They let you do a lot more things with the video, picture and sound in your project than Windows Movie Maker. But they're also harder to use, with a learning curve required.

Importing your photos and video

Bringing photos and video into your computer is easy. For photos, I slip my camera's flash memory card into a drive on my computer, then transfer the photos into a file I set up under "My Videos."

For video, I plug the FireWire cable that came with my camcorder into my computer. A box comes up and I choose to import the video clips using Windows Movie Maker. I follow the program's directions, reviewing and editing the clips as I go.

Finishing the project

Once all of the video and photos are stored in "My Videos," I'm ready to place them in the documentary. This simply involves dragging them onto a panel called the "timeline" in the order I want.

Then I create a title for the documentary, apply a few touches such as transitions between clips and finally add music to the whole thing.

I'm no Fellini, but my short movies capture precious memories.—*Tim Talevich*

OUR TRIATHLON
Summer 2007

Making the most of your camcorder

YOUR CAMCORDER IS not only for vacations and parties. Keep it ready throughout the year for a variety of projects.

Here are ways to use your camcorder that will provide hours of fun and make your life easier.

Create a living history

Interview your grandparents by asking questions about their childhood, school years and marriage before kids came along. Ask about jobs and time in the armed forces. They'll enjoy reliving their memories, and you'll have a living history to enjoy for generations to come.

Make a living record of your child's growth

Videotape your child each year, on holidays or ordinary days, asking the same questions about friends and school and hobbies. You'll both enjoy watching how your child has grown and changed, and stayed the same!

Safeguard your possessions

Videotape your possessions, including car, electronics and jewelry, zooming in on serial numbers and small objects. This can help you to collect insurance in case your valuable property is stolen or damaged in a disaster. Store the tape or a copy in a safe place.

Brighten up a rainy day

Videotape your children acting out a scene from their favorite fairy tale or TV show, and watch it with them while enjoying a bucket of home-made popcorn.

Improve your public speaking

Videotape yourself making a presentation to the PTA or to your book club, and watch it. You'll see if you fidget too much or use fillers (like "um" and "you know"). Then, with practice, you can avoid these pitfalls and give entertaining presentations.

Send the grandparents a birthday video

For the same price as some store-bought greeting cards, you can create and send a videotape filled with your child's smiles and voice as he wishes great happiness on a special occasion.

ADDITIONAL WAYS TO ENJOY YOUR CAMCORDER

- Videotape a crazy-face contest.
- Let your little princess put on a fashion show.
- Record a day in the life of your dog.
- Send a holiday video instead of a holiday card with a still image.
- Make a thank-you video as a teacher's gift.
- Create a video journal of a family trip.
- Let the kids re-create their favorite cartoon—in real life.
- Interview family members for a video family tree.

- Perfect your golf swing.
- Sing and dance in the rain.
- Make a time capsule for 30 years into the future.
- Have a picnic in the living room.
- Plant a flower. Record it for 5 seconds every day.
- Record your new baby for 5 seconds every day for a year.
- Make a music video.
- Create a video scavenger hunt.

Let your child be a star

Whatever your child's hobby or talent is, from playing the piano to cheerleading, videotape him or her weekly and enjoy the performances. Sometimes a child is too shy to perform for relatives, but will be thrilled when you show her the movie where she's the star!

Let your pet be a star

Teach your pet a trick and videotape it. You'll enjoy your talented pet for years to come.

Help your child be a success in school

Videotape your child reading material that will be tested on at school. Then watch the tape a few times. Before long, your child will have it memorized. This technique also works well for learning a new language or memorizing a speech.

Turn everyday events into a vacation

Videotape that memorable restaurant, the walk in the woods and any other adventure that you'll want to relive. ◢

STEPS TO SMART PRINTING

YOU CAN BLOW your budget at home and at the office with wasted printouts from your printer. Save money and time—and get the best results—by taking these steps to make sure you're printing properly.

- Save paper by printing on both sides.
- Save ink by printing in draft mode.
- Print multiple documents on one sheet of paper.
- Use branded inks and papers to ensure the quality of your prints and the life of your printer.
- Before printing photos, check that your print settings are set to "Best" or "Photo quality."
- Use your printer software to expand your ability to print from the Web with options such as text only, print preview and photo editing.
- Use wireless printing to print from anywhere in your home or office. ◢

Video format options for camcorders

TODAY'S CAMCORDER SHOPPERS have more options than ever before, but determining which format to buy can be confusing. Not long ago, all camcorders recorded on tape. Now, you can choose from tape (miniDV or HDV), DVD, hard disk drive (HDD) and flash memory. Each format has distinct advantages, and the decision to go with one or another comes down to your own personal preference and budget.

There's another exciting development with camcorders. High-definition capabilities are arriving in all formats. Being able to record your videos in HD means that the resolution of the pictures is the highest yet and that your video's audio tracks will be in surround sound. This makes for a great presentation on your home HDTV.

MiniDV: Let's go to the videotape

MiniDV is a format that is familiar to many of us. Up to 80 minutes of video can be recorded on a small cassette. These tapes are inexpensive and can be easily purchased just about anywhere (great when you are taking that trip to Tahiti). Compared with other formats, miniDV camcorders are also the most affordable.

DVD: the perfect match for your home theater

DVD camcorders allow you to record your video directly to a 3-inch DVD. This disc is smaller than the larger 5-inch DVD movies you buy or rent from the store. The big advantage of DVD camcorders is their convenience. When you want to watch your video, just pop the disc into your home DVD player, sit back and enjoy. You can record up to 75 minutes of standard video on a single-layer DVD, depending on selected video quality.

Hard disk drive: long recording time

Hard disk drive camcorders do not use tapes or discs. Video is recorded directly to an internal hard disk drive, allowing you to record many hours of video without having to switch media. This means you will never miss a moment when you are recording your child's soccer game. To back up your video in a safe place, you simply download your video to the computer, erase your camcorder's hard drive and start recording again.

Flash memory: Record video in a flash

Flash memory is the newest way to store video. Video can be recorded to a tiny SDHC memory card or, with certain camcorders, directly to an internal flash drive. Since flash memory does not use any moving parts, these camcorders are ultra-compact and lightweight, offer excellent battery life and are shock resistant. Flash memory camcorders are also the most convenient, as a memory card can be easily inserted into a computer's memory card reader or an HDTV's card slot for instant viewing. ◭

Options for using your iPod in the car

IT'S A DILEMMA FOR IPOD LOVERS: how to listen to their beloved music collection in the car. It's not safe (and is illegal in some states) to use headphones while driving. Fortunately, several solutions are on the market. Here are the best options.

Connect via the Aux-In connector. Most new cars now come with an Auxiliary-In (Aux-In) connector. An easy connection by cable will allow you to play your iPod in no time. These cables are known as mini-stereo or 3.5 mm to 3.5 mm cables. Other accessories include mounts and auto-chargers.

Connect through a cassette deck. If your car has a cassette deck, take advantage of it. A cassette adapter allows you to connect directly to your stereo and typically provides good sound. Look for accessories to mount and power your iPod.

Connect through an FM radio. Virtually everyone has an FM radio in their car. Using an FM transmitter turns your iPod into a small radio station, so you can listen through your car's stereo. When you are picking a frequency to transmit on, find one that has no other stations to compete with. Premium FM transmitters will scan and find the best frequency for you. Other features to look for include mounting, charging and memory presets.

Hard-wire the unit. If you are willing to make the commitment, you can get a hard-wire connection for your iPod custom-installed in your car. Many different options are available. Some allow you to control your iPod through the car stereo and display song and artist information. However, this option is often costlier than cables, adapters or transmitters. △

→ THIS&THAT

ROCKIN' AND ROLLIN'

A long drive becomes longer with silence. That's why everyone has his or her favorite tunes to provide the soundtrack. The *Almanac* asked noted rock historian (and Costco member) Paul Grushkin (www.rockindownthehighway.com), the author of *Rockin' Down the Highway* (Voyageur Press, 2006), to compile the quintessential playlist. Here are his top picks.

1. *Born to Run*—Bruce Springsteen
2. *Rocket 88*—Jackie Brenston and His Delta Cats
3. *I Can't Drive 55*—Sammy Hagar
4. *Mustang Sally*—Wilson Pickett
5. *Radar Love*—Golden Earring
6. *Little Red Corvette*—Prince
7. *Drive My Car*—The Beatles
8. *On the Road Again*—Willie Nelson
9. *Highway to Hell*—AC/DC
10. *Detroit Rock City*—Kiss

11. *Freeway of Love*—Aretha Franklin
12. *Built for Speed*—Stray Cats
13. *Arrested for Driving While Blind*—ZZ Top
14. *Dead Man's Curve*—Jan and Dean
15. *Little Deuce Coupe*—Beach Boys
16. *Roadhouse Blues*—The Doors
17. *On the Road Again*—Canned Heat
18. *Rockin' Down the Highway*—Doobie Brothers
19. *Race with the Devil*—Gene Vincent
20. *Maybelline*—Chuck Berry

Unlock your iPod's potential

By J.D. Biersdorfer

SINCE IT HIT THE SHELVES IN 2001, Apple's iPod has become the hottest music player on the market—who knew it could be so easy to fit thousands of songs in your pocket? But if you think the iPod is just a music player, think again. Along with its video capabilities, it can also be used as an electronic organizer, a digital photo album or a pocket projector to pump out a movie or a PowerPoint presentation to a room full of people.

And the best part: You don't have to have a degree in computer science or know a 14-year-old to do all of these things. The key to unlocking your iPod's potential is right there in iTunes. All you have to do is connect the player to your computer, and click a few checkboxes on the iPod's preferences screen in the iTunes window. Most of the features mentioned here work on three of the four current iPod models. (The screenless iPod shuffle has limited powers but is still your best buddy for a demanding gym workout.)

Adding contacts and calendars

Who needs to lug along a personal organizer when you have an iPod? If you've got the addresses of your friends and colleagues stored in Outlook, Outlook Express, Windows Contacts, the Windows Address Book, the Mac OS X Address Book or Entourage 2004 or later, copying that data is just a hop, skip and sync away when you have your iPod connected to iTunes.

Click on the iPod icon in iTunes and then click the Contacts tab (or the Info tab on the iPod Touch) in the middle of the iTunes window. Put a check in the box next to "Sync contacts from" and then select the program you use from the pull-down menu. Click the "Apply" button to synchronize the contact information over to the iPod. Later, when you unhook the iPod from the computer, your contacts will be waiting for you in the iPod's Extras menu (or under the Contacts icon if you have an iPod Touch.)

If you use Outlook, iCal or Entourage, you can copy your computer's calendar in the same way. Click on the Contents or Info tab in the iTunes window, scroll down to the Calendars section and put a check in the box next to the calendar program you use, then click the "Apply" button to sync things up. You can see your schedule by going to the Calendars area of the Extras menu on an iPod classic or nano, or by tapping the Calendars icon on the touch screen. Click or tap on a day to see its events.

The iPod as photo album

Want to show off copies of your favorite digital photos on your iPod without having to print them, smudge them or drag your laptop around? Just click the Photos tab on the iPod's preferences screen.

Here, you can choose to copy photos from your computer's Pictures folder or from a program such as Adobe Photoshop Elements, Photoshop Album or Apple's own iPhoto. You can even select certain albums of photos from these programs. After you check the boxes for the pictures you want, click the "Apply" button to send copies to the iPod. Later, you can corner your friends with your vacation photos by going to the iPod's Photos menu and selecting the pictures you want to share.

The iPod on the big screen

As cool as those photos look on the small screen, they look even cooler when you jack your iPod into a television set to display them. You can do this with the videos you have on your iPod, too. For this, you need an extra bit of hardware: an iPod-compatible AV cable, which sells for around $50 on Apple's Web site. With the iPod tethered to the TV, go to the iPod's Photos or Videos menu, select the Settings area, then hit the "TV Out" option to play your photo slide shows or videos on the big TV screen.

And photos aren't the only images you can show off on the TV or conference-room display system. You can display your Keynote or Power-Point presentations up there as well. To do so, just save your presentation as individual slides in the JPEG format with the "Save As" command and drag them into your photo program or pictures folder. Then sync them in iTunes to the iPod, as you would with regular pictures. Once you connect your iPod to a TV or monitor with the AV cable, you can advance through your slides by clicking or tapping the iPod's controls.

These are just a sampling of the non-music things you can do with an iPod. If you let the device live up to its full potential, life gets simpler—and your bag, pocket or purse can get much lighter. Ⓐ

J.D. Biersdorfer is the author of *iPod: The Missing Manual*, published by O'Reilly Media (*www.missingmanuals.com*). She is also the co-author of *The Internet: The Missing Manual* and *Google: The Missing Manual.*

All about Bluetooth

YOU PROBABLY KNOW Bluetooth® best for cool, futuristic-looking devices that some people use to talk hands-free on their cell phones. But there are more than a billion Bluetooth-enabled devices in the world today, and they extend well beyond the realm of mobile phones.

Bluetooth Wireless Technology allows different compatible electronic products, such as your laptop and your PDA, to communicate wirelessly over short distances. As a result, Bluetooth is popping up all over the place—in cars, homes, businesses and even hospitals.

In short, Bluetooth means the various computers, wireless phones, entertainment systems and accessories in your life are becoming more convenient—and less messy—to use. You can now quickly send files to a printer, easily connect a keyboard to your computer, play music through your stereo from across the room, show favorite pictures from your laptop on a TV or play video games enthusiastically, all without the disorder and restrictions of wires.

Who can benefit from Bluetooth?

Just about anyone who uses a wireless phone or a computer can take advantage of Bluetooth Wireless Technology to make their lives easier and less cluttered. Busy professionals can sync the calendars and address books on their computers with their PDAs, eliminate the desktop clutter of wired peripherals and take calls without dropping what they're doing. People on the go can use it to stay connected in the car without taking their hands off the wheel, a particularly important use considering 25 states have some form of hands-free legislation. Even students can make use of Bluetooth by printing papers from across the room and relaxing to music through a wireless headset.

DID YOU KNOW? The name "Bluetooth" is taken from a 10th-century Danish king, Harold Bluetooth

How do you get connected?

Connecting two compatible Bluetooth-enabled devices is called pairing. It's generally a simple process that involves little setup. For detailed instructions, check the manual specific to each device. Many Bluetooth-enabled devices are completely universal, so your devices can communicate with others regardless of the manufacturer.

The only restriction is that devices must have the same profile in order to communicate. There's a profile for each type of function, and many profiles can exist on a single device. A hands-free profile (HFP) would be found in mobile phones and headsets; the Advanced Audio Distribution Profile (aka A2DP) allows you to play music from your mobile phone through your stereo or computer speakers. If you have a question about the profiles for a specific device, it's best to refer to its manual. △

Why two-way radios?

TWO-WAY RADIOS are proving to be very useful in a variety of settings, from recreational situations to emergencies. These radios have a range of up to 20 miles and can work in places where cell-phone coverage isn't available.

Here's a look at scenarios where two-way radios make sense.

Road trips. When caravanning with a group of family or friends, keeping in touch is important. The lead driver can call the shots in terms of where to stop to eat, etc. Others in the pack can request rest-stop breaks. And if there's a flat tire or other emergency on the road, two-way radios provide a way to communicate. Cell phones can fail in dead coverage spots.

Vacations. Either by plan or by accident, families don't always stay together in theme parks, on beaches, etc., while on vacation. Two-way radios offer a way to make plans to meet for lunch or at a particular ride or ski run. And if somebody gets lost, the radio can help facilitate a reunion.

Outdoors. Many outdoor activities, such as hiking, hunting and fishing, involve long distances. The others in your party are often out of sight in these situations. Two-way radios enable you to keep in touch. They also provide a means to keep in touch during emergencies.

Emergency preparedness. Phone service can fail in a weather-related or civil emergency. Two-way radios work as long as there is power in the batteries. Also, some two-way radios come with a special emergency alert feature, which transmits a signal to other radios and warns of impending danger.

Weather alerts. Advanced models offer access to National Oceanic and Atmospheric Administration (NOAA) channels, which provide weather alerts and continuous local and regional weather broadcasting.

Two-way radio technology has come a long way since the early days. Today's models are more compact and affordable, with improvements such as longer ranges, built-in LED flashlights, improved battery life and even clearer transmissions, so your conversations sound more natural than the original walkie-talkies of past generations.

Whether preparing your family for an emergency or simply a weekend camping trip, don't forget to pack your two-way radios. ◮

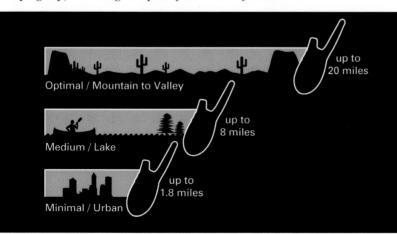

Optimal / Mountain to Valley — up to 20 miles

Medium / Lake — up to 8 miles

Minimal / Urban — up to 1.8 miles

All hands on DECT

HOME TECHNOLOGY IS A FASCINATING, and sometimes frustrating, arena. It seems as if innovations are emerging daily, often creating more consternation than contentment, at least initially. When cordless phones were first introduced, the choice was simple: cords or no cords. But with all of the new options in cordless phone systems today, shopping for a home phone has become much more complicated. And with more homes moving to wireless networking, the wires may not get tangled, but the signals might.

The typical cordless phone system consists of a base and handsets that operate across various radio frequencies. Available platforms include 900 MHz, 2.4 GHz, 5.8 GHz and, more recently, DECT 6.0—the latest advancement to offer superior voice and sound quality.

Along with deciding what features and how many handsets you need, you'll want to consider the right frequency platform, based on the household environment. (The range and sound quality of your phone can be affected by obstructions within the home or other environmental factors.)

What's the difference?

Each cordless phone frequency offers specific benefits, all with varying levels of features and sound quality. The platform chosen can affect the signal clarity and the range your cordless phone can reach from its base station. Here are the options.

900 MHz. Phones on the 900 MHz frequency are fine for household use. They are reasonably priced, although the features offered are limited. Many manufacturers have discontinued production of 900 MHz phones, in favor of newer platforms.

2.4 GHz. Models operating on 2.4 GHz provide better performance and sound quality versus 900 MHz models, and offer more features, such as integrated speakerphones and support for multiple handsets. However, the frequency is increasingly being used by other electronic gadgets, including baby monitors, microwave ovens and wireless networking gear, which may cause interference with phone conversations or vice versa. For instance, while you are on the Internet via a wireless router, a phone call may terminate the Internet connection. If you use any of the items listed above, 5.8 GHz or DECT 6.0 phones may be better options.

5.8 GHz. Phones on the 5.8 GHz frequency offer better clarity than 2.4 GHz phones, as well as a broad variety of extra features, such as color displays. Interference on this frequency is rare at this time, but there is a potential for more incidents if other gadgets start adopting the frequency.

DECT 6.0 phones: superior sound and security

The newest cordless phone platform—one that is growing in popularity—is Digital Enhanced Cordless Telecommunications, or DECT 6.0. Used for a number of years in Europe, DECT 6.0 recently became available in North America and provides enhanced call clarity, security and range.

DECT 6.0 phones operate on the 1.9 GHz frequency, which has been set aside exclusively for cordless phone use. This proven and reliable technology provides superior voice and sound quality. DECT 6.0 also offers high protection against eavesdropping and better range than 2.4 GHz and 5.8 GHz phone systems.

Another benefit of DECT is that you can carry on conversations anywhere in the home or office without the worry of wireless network interference, because the frequency is not used by other wireless technologies. This capability is particularly important in today's digital households, where a variety of Internet and Wi-Fi services are in play.

DECT phones may feature voice-enhancement technology, color displays, speakerphones for hands-free communication, in-house intercom functionality, extended talk time and multiple ring tones so different tones can be assigned to individual callers to immediately recognize who's calling.

In addition, DECT 6.0 cordless phone systems offer dramatically updated designs with beautifully sleek and slim form factors designed to complement the décor of homes or small offices.

Cordless phone tips

- When charging the battery for the first time, before you plug in the telephone line, place the phone on the charger (and don't lift it off the charger) for 12 to 15 hours to ensure the battery is properly conditioned and fully charged.

- Keep the charging contacts clean to ensure a proper charge. Use a pencil eraser to clean the contacts.

- Always read your user guide when setting up your phone to ensure you don't miss any important features. △

→ HELPFUL **HOW TO'S**

HEAR THIS PHONE TIP

Cordless phones are a wonderful invention, but it's smart to have this old-fashioned device around at home and office: a standard, corded telephone. These are an essential part of an emergency kit because they still function during power outages. As long as there is phone service coming into the line, a corded phone will work.

I keep my corded phone in use in my garage. There happens to be a phone jack in the garage, so I use it to get phone service when I'm in the garage doing projects. I like having the corded phone in the garage because it might be easy to misplace the handset among all the tools, storage boxes, etc.

Another option is to keep a corded phone in your emergency kit along with other supplies. That way, you'll know where it is in case of an emergency.

Sometimes old things prove to be very useful!

—*Tim Talevich*

A look at the modern phone

PHONES ARE AN ESSENTIAL part of everyday life. It's amazing to look back at the countless improvements and additional features that have been introduced since Alexander Graham Bell's first phone in the 1870s.

Today, the advancements continue with additional features to help in work situations and at home. Bell would undoubtedly be amazed to see the features found in the latest high-end phone models.

Night mode and call block. Both features are designed to cut down on disruptions for you and your family. With night mode, you can program each handset not to ring, at your discretion. And once you store the numbers of unwanted callers on your phone's "call block" list, those callers will get a busy signal if they call you again.

Talking caller ID. With this feature, a caller's information is announced in between rings so you don't have to get up if it's someone you don't wish to speak to.

Talking alarm clock. With this feature, you can program a multitude of phrases to wake or alert you.

Talking battery alert. This feature reminds you when your battery is low, so you're not left with a dead battery.

Drop- and splash-resistant handsets. Because today's phones are portable, they must be tough. Unlike models of days past, many phones today can stand up to everyday wear and tear and have safeguards against occasional dropping and accidental splashes. ▲

➤ THIS&THAT

DID YOU KNOW?

Alexander Graham Bell's first commercial telephones were called "box" or "long-distance" telephones. The first telephone line was installed in April 1877 between Charles Williams' electrical shop on Court Street in Boston and his home in Cambridge about three miles away. A month later the first rented telephone installations were made, beginning the era of commercial telephone service.

This early phone had no signaling device to determine incoming calls. In June 1877,

Thomas Watson, an electrical designer and mechanic who had worked in Williams' shop, devised a "thumper" that would strike the diaphragm of the box telephone to make a tapping sound on the receiving telephone. This was later replaced by an electric bell, which in one form or another survives today.

Guide to Computing

WHEN WAS THE FIRST computer made? The answer depends on your definition of computer.

Ancients used tally sticks as counting devices from about 35,000 B.C. The Babylonians invented the abacus, an ancient pocket calculator of sorts that did mathematical computations, some five millennia ago. The first modern computers go back to the late 1930s and early 1940s, including the 27-ton ENIAC (Electronic Numerical Integrator and Computer).

And what about the first computer bug? In 1945, a moth reportedly flew into a computer at the Naval Weapons Center in Dahlgren, Virginia. The critter was taped into the logbook alongside the official report, which stated: "First actual case of a bug being found." A

Seven tips to a healthy computer

By Chip Reaves

WHETHER YOU ARE PART of a small business, a multinational corporation or are just trying to find a recipe online at home, you may seem to spend just as much time fixing issues and conflicts on your computer as you do working on it. For the home user, this is merely an inconvenience. But for a business it can add up to tens of thousands of dollars lost to decreased productivity or repairs.

Although the mere thought of trying to fix a computer would cause a cold sweat to break out in most of us, it is in fact the simple little things that even the most timid technophile could prevent that cause the majority of desktop woes. Malware, viruses, identity theft and spyware account for about 80 percent of all computer issues resulting in downtime.

Fortunately, there are certain simple tips everyone can follow—businesses and individual computer users alike—that will keep your computer (and wallet) in tiptop shape.

1. Old hardware

Studies have shown that the likelihood of physical problems with computer equipment goes up significantly after 24 to 36 months. Consider replacing computer systems every three years—considering how inexpensive computers have become, one major repair bill could easily cost more than purchasing an entire new system.

2. Power protection

Surges and power drops can cause data loss and are always damaging to sensitive components, reducing their lifespan. Most people do use surge protectors, but what many don't realize is that surge protectors wear out over time. For the best protection make sure that the surge protectors for all of your computer equipment are replaced every two to three years.

3. Illegal software

Many businesses don't realize that they don't own software—just the licenses to use it on a specific number of PCs. Many software programs automatically report their usage via the Internet, and breach-of-license letters and audits from software manufacturers to businesses are on the rise.

HOW TO RECYCLE YOUR OLD COMPUTER

WHAT SHOULD YOU DO with your old computer when it's time to upgrade? If it's too old to donate to a school or charitable organization, you'll have to recycle. It's not smart (and indeed illegal in many states) to dump them in landfills. Fortunately, many companies and organizations have established recycling programs. To recycle your computer, follow these two steps:

1. Find a recycling program. Costco offers one through the Trade-in & Recycle Program on costco.com. In this program, certain electronics are recycled free—and in some cases you'll actually be paid for them. For details, go to costco.com, click on "Electronics" then on "Trade-in & Recycle."

Some manufacturers are establishing recycling programs for their branded products. Typically, these programs will recycle their branded products free, and take all other products for a fee.

2. Destroy your data. Make sure you "wipe" your hard disk before recycling your computer. Deleting files or reformatting drives is not enough. You must either physically destroy the drive or use a utility called a disk sanitizer or a data shredder. Look for a disk wiping utility that at least meets the DoD 5220.22-M standard. ▲

4. Training

Having to spend money training your staff might sound like a waste, but most employees understand less than 20 percent of the software packages they use. The gain in productivity far outweighs the training costs.

5. Firewall and security

The Internet is full of hackers who regularly try to access computers for nefarious purposes. If they get in (either directly or with the help of malware or viruses) the list of problems they can cause is pretty big, including stealing files or customer records and deleting important data. It's important to be sure that all computers in your organization are updated with the latest security patches from Microsoft or Apple, and that firewalls are installed and maintained properly.

6. Backing up data

It sounds so obvious, but most companies fail to keep 100 percent of their important data backed up 100 percent of the time. There are often gaps in what's being backed up, which are discovered when it's too late. The consequences of lost data can put a company out of business on the spot, and data retrieval is frighteningly expensive.

7. Spam, viruses and spyware

Most service calls are from people with problems directly linked to these issues. You should consider good virus protection, spam filters and anti-spyware programs as mandatory if you want a trouble-free computer.

With a small amount of common sense, weekly maintenance (much of which you can set your computer to do itself) and some small financial outlays, you can have many more trouble-free workdays and spend far less on the repair person. This will allow you more "up" time to complete your work and give you the chance to explore the myriad other technology opportunities that can help you improve your business, or your life. Now that's technology in action. ▲

Chip Reaves is the U.S. director of Computer Troubleshooters, a full-service information-technology service company with 230 locations in North America. Reaves' Web site is at *www.comptroub.com*, and his blog is at *http://technologysolved.blogspot.com/*.

DID YOU KNOW
75% of Americans use the Internet and spend an average of three hours a day online

PROTECTING AGAINST POWER SURGES

POWER SURGES AND lightning strikes are not the only events that can damage your home electronic equipment. Simply switching appliances on and off can create electrical imbalances that will cause cumulative, permanent damage to computers, peripherals and other electronic equipment.

Electrical surges can be small or large. In fact, most surge damage occurs over a period of time without obvious physical damage to equipment. Most often it is small, repetitive power fluctuations that destroy or seriously damage sensitive electrical components.

Electrical surges and spikes don't just enter your household through the voltage power line. Often, computers and televisions are damaged by a surge through the data line or cable connection.

The solution: Look for a surge protector that offers phone/fax and coaxial protection, automatic shutdown, EMI/RFI filtration and a connected-equipment warranty. The higher the joule rating, the longer the surge protector will last. ▲

The right PC for every purpose

HAS YOUR SEARCH for a new personal computer bogged down amid the vast number and complexity of available choices? If so, then take heart, because as complicated as a new PC might be under the hood, finding one that meets your requirements doesn't need to be. The first step, of course, is to decide just what your requirements really are.

One reason PC selection has become so challenging is that we're all doing more with our computers than ever before. With a high-speed connection to the Internet, a personal computer becomes an instant reference library, newspaper, mailbox, shopping mall, flea market, social club, matchmaker, employment service, photo lab, juke box, gaming arcade, movie theater and travel agent. The list gets longer every day, and each new application drives a fresh round of innovations by hardware manufacturers and software developers that make existing tasks easier and entirely new ones possible.

Decision one: desktop or laptop?

The first order of business in choosing a new PC is to decide how you intend to use it, beginning with where you'll use it, because the very first fork in the decision tree—desktop or laptop—divides on whether you want a system to use in a single location (a home office, for instance) or a mobile system for on the go.

Once across the desktop-laptop divide, the next step is to decide what applications and tasks are most important to you. Do you want a multipurpose system for general home and light office tasks? A student machine for homework and online research? A multimedia workshop for enjoying and creating high-definition video? Each of these choices will dictate different priorities for choosing and configuring key components—the processor, main memory, hard disk, optical drives and graphics solutions.

To see how your intended uses can focus the PC selection decision, let's look closely at what you'll need for what you're going to do.

An all-purpose desktop for home multitasking

Let's say you've decided to purchase a new desktop PC for basic home use—primarily Internet browsing, shopping, e-mail, family photo and music

FIVE GOOD REASONS FOR A FAST COMPUTER

Many computer games and applications require far more processing horsepower than an entry-level PC provides. Here are some of the cool and innovative games and applications that make use of the robust processing power of today's higher-performance computers. —*Steven L. Kent*

❶ TOM CLANCY'S SPLINTER CELL: CONVICTION (LATE 2008)
When you are trained like super-spy Sam Fisher, you are never unarmed. In this fifth installment of the *Splinter Cell* series, Fisher starts out empty-handed, but he knows how to blend into the environment, find black-market arms and survive. This version features gunfights and chases, but specializes in stealth and strategy.

❷ BIGSTAGE
Take three digital photos of your face, upload them on the BigStage.com Web site and you can create an avatar: a three-dimensional, highly detailed image of your face that you can use in games, insert into music videos and use for all kinds of mischief.

❸ MOVIEBOX ULTIMATE
Whether you are editing home movies, converting old video tapes to DVD, shooting video clips to upload to YouTube or doing something big, *MovieBox Ultimate* has the hardware and software you need to turn your computer into a video editor's dream.

❹ STARCRAFT II: BLIZZARD (LATE 2008)
Insects, aliens and astronauts go head-to-head in an all-out battle for galactic control in *StarCraft II*, the upcoming sequel to one of the most popular real-time strategy games of all time. What are the processing requirements? Controlling armies with hundreds of autonomous units requires a lot of fast calculations!

❺ EJAMMING
The band that plays together does not necessarily need to stay together, not with eJAMMING, an online service (*http://eJamming.com*) that lets players hook up on the Internet, compiles their tracks in real time and makes long-distance collaborations nearly as smooth and seamless as getting together for a garage session.

HOW COMPUTERS EVOLVE ●⋯⋯

HOW DO COMPUTERS keep getting faster each year? A big part of the answer involves transistors, the tiny switches that process the ones and zeroes of the digital world. The more transistors on a chip, the faster the processing speed.

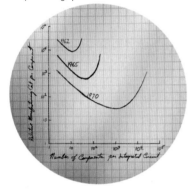

Gordon Moore's original graph from 1965

Intel co-founder Gordon Moore predicted in 1965 that the number of transistors on a chip would double about every two years. This prediction is popularly known as Moore's Law, and it has proven to be fairly accurate.

At any rate, by using different materials and achieving other technological breakthroughs, Intel has been able to increase speeds by phenomenal amounts over the past several decades. For example, an Intel processor in 1976 could hold 275,000 transistors. In 2006, an Intel processor could hold more than 800 million transistors.

That's why today you're able to play high-powered games, surf the Web, edit videos and do dozens of tasks on the computer at very high speeds. ◢

storage, and light home office use at a moderate price tag. A responsive but cost-effective system might be configured as follows.

Processor: A dual-core processor delivers great performance for a wide range of tasks, including more intensive digital photo and music enjoyment. With two cores you'll tackle the longest to-do list.

RAM: Typical installed memory currently ranges from 512 MB to 4 GB, but most users will find noticeable performance improvements with a minimum of 1 GB.

Hard drive: A medium-size hard disk with a capacity in the range of 320 GB should provide ample storage for most general-purpose home machines. A second drive might be considered to simplify backup.

Optical drives: A CD-write/DVD-read combo drive is almost indispensable, both for inexpensive backup and for sharing slide shows and other content.

Software: Many systems in this category come with the Microsoft Windows Vista Home Basic operating system and the Microsoft Works productivity mini-suite. You might consider the additional multimedia features of Vista Home Premium, such as Windows Movie Maker, and one of the more fully featured Office 2007 productivity suites.

A mobile study hall

Perhaps you're seeking a new PC for a college-bound student, and you've decided on a notebook that can easily make the rounds from dorm to lecture hall, library and lab. For an intellectually stimulating computing experience, you might consider a system outfitted as follows.

Processor: This is another job for a dual-core processor, which provides a combination of high performance, great battery life and advanced wireless connectivity to get the job done.

RAM: 2 GB or more.

Hard drive: 80 GB or more.

Optical drives: A CD-write/DVD-read combo is adequate. A DVD burner is better.

Software: Windows Vista Home Premium is the operating system typically provided with systems like this, but an upgrade to Office Standard 2007 or another of the Microsoft Office suites should be a priority.

A desktop for digital content creation

Perhaps digital video and photography are your passions, and you're seeking a PC that will not only let you enjoy them at their high-definition best, but will help you turn your own raw images into polished works of art. You need a system with the power and performance to handle the largest files and run the most heavily threaded, computing-intensive applications. You'll know you've found it when you see specs like these.

Processor: A quad-core processor is the best tool here. It delivers blockbuster performance for breathtaking high-definition digital media experiences and production capabilities. With four cores you'll fly through heavy processing tasks, so you'll create more, wait less.

RAM: 3 to 4 GB.

A PROCESSOR RATING SYSTEM

INTEL HAS CREATED a rating system to help computer buyers choose the right processing power to meet their needs. The rating system below offers three simple ways to compare

options. To find the processor with the right amount of "smartness" for what you want to do, just look for the new Intel brains.

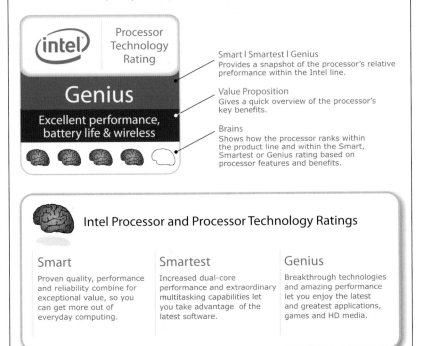

Smart | Smartest | Genius
Provides a snapshot of the processor's relative preformance within the Intel line.

Value Proposition
Gives a quick overview of the processor's key benefits.

Brains
Shows how the processor ranks within the product line and within the Smart, Smartest or Genius rating based on processor features and benefits.

Intel Processor and Processor Technology Ratings

Smart	Smartest	Genius
Proven quality, performance and reliability combine for exceptional value, so you can get more out of everyday computing.	Increased dual-core performance and extraordinary multitasking capabilities let you take advantage of the latest software.	Breakthrough technologies and amazing performance let you enjoy the latest and greatest applications, games and HD media.

Hard drive: Bigger is better for these systems, up to 750 GB.
Optical drives: HD optical drive plus a CD/DVD burner are recommended.
Graphics: Make sure to get a high-performance video card.
Software: Look for Windows Vista Ultimate, Office 2007 and advanced graphics applications such as Adobe Photoshop.

Let your purpose be your guide

Choosing the right PC can seem bewildering when you first begin the search: The number of choices is almost infinite. But the search gets simpler if you start the process with an eye on the end result. First decide how you want to use your new system and what you want to do with it. Then pick a machine with the processing capacity and other resources for the tasks that are most important to you. Add some performance margin for future growth and you're well on your way to a PC that's perfect for your own personal purposes. ▲

CHOOSING THE RIGHT MONITOR

FROM WORD PROCESSING and spreadsheets to blockbuster shoot-'em-up games and movies, today's computer monitors are true gateways to productivity and entertainment. To fully experience immersive multimedia computing, users are turning to large, flat LCD panels as the choice of display. Do some homework to choose the best monitor for your needs.

- Look for the largest wide-screen within your budget, but also pay close attention to its resolution. For example, a 20-inch LCD offers only 1 inch more than a 19-inch LCD, but offers 36 percent more resolution at 1680 x 1050—the same as a 22-inch. This means you can fit the same amount of data on-screen as a 22-inch, including 1080p high-definition input.

- Look at contrast ratios and response time. High dynamic contrast ratios and low response time will improve picture clarity, especially in movies and games, and Windows Vista premium certification will assure that everything works seamlessly.

- An insider hint: For video inputs, you can use a simple HDMI-DVI adapter to connect HDMI output from set-top and gaming boxes to your monitor's DVI input. ▲

What to know about quad-core processors

By Marc Saltzman

IT CAN BE TOUGH to keep up with all the techno-babble these days—megapixel this, gigahertz that, terabyte the other—so it's no surprise that many people are confused about the biggest thing to happen to computers in a long while: quad-core processors.

Wait! Before you roll your eyes and flip the page, hold on. This is pretty cool stuff.

If a computer were a car, its engine would be the processor (also referred to as the central processing unit, or CPU). Whenever something needs to be computed—whether it's a simple task such as opening a document or more complex functions such as rendering animation—the instructions are sent to the CPU to be processed. Generally speaking, the faster the processor, the faster your PC experience will be, which is a good thing.

Now imagine you have four engines under the hood of your car instead of one. This is a good way of understanding quad-core processors. With four independent cores on a single die (chip), your computer can do some amazing things.

As alluded to above, one advantage is incredible speed and smooth performance, especially for demanding applications such as home movie editing, computer gaming or compressing DVDs into portable video files. Think of it like this: Quad-core is like pushing gallons of water down four individual hoses at once, instead of waiting for the water to make its way through just one hose, which would obviously take longer.

Quad-core processors also make multitasking a breeze for those who like to open and use multiple programs simultaneously. Watch teenagers using a computer these days and you'll likely see them listening to music, surfing the Web, downloading files, chatting via instant messenger and writing documents—all at once! Businesspeople are pros at multitasking as well, with spreadsheets, Web browsers, mail managers and more open all at once.

Despite this newfound power and speed, quad-core processors have been engineered to be more energy efficient. This is good for the environment—and your utility bill—because it can cut down on power consumption.

The time is ripe to take a hard look at quad-core. Considering that video is moving to high definition, audio is going multichannel (six speakers instead of two) and fast wireless connectivity is becoming commonplace, you may want a seriously fast processor to handle it all.

Best of all, you're preparing for the future by picking up a quad-core PC, because quad-core's capabilities will grow. ▲

Marc Saltzman is one of the leading technology experts in the United States and Canada. Along with his regular tech column for *The Costco Connection*, Saltzman writes weekly syndicated columns for Gannett News Service, CNN.com, USAToday.com and CanWest Media. He also hosts two radio shows focusing on technology and has written 13 books, including *White Collar Slacker's Handbook: Tech Tricks to Fool Your Boss* (Que Publishing, 2005).

The latest in LCDs

TODAY'S LCD MONITORS are more than just workplace or home office peripherals. They are the centerpiece of your digital entertainment world. Many LCD technology innovations that have come about in the last year make it easier than ever to find an LCD that gives you an incredible picture regardless of your budget.

Here are some of the technologies to look for when choosing your next LCD, and what they mean to you.

Image enhancement

Many LCD panels today are coated with a film to avoid glare from the screen. However, this coating results in reduced brightness and less vivid colors. Some LCDs offer an alternative technology that makes colors stand out more sharply and produces improved image clarity. In this case, a special treatment of the screen allows more light to pass through the glass panel, boosting color saturation and producing brighter and more vivid colors.

Color enhancement

High-performance LCDs feature color-enhancement technology that extends the available National Television System Committee (NTSC) color gamut. Color gamut is the range of color a display can reproduce and is commonly expressed as a percentage of NTSC.

The average LCD displays 70 percent to 80 percent of the NTSC color gamut. For the best possible color, look for LCDs that display higher color gamuts—from 98 to 116 percent.

Surround sound

For monitors with integrated speakers, SRS WOW is a sound technology that provides a higher level of performance. SRS WOW HD offers a surround-sound experience on your desktop with panoramic three-dimensional sound and improved low frequencies. SRS WOW HD allows you to adjust the bass, treble, EQ, 3-D space level and definition level of the speakers. If you can't have a high-end external speaker system, SRS WOW is worth considering.

Dynamic contrast ratio

Advanced LCDs feature dynamic contrast and offer superior front-of-screen performance. With dynamic contrast ratio (DCR) you don't have to turn up the LCD's backlights all the way to show darker images. DCR touts performance up to four times greater than the traditional contrast ratio.

Fast video response

Just a few years ago 12 milliseconds (ms) was considered a really fast response time. Now high-performance LCDs feature response times as fast as 2 ms to meet the demands of today's work and entertainment options.

Super HD resolution

Today's LCDs offer higher resolutions than ever, with some of the best LCDs offering 1920 x 1200 resolution that supports a true 1080p HD experience. If you're in the market for a truly high-performance desktop LCD, look for one that offers full HD 1080p performance. ▲

All you need to know about CDs and DVDs

LIKE MANY TECHNICAL PRODUCTS, CDs and DVDs can be confusing. What do those plus (+) and dash (-) symbols mean? What's the best format to use for certain projects? Here's a look at how optical disc technology works.

How optical disc technology works

Compact discs (CDs) and digital video discs (DVDs) generally come in two choices: recordable (R) and rewritable (RW).

Recordable discs can be written to only once because marks are "burned" into the disc with a laser during the writing process. As a laser passes over the disc during the reading (playing) process, it reads a zero when hitting one of these burned marks and a one when the laser hits an area of the disc that was not burned. These zeros and ones are referred to as "bits," or binary digits, and are the basis for digital technology—the technical way information is stored.

With rewritable (RW) discs, the marks are not "burned" into the disc. Once a mark is made on the disc, the laser has the ability to change or reverse the mark. This is why these discs can be overwritten multiple times.

Choose discs according to your applications

It is highly recommended that you back up files, whether they are photos, videos or documents. CDs and DVDs can safeguard your data in case of a catastrophic loss, such as when a hard drive crashes.

The amount of data that you want to back up will determine how many discs you need. The chart at right shows the capacities of today's most popular optical discs. CDs store 700 MB (736,819,200 bytes) and DVDs can store 4.7 to 8.5 GB (1 GB equals 1 billion bytes). The newest format, Blu-ray Disc™ media, can store an amazing 25 to 50 GB.

If you want to back up the hard drive on your computer, RW discs are a good choice because they can be reused. On the other hand, R discs are more

→ **TIPS** &TRICKS ⌐

CLEANING OPTICAL DISCS

• Gently wipe disc with a soft, dry lint-free cloth, commercial CD cleaner or ethyl alcohol.
• Always wipe in a straight line from the center of the disc out, in radial fashion.

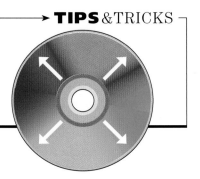

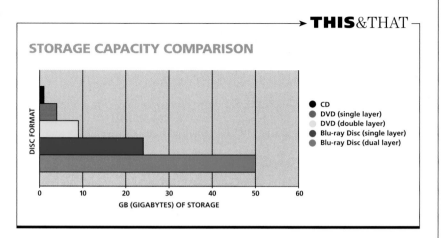

STORAGE CAPACITY COMPARISON

CD
DVD (single layer)
DVD (double layer)
Blu-ray Disc (single layer)
Blu-ray Disc (dual layer)

DISC FORMAT

GB (GIGABYTES) OF STORAGE

widely compatible with drives and set-top players—the type you have connected to your TV—and also last longer compared to RW discs. If you plan to save your backups or record events on video to share, R discs are your best choice because more people will be able to play them in their own equipment.

Discs are available in different colors, which can help you organize your recordings. Printable discs are great for customizing your data or movies, when used with a compatible inkjet printer for professional-looking results.

Speeds and recording times

Recordable DVDs have a speed, such as 16x, noted on the package. This means that if your computer's drive can record at 16x, a video will record 16 times faster than it takes to watch it; e.g., it would take one minute to record a 16-minute video. However, if the DVD drive speed is lower—4x for example—even a disc marked 16x will record only four times faster; e.g., it would take four minutes to record a 16-minute video. Regardless of the speed of the disc, the recording speed can be no faster than the speed of the computer's drive.

What is the difference between DVD+R and DVD-R?

The truth is, not much. Over the years the differences between the plus and dash formats have narrowed. The most important factor when making a disc purchase is to match the drive recorder format in a particular computer to the disc.

If the drive recorder is a combination unit, either format will work. When time is the main concern, the DVD+R is a good choice because +R discs have a faster finalization time (the time needed to write system information to the disc at the end of the recording process). If playback compatibility is your main concern, DVD-R is more often compatible because it has been around longer than the DVD+R format. ◪

CREATE A COMPELLING SLIDE SHOW

WHY DISPLAY YOUR photos statically on your computer screen or TV when you can instead present them in an interesting slide show with music? Here's how, using common slide-show-creating software on your computer.

1. Shoot an entire event, such as a school musical or a whole season following your child's sports team, and then select highlights for your disc. Capture backstage or sideline action as well as the actual games or performances. The stage managers, set designers, coaches and water carriers are important too!

2. Identify the people in the pictures using the program's titling capabilities, or simply label photos with the names of the people in them.

3. Ask other photographers, such as parents, for their photos and video to supplement your own, and choose the best material for your production. You don't need to do all the shooting.

4. Most programs have tools to add special creative effects and transitions between slides. You can even combine them with video tracks.

5. Add a title, music and credits, and you've created a masterpiece. Then share it on a DVD or online. ◪

Backing up your digital documents

EVERYTHING IS IN DIGITAL format these days—family photographs, video clips, music collections, address books and more—but they may be lost forever if your computer crashes. To save these precious documents and files, back them up. Here's how.

Get organized. Put all of the documents you create, the pictures you take and the music you buy in a single master folder in your computer. Divide that master folder into subfolders to keep your files organized. Backing up your data becomes much easier if everything is in a single master folder.

The "My Documents" folder is a good place to store files on any computer with Microsoft Windows.® When all of your personal files are in one place, you're less likely to forget a file when you back up.

Back up regularly. Back up your files regularly. If you work on your computer daily, you should back up important files daily. Then, back up everything at least once a week. Better still, look for backup software that will back up your data automatically in addition to manual backups.

Be selective. You don't have to back up your entire system. That's a time-consuming task that only duplicates all of the problems that have built up on your hard drive. Instead, save original copies of your software. Then you can reinstall your operating system and clean copies of your software if your system crashes.

Back up what's important to you. The most important things to protect are files you create. Whether they are text documents, e-mail messages, pictures, music, videos or game saves, if you made them you will want to save them and keep them nearby. It's also helpful to back up the configuration settings for any programs you use, along with critical Windows data such as the registry. And don't forget to back up data you have stored on external hard drives.

Where to back up. You can back up to CDs or DVDs, but this is a slow, manual process. And some low-priced CDs and DVDs wear out.

The best backup medium is an external hard drive. High-capacity external drives are very fast and allow you to keep your backed-up data in one place. For extra safety, get a two-drive external storage system and dedicate half of the capacity to automatically backing up your backup. ◪

The HDTV Guide

THE HISTORY OF TV has several distinct milestones: the first flickering pictures in 1926, the first color shows for the U.S. public in 1950, the first practical remote control in 1956, to name just a few. The latest significant development is one of the most exciting—high-definition television (HDTV).

Millions of people have joined the HDTV crowd. According to the Consumer Electronics Association, 39 percent of American households have an HDTV, and sales of 25 million units are projected for 2008. HDTV is taking over, just as color TVs replaced black and white in the 1960s.

If you are considering the purchase of an HDTV, this guide is meant to explain the lingo, offer setup tips for the complete home theater and help you make the right choice for your needs. You'll be left with only one question: Why didn't you switch earlier?

THIS CHAPTER SPONSORED BY

DIRECTV	Philips	Simplicity
Mitsubishi	Quest Group	TEAC
Panasonic	Samsung	Tripp Lite
Peerless	Sharp Electronics	Vizio

The complete guide to HDTV and your home theater

By Alfred Poor

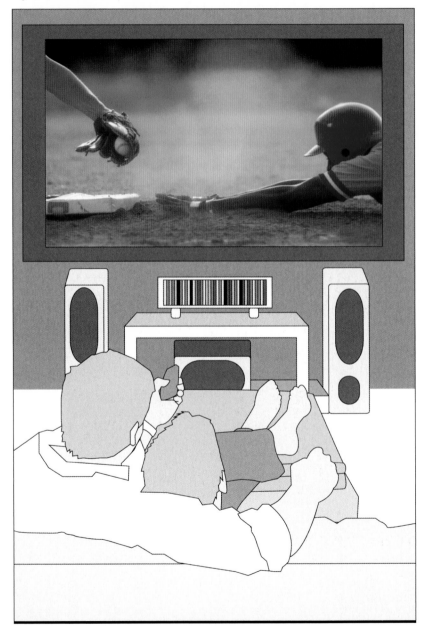

HDTV IS THE BIGGEST THING to hit television since color TV. It's nothing less than a technological revolution that delivers a more exciting and life-like image, bringing the immersive experience of a movie theater right into your home.

HDTV also can be confusing. Almost everyone has heard of it, but not everyone is quite sure what it is and what they need in order to get it. To complicate matters, a number of separate but related factors can make choosing the right HDTV setup for your home more confusing.

This guide will help to lead you through all the issues so that you can make a confident choice about a new television and the other components and services that you'll need to get the full HDTV experience.

HDTV basics

HDTV stands for "high-definition television." Definition in this case simply refers to how much detail is in the image. You'll hear terms such as "pixels" and "resolution" in discussions of HDTV (and those terms will be explained later on), but here's the basic idea: A high-definition television uses more dots to create the image than a regular television does. In fact, an HDTV image uses about three to six times as many dots as a standard television image.

What does that mean in terms of your experience? Think about a snapshot of someone that you might take using an instant camera. You'd get a nice picture that would be a recognizable image of that person. But now imagine taking that same photo with a high-quality 35 mm film camera and having a professional print made the same size as the snapshot. The 35 mm print will be much sharper and with more detail, so it will look more realistic. In the same way, a high-definition television image looks much more realistic than a standard television image because of the extra detail.

IT'S IN THE PIXELS

ANALOG TV

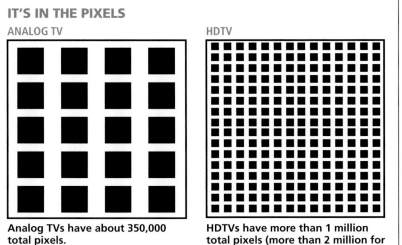

Analog TVs have about 350,000 total pixels.

HDTV

HDTVs have more than 1 million total pixels (more than 2 million for 1080p models).

What you need for an HDTV home theater

In order to get the HDTV experience, you need three things:

1. An HDTV

2. HDTV content from a digital signal source or a digital player

3. Audio equipment to complete the system

Let's explore each of these different pieces in turn.

Step 1: The HDTV

Most people immediately think of a flat-panel television, but you should know more details about the choices. To be called an HDTV, a television must meet certain standards relating to screen format, picture quality and sound quality.

The wide-screen look

First, all HDTVs must have a wide-screen format. This means that their width-to-height ratio—called the aspect ratio—is typically 16:9. This is wider than a traditional television's 4:3 aspect ratio and looks more like a movie screen.

THE WIDE-SCREEN FORMAT

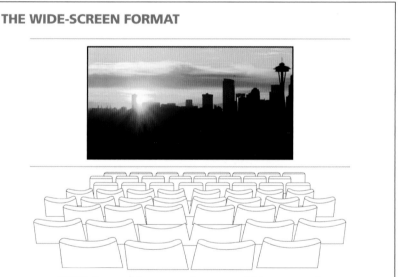

HDTVs have wide screens, known as 16:9 aspect ratio.

Older TVs are boxy, with a 4:3 aspect ratio.

Resolution: 720p and 1080p

Next, an HDTV must have a certain minimum resolution. Resolution refers to the total number of pixels on the screen; a pixel is simply the colored dot used to create the image. Resolution is expressed as the number of vertical lines of pixels times the number of horizontal lines of pixels. So, you'll see such specs as 1366 x 768 or 1920 x 1080. The higher the numbers, the sharper the resolution.

To be considered an HDTV, a set must have at least 720 horizontal lines of resolution. A new generation of HDTVs has at least 1,080 horizontal lines, which works out to more than 2 million total pixels. These are called 1080p (or "full HD"). Both 720p and 1080p screens will produce an excellent image, but 1080p will typically cost more.

Here are some other terms you'll come across when researching HDTVs.

Refresh rate. This is the number of times a display's image is repainted or refreshed per second. The refresh rate is expressed in hertz (Hz), so a refresh rate of 60 Hz means the image is refreshed 60 times in a second. The higher the rate, the better. New technology features a "frame rate conversion" process (available in 120 Hz) for superior fast-motion image processing.

Contrast ratio. This refers to the difference between the "whitest" image the set can produce divided by the "blackest" image. Typically, the higher the contrast ratio, the better the black levels, but let your eyes be the ultimate judge.

Progressive and interlaced. You'll see references to 720p and 1080i signals. The letters refer to progressive and interlaced—the way the program is presented on the screen (see box below). The latest TVs can handle both signals. LCD, plasma and rear-projection HDTVs display images progressively.

→ **TIPS** &TRICKS

THE ARGUMENT FOR 1080P

Should you opt for an HDTV with a resolution of 1080p, or go with a 720p model? There are some compelling reasons to choose a 1080p set.

The "1080" refers to the number of horizontal lines of pixels filling the screen. The more lines, the higher the resolution. A 1080p screen has 1,080 horizontal lines of pixels and typically 1,920 vertical lines of pixels. This resolution is referred to as 1920 x 1080.

A "720p" HDTV has at least 720 lines of resolution, and typically 1,024 to 1,366 vertical lines. So a 1080p HDTV has more pixels than a 720p HDTV, and more pixels equates to a higher resolution.

The other advantage is how 1080p works. Not long ago, the best tube TVs used a 1080i process. The "i" indicates that the images were conveyed in an interlaced format: The images get painted on the screen sequentially,

with the odd-numbered lines appearing first, followed by the even-numbered lines, all within one-thirtieth of a second. This method can produce the kind of flickering seen on older TVs.

In comparison, 1080p systems use a progressive-scan format. All of the lines of resolution are sent sequentially in a single pass, making for a smoother, cleaner image. This is especially apparent when viewing sporting events and other fast-moving situations.

The new Blu-ray Disc format produces images in the 1080p format. When you watch movies in this new format with a 1080p set, you'll be getting the sharpest resolution available in the HD world today.

HDTV choices

HDTVs are available in a variety of types and sizes utilizing various technologies. The two most popular are LCD and plasma. But rear-projection HDTVs and projectors, popular for sets 60 inches and larger, are also worth considering for their features and value.

Plasma and LCD. Plasma and LCD TVs both offer fantastic images, created by two different technologies. Plasma models use a process involving electrically excited inert gases (known as "plasma") to create the images. LCDs use liquid crystals to create the images.

The general rule of thumb has been that smaller HDTVs have been LCD, while larger models have been plasma. This is changing, as LCDs are getting larger and plasma TVs smaller. It makes doing your homework even more important before buying.

One rap on LCDs is that fast-moving images might not be as sharp as they would be on a traditional picture-tube television or a plasma HDTV. New technologies have helped improve LCD performance, however. Sets with 120 Hz refresh rates create new images twice as often as traditional LCD sets, which makes moving images much smoother.

A plasma set can look better than an LCD set if you can darken the room, but an LCD set has an advantage in a well-lit room or one that has windows that let in light during the day. This light can cause glare on the TV.

Some buyers are concerned about short life and "burn-in" on plasma displays. These were problems with early plasma models, but not anymore.

Rear-projection HDTVs. Rear-projection HDTVs use microchips and a bright light source to create the image. The thumbnail-size microchips can use DLP, LCD or LCoS technologies.

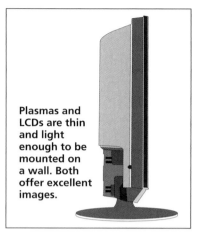

Plasmas and LCDs are thin and light enough to be mounted on a wall. Both offer excellent images.

→ **TIPS** &TRICKS

WHAT SIZE SCREEN SHOULD YOU GET?

Everyone wants a big screen, but many people have a hard time figuring out how big the screen should be. The short answer is "bigger than you might think." Think about a movie screen at your local cinema. You don't sit way in the back so the screen looks small; you probably sit in the middle so it fills a large portion of your field of view. You want the same effect with your HDTV.

Here's a good rule of thumb to calculate a minimum viewing distance: For sets with 720p resolution, divide the distance (in inches) that you are going to sit from the HDTV by 2.5. For 1080p sets, the figure is 1.5. When in doubt,

go larger. Some examples for 1080p sets:
• 8 feet away, 64-inch screen
• 6 feet away, 48-inch screen

However, the best tool is your own eyes. When researching HDTVs, stand back and see what looks best to you. Another tip is to tape an outline of the HDTV on your wall at home with easy-peel painter's tape to get an idea of the set's dimension.

WHAT IS 120 HZ?

One exciting feature emerging in the world of LCD HDTVs is the 120 Hz refresh rate. What does this mean, and what difference does it make on the screen?

Many LCDs today have a refresh rate of 60 Hz. This means that the image on the screen is refreshed 60 times a second. That's a wonderfully fast refresh rate, but it can result in motion blur in fast-moving scenes, such as sporting events and movies.

A faster refresh rate can make the picture smoother in such scenes. An LCD with a 120 Hz rate refreshes the images at twice the speed of one with a 60 Hz rate.

Watch for "120 Hz" to become mentioned more frequently in discussions about hot specs for LCDs.

In many cases, these sets are only a few inches deeper than an LCD or plasma set of the same size. Rear-projection models can represent an excellent bargain if you want a large screen. The lamps used in these models will have to be replaced when they get dimmer, typically after a few years. The lamps can cost $200 to $300, which adds to the cost of ownership. But these sets use less energy than other TVs in this size category, and a new lamp restores the TV to an almost new condition.

Projectors. The other choice is a projector. Once limited to high-end home theater installations costing five figures or more, high-definition models are now available for less than $2,000. You do need to be able to control room lighting, but a projector can give you an enormous image at a reasonable price. Projectors use lamps similar to those in most rear-projection HDTVs. They need to be replaced every few years, depending on usage.

So how do you decide?

The best advice is to look at the sets for yourself. Pay close attention to the black areas of the images. Crisp, sharp blacks bring all images to life.

Although studying specs is important, the best advice is to use your eyes. Do your homework on various manufacturers and ask advice from friends who already have an HDTV. Look at the room where the HDTV will be placed to see how big you can go. Size and budget are big factors.

KEEPING THE BIG NEW SCREEN CLEAN

A COMMON QUESTION for HDTV owners is how to keep the new big screen clean. Big screens attract dust, which can dull the picture. However, keeping them clean requires very careful handling. The problem stems from the fact that many plasma and LCD TVs have a special antiglare coating that can be damaged by the wrong cleaning materials and techniques.

For information on your specific model, the first step is to check the user's guide or the manufacturer's Web site.

Here are some guidelines for keeping your TV clean.

1. Unplug the power cord from the wall or surge protector before cleaning the TV.

2. Use a soft, dry cloth to remove dust from the TV screen. Do not use an abrasive material such as a paper towel to do this.

3. Don't use liquid or aerosol cleaners unless they're specially intended for this purpose.

4. For tougher dirt or fingerprints, proceed with caution. Some manufacturers say you can use a slightly damp cloth with mild soap to lightly clean the screen's surface. Others say you should never use anything but a dry cloth. Check your user's manual.

5. Do not press hard on the screen while cleaning it. ◢

Rear-projection HDTVs come in large screen sizes and can represent a great value. Some are not much wider than a flat-panel HDTV.

Step 2: The HDTV signal

Now that you've chosen your HDTV, you need HDTV content: movies, TV shows and games. Standard analog broadcast signals cannot carry enough information to transmit high-definition images. As a result, you must have a digital signal source to get HDTV. Keep in mind that not all programming with a digital service will be in high definition, but if you don't have a digital source you won't get any high definition. You have four main choices:

1. Free digital broadcasts over the air

2. A digital cable subscription

3. A satellite subscription

4. A Blu-ray Disc player

➤ **THIS**&THAT ─

THE BENEFITS OF BLU-RAY

What's all the buzz about Blu-ray? The answer is that if you're looking for the sharpest resolution in your HDTV, you'll need two essentials: an HDTV with 1080p resolution and a Blu-ray Disc player. Well, three: You'll also need an HDMI cable to connect the two.

Blu-ray is the new generation of optical disc formats. The format has more than five times the storage capacity of traditional DVDs and can hold up to 25 GB on a single-layer disc and 50 GB on a dual-layer disc. This unrivaled storage capacity means discs can hold enough information to deliver full 1080p resolution to a compatible HDTV. Blu-ray delivers six times the resolution of a standard DVD and up to 7.1 channels (compared to the 5.1 channels of standard DVDs) of high-quality audio.

It's called Blu-ray because the laser beam that reads the data from the new discs is blue instead of red, which is used for DVDs and CDs. These new discs are the same size as traditional DVDs and CDs. That enables a Blu-ray player to play traditional DVDs (but a traditional DVD player will not play a Blu-ray Disc).

To take advantage of this new technology, you'll need a Blu-ray Disc player, either as a stand-alone player or as a computer drive. Also, the Sony PlayStation 3 has a fully functional Blu-ray Disc player.

True 1080p resolution is just one of the features of a Blu-ray system. Movies being made in the Blu-ray format feature movie notes, menus, interviews with directors and actors, etc., all of which can be easily accessed while you're watching the movie. In the works is another feature: Internet access for Web-enhanced movie viewing. For more about Blu-ray, see *www.blu-raydisc.com*.

Free digital broadcasts. These are available in just about all major TV markets. All you need to receive these signals is an antenna attached to a TV with a digital tuner or a digital set-top box. If you live close enough to the transmitters, simple "rabbit ears" will do the job. If you live farther away, you may need a larger rooftop antenna, sensitive enough to pick up digital signals, or even a signal amplifier. You can find out what type of antenna you need at *www.antennaweb.org*. Just enter your address and it will tell you the direction of local TV stations and what kind of antenna you need. Note: Changes are coming for people who use an antenna for TV service. See story on page 54.

Digital cable service. Cable is available in many—but not all—markets. In some cases, you will need to pay a premium for a high-definition set-top box. Typically, cable offers channels with standard-definition programming and an additional set of channels that carry the HD versions, as well as a wide range of on-demand HD programming, such as movies.

Also, if your TV has a QAM (quadrature amplitude modulation) tuner, you can receive HD channels directly from the cable to the TV. However, you won't get much variety, nor will you be able to view premium channels without a set-top box or cable card.

Satellite service. These digital services, such as DIRECTV, are available even in areas where there is no local broadcast or cable service. In general, you will pay a premium for high-definition service. All satellite TV channels are broadcast in digital format. Also, satellite TV services offer local channels in many markets and more national HD channels than cable, and feature a big selection of regional sports networks, sports packages and pay-per-view events.

Which service is right for you? The free local broadcasts are the most limited, as you will have access only to a few unscrambled stations. A limited portion of the programming will be in high def: generally prime-time programs, movies and some sporting events. You can find an offering of HD channels in your area at *www.whereishd.com*.

High-definition DVD player. This choice was simplified after the industry settled on Blu-ray Disc technology as the way to deliver high-definition movies. You can buy a stand-alone Blu-ray Disc player, or you can buy other devices that include a Blu-ray Disc drive, such as a personal computer or a Sony PlayStation 3.

→ TIPS & TRICKS

HOW HIGH TO MOUNT YOUR HDTV?

The height of your flat-panel TV will greatly affect your viewing experience. Mount your TV so that, while sitting, your eyes are level with the middle of the screen. Resist the urge to mount your TV at the same height as a picture. You don't want to strain your neck looking up at a TV that is mounted too high. Purchasing a tilting or full-motion mount will allow flexibility in viewing angles and seating positions.

● TIP SPONSORED BY

simplicity™

Protecting your equipment

Your new HDTV is a complex electronic device, similar to a personal computer in terms of its processing power and internal components. As a result, it's a good idea to provide power protection for it and any other components in your home entertainment system. At the very least, you should have a good surge protector between the set and the power outlet.

You should also consider getting more extensive protection, such as that offered by many uninterruptible power supplies (UPS). These can protect against several problems:

• Power surges and spikes, which can interrupt recording, erase settings and data, and even damage or ruin hardware and sensitive components

• Power sags or "brownouts," which are a decrease in voltage, often experienced during periods of peak demand for power

• Electronic line noise, which is created by household appliances. This noise in the line can degrade sound and picture quality and interfere with recordings.

• Blackouts, which are complete losses of power. These are bad news for projection bulbs, which can burn out if their cooling fans lose power. And blackouts can erase data and settings throughout the system.

In the event of a power failure, a UPS will keep the HDTV running so that you can shut it down properly.

Step 3: Completing the system

If you have an HDTV and a source of high-definition content, you've got the basics covered. You will want to consider a few other items, however.

First, you need a place to put the new television. Unfortunately, chances are good that your new set won't fit your existing entertainment center, which was likely designed for a standard TV. As a result, you may want new furniture for your HDTV, or, if it's a flat panel, you may want to hang it on the wall.

→ **THIS**&THAT

WHAT'S AN UPSCALING DVD PLAYER?

Note that there are "upscaling" DVD players that will take a standard 480p DVD and produce an image in high definition: either

Some DVD players can "upscale" standard DVDs to HD. The new Blu-ray players offer true HD.

720p or 1080p. This is the same scaling that your HDTV does with any standard-definition signal. The upscaling DVD players may have a higher-quality scaler than the one in your HDTV, which could result in a better-looking image. But in either case, the original DVD is standard definition, and either the player or your HDTV will "interpret" the missing dots to fill out the high-definition image. To get high-definition movies on your HDTV, you will need a Blu-ray Disc player.

WHERE DOES THE SUBWOOFER GO?

Subwoofers are an essential part of a home theater package. They make those deep, throbbing sounds that are part of a movie or show's audio mix. Here are tips to help a subwoofer sound best.

1. Keep the subwoofer low in the room. Don't try to mount it or place it on top of something. Bass likes to be "down low."

2. Placement in the corner of a room is usually best. Sit in your favorite listening position and have someone move the subwoofer around the room. You'll probably find that a room corner gives the nicest, deepest, most detailed bass.

3. Make sure the subwoofer is placed on a hard surface, such as the floor or a hardwood board. Carpet will absorb the sound. Most subwoofers use quite a bit of electricity, so make sure the electrical outlet is stout enough to handle the load.

4. Turning it up too loud can damage the subwoofer's internal speaker or power supply. If you hear a "clacking" noise coming from the subwoofer, turn it down. That is most likely the speaker's voice coil banging against metal pieces in the speaker.

5. Some subwoofers have a "crossover frequency" adjustment on the back. The rule of thumb is, the larger your front speakers are, the lower the crossover frequency can be set. If you have tiny front speakers, turn the crossover frequency up to its maximum position. Large speakers easily work down to low frequencies; little speakers don't. With small speakers, you need the subwoofer to do more of the work, so turn the crossover setting as high as it will go.

● TIP SPONSORED BY

Some people opt for professional mounting, but it can be done by a do-it-yourselfer.

Mounting an HDTV

You can hire a professional to hang your HDTV, but you can also get wall mounts for flat panels for the do-it-yourselfer. In general, you will need only a few standard tools, and the kit will include all of the details about how to install the mount so it will hold your screen safely.

Keep in mind that a large flat-panel TV can weigh 100 pounds or more, so follow the directions carefully. It's a good idea to have at least one other person on hand to help with the installation.

Hanging an HDTV on the wall creates the problem of where to run the cables. An easy alternative to snaking the cables behind the wall is to get plastic cable channels to conceal them. These channels can often be painted to match the wall, which makes them all but disappear. Important note: Don't snake electrical power cords through a wall—leave any adjustments to your power supply to professionals.

Setting up the sound system

Most HDTVs come with built-in speakers, and compared with the speakers found in many traditional picture-tube televisions, they can do a pretty good job. However, you may be missing out on a major part of the HDTV experience if you limit yourself to the two speakers in the television.

Most HDTV content comes with an audio signal in 5.1 format. Where a standard stereo signal has two channels—left and right—the 5.1 format provides for five separate channels, plus a subwoofer. You get the front left and right channels, plus a center channel that helps deliver movie dialogue with a clarity that can be surprising. You also get left and right rear channels, which help complete the surround-sound system (and let you know when something creepy is trying to sneak up behind you in a scary movie).

The subwoofer adds the gut-shaking low-frequency sounds that make all the difference in an action sequence or in delivering realistic background noise in a scene. (You can now find systems with 6.1 or 7.1 channels that add even more surround-sound speakers to the configuration.)

You can experience the full excitement of surround sound through a home theater sound system. This is the next generation of the home stereo and includes equipment such as an integrated DVD player and an AM/FM tuner.

Another feature that can be handy is wireless surround speakers. These let you set up the rear left and right speakers without having to run wires to them from the home theater box, which can greatly simplify installation (they still require power). Home theater systems are available with a wide range of features and corresponding prices.

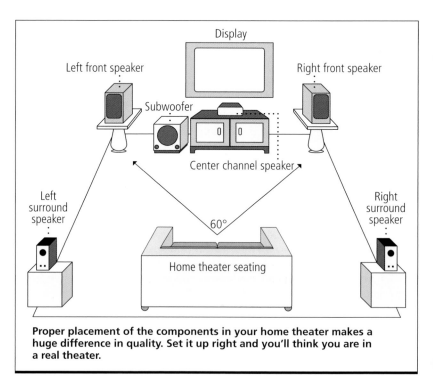

Proper placement of the components in your home theater makes a huge difference in quality. Set it up right and you'll think you are in a real theater.

DO CABLES REALLY MATTER?

You go in one store and see a 6-foot HDMI cable for $120; you visit another and see a seemingly similar cable for $49. Can there be that much difference in something as innocuous as a cable?

The short answer is that there are differences in cable design, materials, manufacturing quality and quality-control testing disciplines. A cable's job is to transfer information with minimal or (ideally) no distortion or loss. How it achieves that can vary.

Take, for example, an HDMI cable. These cables are hard to make. There are 19 separate connections at each end of the cable; precise construction techniques are vitally important. Many manufacturers manually solder these delicate connections.

This means 38 solder joints made by hand for each cable, greatly increasing the likelihood of error. Higher-performance (and inherently more reliable) HDMI cables are constructed using techniques other than hand-soldering, such as crimping and wave-soldering.

Quality-control testing of HDMI cables is extremely important. While many manufacturers use an eye-pattern wave test, better manufacturers also employ a bit error rate test. Ensuring minimal information loss is best verified by actually counting the bit error rate.

A tremendous amount of information runs from your signal source to your HDTV, especially with the newer 1080p requirements. Look for cables that are specified as "HDMI 1.3" or "full HD."

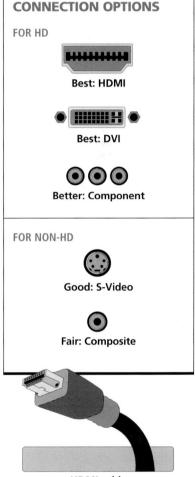

CONNECTION OPTIONS

FOR HD

Best: HDMI

Best: DVI

Better: Component

FOR NON-HD

Good: S-Video

Fair: Composite

HDMI cable

Making the connections: a look at cables

All you have left to do is connect all the pieces. Cables can be confusing—and if you use the wrong ones, you won't get the full HDTV experience. Also, the type of cables you can use depends on your system. Here's an overview of cable types and where to use them.

HDMI (high-definition multimedia interface). HDMI delivers uncompressed 1080p HD video and up to 7.1 channels of surround sound. You get top-quality video and sound—all in one cable. HDMI should be your first choice; it's a digital connection and is closely related to the DVI connections found on many PCs and monitors. Plus it's a big step up in convenience.

DVI (digital visual interface). DVI can carry 1080p HD video, but not audio.

Component. These are red, green and blue video cables that can handle high-definition resolution. Before the arrival of HDMI, component cables were the preferred way to transmit HD video signals. If you are like many people, you haven't bought a Blu-ray Disc player yet but you probably already own a DVD player. Most of these players use component video outputs, so you may need a quality component cable with your system.

Of course, DVI and component cables carry only the video signal. You'll need audio cables to complete the connection. You can use the standard analog audio connections (a red and white pair of RCA connectors), but for best results, use a digital connection if one is available. The choices are digital optical or digital coaxial cables.

S-video. This cable breaks video information into two parts: one for color and one for brightness. Use S-video only to connect to standard-definition devices, such as VHS players, DVD players or video camcorders. (Note that some digital camcorders now record high-definition images, so you don't want to use S-video or composite connections with them.)

Composite. This cable has a yellow connector for video and red and white connectors for stereo sound. They can't handle HD signals.

HELPFUL **HOW TO'S** •·······

GETTING HELP

IF YOU PURCHASED your HDTV or components from Costco, either in the warehouses or online at costco.com, your purchases are covered by Costco Concierge, a free tech-support program for TVs and other consumer electronics. Costco Concierge can answer setup questions if you get stuck. It can be reached toll-free at 1-866-861-0450.

HDTV RESOURCE LIST

- Samsung HDTV guide: Enter "Samsung HDTV Guide" in Google, then select "The HDTV Guide."
- Consumer Electronics Association Connections Guide: *www.ceaconnectionsguide.com*
- CNET Home Theater Guide: *http://help.cnet.com/home-theater-learning/*
- Alfred Poor's HDTV resource center: *www.hdtvprofessor.com/*
- Philips HDTV Video Learning Center: *www.youtube.com/philipstvman*
- *HDTV for Dummies,* by Danny Briere and Pat Hurley (Wiley Publishing Inc., 2005)
- *HDTV Magazine's* An HDTV Primer (*www.hdtvprimer.com*)
- *The Home Electronics Survival Guide,* by Barb Gonzalez (*www.home-electronics-survival.com*) △

COMING SOON: THE DIGITAL TV CONVERSION

The digital revolution is coming to television broadcast transmissions. If you rely on an antenna to receive your TV signal, you may have to make changes before February 17, 2009.

At midnight on that day, all full-power television stations in the United States will stop broadcasting in analog and switch to 100 percent digital broadcasting. Digital broadcasting promises to provide a clearer picture and more programming options, while freeing up airwaves for use by emergency responders.

A simple checklist can determine whether your TV will be affected by this change. You will not be affected if:

- You subscribe to cable programming (with or without a cable box).
- You subscribe to satellite TV programming.
- Your TV was manufactured after March 1, 2007, ensuring that it has a built-in digital TV tuner.
- Your TV set was manufactured before March 1, 2007, but you are certain that it has a built-in digital TV tuner.

On the other hand, you will need special equipment if:

- You receive TV programming via rabbit ears or an outside antenna.
- You do not subscribe to any pay TV service such as cable or satellite.
- Your TV does not have a built-in digital TV tuner.

So what do you do? You have two options:

- You can purchase a TV converter box. This box plugs into your TV and will keep it working after February 17, 2009. Note that a digital over-the-air signal may not reach your area as the analog signal did.
- You can upgrade to a subscription service.

Fortunately, the government will help you purchase a TV converter box. Thanks to the TV Converter Box Coupon Program, U.S. households wishing to keep using their analog TV sets can obtain up to two coupons, each worth $40, that can be applied toward the cost of eligible converter boxes at participating retailers.

Other options are to connect to cable, satellite or other pay service, or purchase a TV with a built-in digital tuner.

For complete details on the digital TV conversion plan, see these Web sites:
www.dtv2009.gov
www.dtv.gov
www.dtvanswers.com

Step 4: Ready, set ... action!

With your system all set up, it's time to enjoy the HDTV home theater experience. Read the owner's manuals for your components to make sure everything is configured together, such as your DVD player and your HDTV. Often, the basics are covered in a "quick start" guide.

Make sure you indeed have an HD signal, either from a cable or satellite TV service or an over-the-air antenna, or from your Blu-ray Disc player. Non-HD content is not as impressive on your new HDTV. And make sure you're tuning to an HD channel; it may have a different number than the analog channel.

Once everything is in place, sit back and enjoy the show. △

Alfred Poor is an independent expert in the display industry, and is the author of the HDTV Almanac, *http://hdtvprofessor.com/HDTVAlmanac*, a free online site with daily news and commentary about HDTV and related home entertainment topics.

Office Basics

THINK OF "OFFICE" and what comes to mind? For many, it's *Dilbert*. The popular comic strip now appears in some 2,000 newspapers in 65 countries and 25 languages. It wasn't always that way. When creator Scott Adams sent packets of sample cartoons to major cartoon syndicates in 1988, response was lukewarm. Here's one representative rejection letter:

Dear Mr. Adams:

Thank you very much for sending us your interesting feature, "Dilbert." We were impressed with the quality of the work and in your obvious credentials. After carefully evaluating your material, however, we don't feel that we can successfully syndicate it at this time. This is no reflection on the quality of your work or of your ideas. Rather, it is our assessment of what will sell in today's newspaper market. Wishing you the very best ... ▲

An office chair primer

IF YOU SPEND MOST of your workweek at a desk, a comfortable chair—one that provides sustained orthopedic well-being—is an essential piece of equipment. An ill-fitting chair will cause lower back pain and dramatically increase existing back or neck problems. This is because, even though sitting is a static activity, it's physically stressful on your back, neck, shoulders, arms and legs.

Sitting for prolonged periods places undue pressure on back muscles and spinal discs because the muscles you use for good posture tire over time. Slouching is a natural response, but this posture tends to stretch spinal ligaments and strain the discs and surrounding structures of the spine. This scenario eventually leads to back problems and pain.

A comfortable chair that works well ergonomically will maximize back support and help you maintain good posture while sitting. The upshot is that you won't be plagued by back pain and fatigue, leaving you physically unencumbered where work is concerned.

It's a good idea to "test-drive" different office chairs to see which feels best. Simply buying an "ergonomic" chair will seldom provide a good long-term fit. A good chair will fit your individual body type as well as dovetail with

 **TIPS** &TRICKS

FINDING A SEAT THAT FITS

If it's true, as the adage says, that "people come in all shapes and sizes," how do you find an office chair that fits? Here's an office chair overview that groups chairs into three general types.

HEAVY-USE CHAIR

This type is for people who are glued to their chairs for long hours each day—e.g., computer programmers, receptionists and so on. If you're in this group, look for a chair with a synchro-tilt mechanism, a fatigue-reducing device on the underside of the chair's seat. Thanks to this device, whether you lean forward or back, the chair back moves with you to provide continuous support.

MODERATE-USE CHAIR

If you're a typical middle manager—up and down a lot, alternating between work-

ing at your computer and spending time in meetings—a chair with a knee-tilt mechanism is worth considering. This mechanism allows you to lean back in the chair while keeping your feet on the ground. In chairs without this device, your feet typically are lifted when you lean back, leading to discomfort over time. One additional note: This type of chair typically has more style to convey management status.

EXECUTIVE CHAIR

This model has the same mechanical features as the moderate-use chair, but is typically larger, more comfortable and more elegant for the executive. It's designed for the person who spends time going from conference room to conference room, and spends more time on the phone than on the computer while at his or her desk. Think comfort, style and status (and a higher price tag).

1. ELBOW MEASURE

Begin by sitting comfortably as close as possible to your desk. Your upper arms should be parallel to your spine. Rest your hands on your workstation. Adjust the height of your seat so that your elbows are at a 90-degree angle.

2. THIGH MEASURE

The goal here is to be able to easily slide your fingers under your thigh at the front edge of your seat. If the chair is too high, prop up your feet with an adjustable footrest. If you're on the tall side and you've got more than a finger's width between your thigh and the chair, you will need to raise the height of your desk so that you can raise your chair into proper adjustment.

3. CALF MEASURE

With your back against the backrest and your bottom all the way back in the seat of your chair, lean forward and try to pass your clenched fist between the back of your calf and the front of the chair. If can't do this easily, the chair seat is too deep. You'll need to adjust the backrest forward; insert a lower back support such as a lumbar support cushion, a pillow or a rolled-up towel; or consider buying a different office chair.

4. LOWER BACK SUPPORT

Your back should be pressed against the back of the chair, and there should be a cushion that causes your lower back to arch slightly so that you don't slump forward or slouch down in the chair as you tire. This support is crucial to minimize strain on your back. Slouching and slumping in your chair adds stress on your lower back and your lumbar discs.

5. RESTING EYE LEVEL

Close your eyes while sitting comfortably with your head facing forward. Slowly open your eyes. Your gaze should be aimed at the center of your computer screen. If your computer screen is higher or lower, you will need to adjust it to avoid neck strain.

6. ARMREST

Adjust the armrest of the office chair so that it just slightly lifts your arms at the shoulders. Use of an armrest on your office chair is important to take some of the strain off your neck and shoulders, and it should make you less likely to slouch forward in your chair.

7. JUDGMENT

There is not one type of office chair that is optimal for all people. You should determine your individual preference for comfort while following these guidelines to promote good posture and back support while sitting in an office chair.

the space in which you work. The following points will help you buy the right office chair.

Choosing a high-quality chair

A good office chair enables you to work day in and day out in comfort. High-quality chairs are made using ergonomically correct plywood forms that adhere to ergonomic guidelines for seat height and depth, arm height, and back and seat angle, as well as contoured foam to provide support.

In addition to all of this, good chairs offer a wide range of ergonomic features that enable you to adjust and customize the chair to your body shape and support needs. Keep the following features in mind before you buy a new chair.

- Gas lift offers the best adjustment to seat height, which helps maintains correct position of feet and knees.
- Adjustable-height arms allow for correct shoulder and back posture.
- Adjustable-width arms enable proper positioning of elbows and straight posture.
- Pivoting arm pads offer support in typing position as well as when reclining.
- Gel or memory-foam arm pads distribute weight evenly, reducing pressure on elbows.

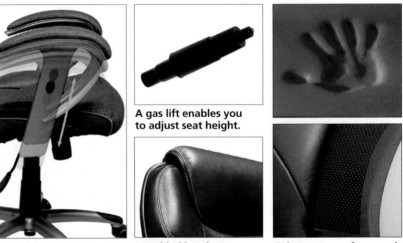

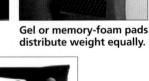

A gas lift enables you to adjust seat height.

Adjustable-height arms aid the shoulders and back.

A padded headrest provides neck support.

Gel or memory-foam pads distribute weight equally.

Lumbar support mini-mizes stress on the spine.

A knee-tilt seat plate helps reduce fatigue.

- Memory-foam seat and lumbar cushioning will conform to your body's exact contour, providing evenly distributed support and reducing stress on pressure points.

- Padded and/or adjustable headrest provides proper back and neck support.

- Adjustable lumbar support caters to your individual support needs, minimizing stress on the spine. This feature allows change in support position periodically to reduce back fatigue.

- Center-pivot and tilting seat plate allows for change in leg angle while reclining, reducing leg fatigue and increasing circulation.

- Knee-tilt seat plate allows for change in leg angle while reclining, reducing leg fatigue and increasing circulation. Forward-pivot designs allow feet to remain flat on the floor and enable you to maintain proper posture.

- Synchro seat plate allows for change in leg angle while reclining, reducing leg fatigue and increasing circulation. This feature also allows you to recline the backrest at a 2:1 ratio in relation to the seat, which provides an added ergonomic benefit in that the body angle is allowed to open up during recline, allowing for increased circulation in legs and back while reducing fatigue. (With a center-pivot or knee-tilt seat plate, the body angle remains constant.)

- Multi-paddle mechanism provides all of the benefits of the synchro seat plate with the added benefits of adjustable seat angle, adjustable back angle and adjustable back height for custom fit of lumbar support and headrest.

- Waterfall seat-edge design promotes leg circulation.

- Fingertip controls on arms reduce the need for bending and straining to adjust components. ◪

→ **THIS**&THAT ⌐

THE FIRST CHAIRS

In ancient times, the best chairs were a privilege of deity or state, and thus were characterized by rich and ornate designs. For example, ancient Egyptian chairs were made of ebony and ivory and covered with costly materials. The legs often were carvings of beasts or lion's claws. It wasn't until the Renaissance that the chair became a piece of furniture available to whomever could afford it. From then on, the chair commonly became a reflection of style from period to period.

TIPS&TRICKS

CHAIR MATS SAVE FLOORS AND BACKS

ROLLING AN OFFICE CHAIR around a carpeted floor in the home office or at work can be a real pain—for both the floor and you! Casters can cause serious, permanent damage to the floor or carpet. What's more, constantly pushing the chair around during the typical workday can lead to leg fatigue and lower back strain.

The best and simplest solution is a chair mat. You can instantly improve the ergonomics of your work space, reducing the effort required to roll your chair by as much as 82 percent (compared to rolling on unprotected carpet). In addition, you'll lessen the chance of floor damage, extend the life of your flooring surface and even protect it from the occasional spill. ◪

Taking steps to avoid identity theft

By Mari Frank

WHEN A WOMAN I'd never met took my identity in 1996, I was shocked. She stole more than $50,000 in my name; used my good reputation to obtain credit to buy a convertible; totaled a rental car, for which I was sued; and, worse, assumed my profession as an attorney, distributing business cards with my name on them. It took me 11 months and 500 hours of my time to regain my identity.

When I learned that there were no laws to assist victims of identity theft, I took action by helping to write legislation and testifying in Congress to create laws to protect consumers. It is now my mission to support thousands of victims and protect good people from identity theft.

A recent survey conducted by Impulse Research Inc. found that approximately 57 percent of Americans have experienced some form of identity theft, or the crime has affected someone they know. While millions of people have lived the nightmare of identity theft, the survey shows only 34 percent of Americans are concerned about becoming a victim.

One traditional form of identity theft still popular today is check fraud. Ernst & Young estimates that more than 500 million checks are forged annually in the United States. In one common crime, the fraudster erases information on the check with household chemicals and replaces it with new information. According to a recent *Los Angeles Times* article, this decades-old process is known as "check washing" among con men, and in an era of high-tech crimes it seems almost quaint. Except that it's back, along with other check crimes.

DID YOU KNOW?

Check fraud is growing at a rate of 25 percent each year

The buzz today is about online identity theft. But traditional methods of fraud are still happening, so take action now. For example, when writing checks or signing important documents, use a pigmented gel ink pen. The pigments in such pens get embedded within the fibers of the paper, helping to prevent criminals from washing off sensitive information.

It is vital to take privacy and identity theft issues seriously and empower yourself with knowledge. Before you provide your private information offline or online, stop and consider your privacy—be vigilant and exercise caution. Protect yourself from this faceless crime. Ⓐ

Mari Frank is an identity theft expert, attorney and author of *Safeguard Your Identity: Protect Yourself with a Personal Privacy Audit* and *The Identity Theft Survival Kit*. As a certified information privacy professional, Ms. Frank provides training and consulting on privacy issues for law enforcement, government agencies and top corporations and financial institutions. She has also appeared on *Dateline* and *48 Hours*, and hosted her own PBS television show. For more information, visit *www.identitytheft.org*.

A safety check

HERE'S A STARTLING FACT: More than 500 million checks are forged annually. Fortunately, sophisticated security features can be built into checks to help consumers, businesses and banks avoid check fraud. Here's a look at the top safety features.

Microprint signature line
The signature line appears as a solid line and contains the words "AUTHORIZED SIGNATURE," printed in a small font that is legible when viewed closely or with a magnifying glass. If scanned or photocopied, the microprint text is not legible and appears as a broken line.

Padlock icon
A padlock symbol is printed on the check face to indicate that at least two overt (easily seen) security features are present. The icon alerts check handlers and criminals that security features are present.

Security warning box
A warning box printed on the back of the check indicates the security features present and what happens when a check is altered.

Original document
"ORIGINAL DOCUMENT" is printed in very light ink on the back of the check so that it cannot be easily copied or scanned.

Costco members can rest assured that checks ordered through the Costco Check Printing program have all of these safety features and more. The program offers personal and business checks at savings of up to 50 percent over bank prices.

Ordering is easy. Just go to costco.com and enter "Buy Checks" in the Search box. Executive Members receive an additional 20 percent off their orders. ▲

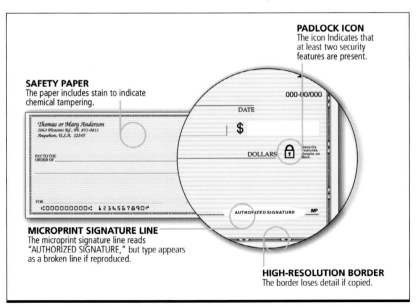

SAFETY PAPER
The paper includes stain to indicate chemical tampering.

PADLOCK ICON
The icon Indicates that at least two security features are present.

MICROPRINT SIGNATURE LINE
The microprint signature line reads "AUTHORIZED SIGNATURE," but type appears as a broken line if reproduced.

HIGH-RESOLUTION BORDER
The border loses detail if copied.

Surveillance to keep your business and home safe

KEEPING YOUR BUSINESS and home safe is critical for peace of mind, as well as to protect invaluable assets: your family, belongings, employees and products. A few smart steps, using the latest in surveillance technology, can help.

What does security mean to you?

The newest generation of professional-grade integrated surveillance systems are not only making it easier and more affordable to secure your home or business with the latest digital video technology, they are also being designed to serve you in ways you might never have imagined.

The best surveillance systems start by recognizing that your needs and expectations for security are unique to you and your home or business—and offer the best range of advanced features available to serve you.

Video surveillance basics

Video surveillance enables you to monitor a person, place or possession when you're in another area, in another room or traveling to another country. For this, you'll want to choose a system that has high-resolution cameras (for the best image quality), a high-quality LCD monitor with multiple display viewing options and real-time recording capabilities. It's important that the system can be connected to the Internet for remote viewing, playback and control from any computer, and can be expanded to accommodate more cameras.

Studies have shown that surveillance cameras significantly reduce crime in a monitored area. Whether you want to reduce the likelihood of your home being burglarized or reduce "shrinkage" at your store or warehouse, you'll want to select a system with multiple professional weatherproof cameras with night-vision capabilities that can be installed both indoors and outdoors.

Instant notification is key

Being notified when your security is potentially threatened will empower you to take action quickly. If this is important to you, purchase a system that offers a video motion-detection feature and can notify you of an alarm event by sending an e-mail to your handheld device or laptop.

Digital video recorders (DVRs) with advanced video compression technology will provide you with longer recording time, measured in weeks of continuous recording. For this, choose a system that offers programmable recording by channel/camera and a security-certified recording hard drive. The option of easily transferring video footage to an external storage device via USB will allow you to provide vital evidence to police for investigation and prosecution of a crime.

One closing note: You don't have to sacrifice beautiful interior design or your lifestyle to have professional-grade security. New surveillance systems offer incredibly thin LCD designs and a new range of performance. ◭

Resources for fighting scams

SCAM ARTISTS HAVE claimed millions of victims with various schemes over the Internet, on the telephone and through the mail. Here's a list of handy resources to get information on various scams, along with tips on avoiding them.

Better Business Bureaus alerts
The Council of Better Business Bureaus posts warnings to notify consumers and businesses about recently discovered fraudulent business scams, and also helps resolve buyer/seller complaints against a business, including mediation and arbitration services. Contact: *www.bbb.org*.

Bureau of Public Debt
Is it really a security and is it really backed by the U.S. government? Many schemes have been directed at banks, charities, companies and individuals by others seeking payment on fraudulent securities. The Bureau of Public Debt alerts people to these scams and helps protect them from being taken in. Contact: *www.treasurydirect.gov/instit/statreg/fraud/fraud.htm*.

Centers for Medicare & Medicaid Services
Fraud and abuse in the Medicaid and Medicare programs cost taxpayers billions of dollars each year and can pose a threat to patient health and safety. Learn about some of the most common ripoffs and schemes and how you can protect yourself. Contact: *www.cms.hhs.gov/FraudAbuseforConsumers*.

Coalition Against Insurance Fraud
The Coalition Against Insurance Fraud is a national organization dedicated exclusively to fighting insurance fraud through public advocacy and public education. Contact: *www.insurancefraud.org*.

Consumer Sentinel
See how law enforcement agencies all over the world work together to fight fraud, using Consumer Sentinel, an innovative international law enforcement fraud-fighting program. Contact: *www.consumer.gov/sentinel*.

Fight Back!
Since 1972, Fight Back! has provided information and raised awareness to help consumers help themselves in the marketplace. Some services require a fee. Contact: *www.fightback.com*.

National Consumer League's (NCL) Fraud Center
The NCL's Web site offers tips and instruction on avoiding a variety of scams on the Internet, over the phone and elsewhere. If you think you've been a victim of fraud, you can file a complaint through an online complaint form. Contact: *www.fraud.org.—Tim Talevich*

DID YOU KNOW? The best defense against fraud is being an informed consumer

THE ADVANTAGES OF MECHANICAL PENCILS

THERE ARE SEVERAL good reasons for using a mechanical pencil:

- They use refill leads so you don't have to throw them away. This is better for the environment.

- They never need sharpening, which means they're always ready to go.

- If the lead breaks, you can quickly click to advance another lead and keep on writing.

- They come in various lead diameter sizes to accommodate all types of writing styles.

- Most have a soft grip that helps reduce hand fatigue.

- They contain refill lead equivalent to a No. 2 lead pencil, which makes them perfect for taking scantron tests.

- They come in a variety of styles, meaning that you're certain to find one that's right for you.

Workplace ID theft: Are you at risk?

EVIDENCE SUGGESTS THAT identity theft in the workplace is more common than we think. Criminals can steal trade secrets, marketing research, consumer data and confidential employee information simply by Dumpster diving or accessing stolen laptops. The release of this proprietary information can have disastrous consequences for a business.

In the last two years, according to Ponemon Institute's "The Business Impact of Data Breach Survey" of May 2007, 85 percent of businesses experienced a data breach with startling financial implications. In 2005 alone, the theft of proprietary information cost businesses and consumers an incredible $56.6 billion, according to the report.

The first step toward safeguarding proprietary information is to shred all documents, discs or CDs before disposal. Shredding in your home office or small business is convenient, and it provides a greater sense of security because you know the information has been destroyed immediately.

In addition to shredding, follow these tips to help protect your business from the threat of workplace identity theft.

- Keep sensitive information and files in locked drawers or file cabinets.
- Limit access to electronic files—all files should be password protected and encrypted.
- Use updated anti-virus, anti-spyware and firewall software on all computers.
- Make sure wireless networks are protected with the proper security settings.
- Limit the use of Social Security numbers in the workplace and on items such as ID badges, time cards and paychecks.
- Conduct thorough background checks of potential employees.
- Use a locked mailbox to prevent mail theft.
- At the end of the day, log off computers and lock workstations or office doors.
- Pay attention to your surroundings when you travel and when you use a cell phone, laptop or BlackBerry. ▲

•**TIPS**&TRICKS

WHAT TO SHRED

INDIVIDUALS	BUSINESS ORGANIZATIONS*
ATM receipts	Accounts receivables
Bank statements	Client contacts
Canceled checks	Financial documents
Credit-card statements and receipts	Insurance records
Insurance policies	Medical records
Investment statements	Obsolete legal files
Junk mail	Occupational and Safety Health Administration 300 logs
Pay stubs	Payroll records
Retirement-plan contributions	Personnel files
Tax returns	Trade secrets
Wills and other legal documents	

* Depending on the laws in your area or the nature of your business, there may be privacy, retention and destruction guidelines that you are required to follow.

CHOOSING THE RIGHT SHREDDER

ASSESS YOUR POWER NEEDS

Because people tend to shred twice as much as they think they will, they often choose an underpowered shredder and end up frustrated by its inability to keep up with their work flow.

Choose a shredder based on sheet capacity, machine speed per shred and power rating, which is the amount of paper a machine can shred before the motor needs to rest (one cycle). Though a shredder may have a high sheet capacity per pass, it may not run very long or very fast—which means you get little power or value for your dollar.

Select a shredder that's powerful enough to destroy credit-card offers, unopened junk mail and even CDs.

ASSESS YOUR SECURITY RISK

Security level is determined by cut type. A strip-cut shredder typically slices paper into ¼-inch strips. Though strip cutters are better than tearing by hand, identity thieves could still reassemble and read your information.

Cross-cut and micro-cut shredders cut paper into secure particles more than 89 percent smaller than strip-cut shreds and are virtually impossible to reassemble and read.

CONSIDER ANY SPECIAL NEEDS

Because paper shredders have become more common in businesses and households, concerns have been raised about shredder safety. Look for brands with built-in safety features such as sensors that automatically stop a shredder from shredding if a user comes in contact with the paper opening.

If you have owned a shredder before, you are probably aware of features you are looking to improve upon in your next model. Jamming or noise may have been a frustration with your previous shredder. Consider choosing a shredder with an anti-jam feature to prevent jams and ensure quiet operation.

If emptying shredded waste neatly is a problem, choose a shredder with a pull-out bin for hassle-free waste disposal.

TIPS & TRICKS

SHARPEN THEIR FOCUS

IT'S TOUGH AT the best of times to keep younger students focused: They will look for any excuse to get up and move around the classroom. Young students are fascinated by pencil sharpeners, and have a tendency to spend a great amount of time sharpening their pencils. They will then break the pencil lead and need to sharpen again.

To stop this distraction, sharpen a bunch of pencils and keep them on your desk, in a flowerpot or a decorative cup. Once a day have one child come into the classroom early and take on the task of sharpening the class pencils. Sharpening 20 or more pencils in one sitting will soon have that pupil losing his or her appetite for this chore! ◪

Five steps to tame the paperwork monster

PILES OF PAPERWORK can be among the worst evils in any office. With today's offices being extremely hectic, most people cannot seem to find the time to file on a regular basis. So the piles build up, just like laundry or dirty dishes—and the more you allow them to build, the harder it is to work efficiently.

Organizational experts suggest filing your paperwork right away. As difficult as it can be sometimes, make a decision about each paper that crosses your desk immediately. If it is destined to be filed, do so right away. Here are five reasons why this strategy is a good one.

1. Prevent lost files and misfiles. The longer a document sits around on a desk, a shelf or anywhere else, the more chances it has of being misplaced, covered up, hidden or otherwise lost. If you let papers sit idle until you have a mountain of documents to put into the file, misfiling is likely to occur. Keep your papers filed and your mind will be at ease.

2. Keep confidential information secure. Many files contain sensitive information, such as priority data about budgets and personal information about employees and customers. Filing helps keep these documents secure.

3. Raise productivity. If everything that is supposed to be in a file is there when you or your co-workers need to access it, less time will be wasted searching for documents in the file drawer. This will help make your company more efficient and more productive. Devote 10 minutes at the end of each day to cleaning up your desk.

4. Avoid confusion. When papers are placed into a file immediately instead of being allowed to sit idle, the likelihood of grabbing the wrong document is decreased substantially, eliminating the possibility of confusing your documents. In a file, each paper should be neatly organized in its place with a file heading that clearly identifies what it contains. It will be a relief to know that everything is where it's supposed to be, and that if you need that particular document you know exactly where it is.

5. Create a cleaner desktop. Putting papers into a file right away means that you will have more room on your desktop—and that can change your whole outlook every morning when you start your day! ▲

➤ **TIPS**&TRICKS┤

FILING TIPS FOR TO-DO LISTS

Using a simple filing system can help you manage your projects.

• Decide on priority by dividing your projects into groupings for "this week," "this month" and "future projects."

• Label three file folders to hold project papers. Label the first folder "THIS WEEK," the second folder "THIS MONTH" and the third folder "FUTURE PROJECTS."

• Write a project list of the steps to be completed for each project and place it in the front of the appropriate folder.

• Review the folder contents each week, moving project papers to more active status as desired.

• As new projects arise, place the information and list of tasks in the appropriate folders.

Following these few easy steps will quickly take the hassle out of home projects.

Pop quiz for work-at-homers

OCCUPATIONAL HAZARDS IN the traditional workplace tend to be things such as heavy-machinery accidents, slippery floors or pulling a back muscle. But for work-at-homers, there's a different type of hazard: overwork.

While we tend to give kudos to hard-driving self-starters, too much work has many downsides—including, oddly enough, a potential decrease in productivity. To check if you've crossed the line, the *Almanac* offers this work-habit quiz.

1. Do you think of work all the time, even on weekends and vacations and right before falling asleep?
 ❑ Yes ❑ No

2. Do you get really angry when somebody disrupts you with a simple question or request, such as your kid wanting to play catch?
 ❑ Yes ❑ No

3. When you're not working, are you bored and restless and do you pace nervously around the house?
 ❑ Yes ❑ No

4. Do you fail to have a good laugh at least three times a week?
 ❑ Yes ❑ No

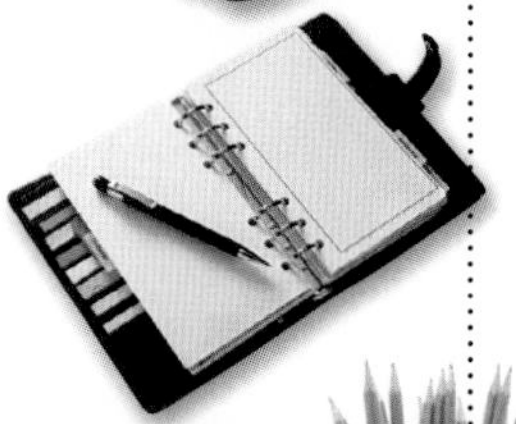

5. Do you have a conversation of more than three sentences about something other than work at least three times a week?
 ❑ Yes ❑ No

6. Are your pants or dresses more than one size bigger this year than a year ago?
 ❑ Yes ❑ No

7. Do you answer after-work phone calls "ABC Consulting," even if it's your mom calling?
 ❑ Yes ❑ No

8. Is your staple breakfast a chocolate-chip cookie and double-tall latte?
 ❑ Yes ❑ No

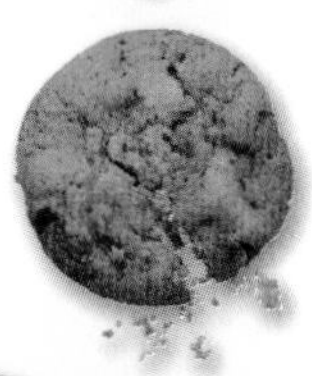

Test results:

5–8 "Yes" answers: Not good. It's time for a vacation, a meditation course and some serious soul-searching about getting a life.

3–4: You're pretty well balanced.

1–2: Slacker—get serious or get broke.—*Tim Talevich*

● MEMBER**TIP**

COURTESY OF
RUSS ALLEN
MARIETTA, GA

OFFICE SPACE IS always at a premium. To put more office tools in easy reach I had to reach out to the dining room for my solution. Now in a corner on my desk a lazy Susan puts most of my small office tools in easy reach. On mine, I have a three-hole punch, stapler, tape dispenser, scissors, rulers, white paper correction fluid, a paper clip holder, a Post-it holder, a stamp container, Kleenex and hand lotion. **Ⓐ**

The benefits of printing labels

ON AN AVERAGE DAY, the U.S. Postal Service (USPS) handles enough mail to circle the globe three times. But on the busiest day of the year (at holiday time), the mail could take an extra spin around the Earth!

Aside from being a mind-boggling pile of letters and packages, what does this actually mean for you and your mail?

Better than handwriting

With that much volume, a small amount of mail may get lost or not arrive in time. So you should do everything possible to make sure that doesn't happen to your mail. One way to lessen the risk of loss is to use printed labels. Why?

- They're easier to read than handwriting.
- You can include a complete ZIP code on every package and letter for more efficient machine processing.
- It's faster than doing it by hand.

Standing out in a crowd

It's always nice to help your mailings stand out—in a good way. People form impressions based on appearance. You want your mailings to set the right tone, whether it's formal and businesslike or warm and friendly.

Does it sound like a lot to think about? None of it's difficult, yet it can be time-consuming and labor intensive. But with the right tools, you can organize your mailing list, print labels that are up to USPS specifications and even give your mailings a customized look in very short order.

You can create a return-address label at the same time for a complete professional look (and timesaver).

• MEMBER**TIP**

COURTESY OF
ROBERT PASSARETTI
RIVERSIDE, CA

MOVING? I discovered a great tip while I was wrapping my collectibles. I happened to use up all my Scotch tape. It occurred to me that I had no use for all my old address labels: Why not use them in place of tape? The address labels worked great. ▲

Easy to do

If you use Microsoft® Office, help is available through the Mail Merge tool. Add-on software programs are available to simplify the label process. One such program is the Avery Wizard—offered free on the label maker's Web site, *www.avery.com*—which removes some of the steps from Mail Merge. The Avery Wizard can be launched from wherever you keep your mailing list, whether it's in Microsoft Word, Excel,® Outlook® or Access.® △

→ HELPFUL **HOW TO'S**

TIPS ON USING COMPUTER LABELS

- Only labels designed for inkjet printers should be used with an inkjet printer and only labels designed for laser printers should be used with a laser printer. Manual, copier and inkjet labels will not feed through consistently and may damage laser printers. Most laser labels are designed to work when printed directly from the automatic-feed tray.

- Before printing onto a label sheet, first print onto a blank piece of paper. Place the printed sheet in front of a label sheet, then hold the sheets up to a light to make sure the positioning is correct.

- Refer to the printer manual for loading and feeding recommendations. Many printers have special instructions for loading labels.

- Fan the label sheets before loading them into the paper tray. Do not bend the corners.

- For easier feeding in most printers, place label sheets in the paper tray on top of 25 sheets of plain paper.

- Store unused label sheets flat in the original box in a cool, dry place.

- Adjust the paper-width lever so that it barely touches the edge of the label stack and the labels don't buckle.

- For best results, after the labels are printed let the ink dry completely before removing the labels from the sheet.

- Sheets of inkjet and laser labels can be passed through a printer only once. The tight paper path of an inkjet printer can cause the label to curl on multiple passes through the printer. This could cause the label to jam or peel off inside the printer, resulting in an expensive repair bill.

- Sheets of laser labels can be passed through a laser printer only once because the heat of the printer causes the adhesive to soften. If a sheet of labels is passed through the printer a second time, the adhesive could ooze and adhere to the inner workings of the printer, causing the labels to jam or peel off.

- For trouble-free label printing, have your printer thoroughly cleaned on a regular basis.

Compressed gas: a smart cleaning solution

EXCEPT IN THE WORLD'S most controlled environments, such as certain laboratories and research facilities, dust is everywhere in our lives. One of the most effective ways to dissipate dust, particularly in sensitive areas, is through a compressed-gas cleaning duster.

The market for these dusters grew with the proliferation of computers and other high-tech equipment. Dust and dirt buildup in computers can lead to overheating and complete breakdown. But there are many other situations where compressed gas is the best cleaning solution.

Keeping your computer clean

Many people don't realize the importance of cleaning their computer on a regular basis. Here's how.

- Before starting any cleaning project, make sure your CPU and/or other equipment is turned off and has had a chance to cool down.
- Make sure the room you're working in is well ventilated.
- Blow compressed gas into the keyboard and gently around the monitor to dissipate dust and crumbs. You can also gently blow away dust from the ports in the back of the computer. Remember to never spray directly into the unit; doing so could damage the computer.

Cleaning equipment and photos

Compressed gas can be effective in cleaning equipment that might be damaged by normal dusting measures. Examples include:

- Photographic negatives, which attract dust and lint.
- Slides, which are fragile and shouldn't be touched. Cleaning is an important step before digitizing your slides.
- Cloth speaker grilles, which can be damaged or spotted by a wet rag.
- Smoke detectors, which should be cleaned twice a year.
- Pictures being prepared for framing. Remove the dust that clings to the glass.

Around the house

Compressed gas has useful applications around the house and the office. This option often saves time over traditional dusting methods and is more effective. Compressed gas can be useful for cleaning:

- Silk flower collections. It can be very time-consuming to wipe down flower collections with a cloth.

THE DO'S AND DON'TS OF USING COMPRESSED-GAS CLEANERS

Because compressed gas is an aerosol product, the contents can be hazardous if used improperly. One big danger is inhalant abuse, or "huffing." It's critical that people who use aerosol products, parents and children understand the seriousness of this practice. To discourage huffing with its aerosol products, Falcon has added an invisible, bitter agent to Dust-Off and has been an industry leader in warning consumers about the dangers of huffing.

Other safety tips to follow when using compressed gas are:

• Read the back-panel warning information carefully before using.

• Clear the nozzle prior to use by pulling the trigger in a series of short blasts.

• Hold the can in the most upright position during use.

• Use in a sufficiently ventilated area.

• Contact a physician in cases of inhalation or contact with eyes or skin.

• Don't tilt excessively or shake the can before or during use.

• Don't leave in direct sunlight or enclosed vehicles.

• Don't use near potential ignition sources, open flames or spark-producing equipment (for example, a paper shedder).

• MEMBER**TIP**

COURTESY OF
CYNTHIA FALTER
RANCHO PALOS VERDES, CA

THOSE BOXES THAT your checks come in are a handy size to help organize office drawers by holding pens, pencils, folder tabs, paper clips, rubber bands, etc. △

• Collectibles, such as figurines, dishware, model trains, holiday displays and wicker baskets. Cleaning collectibles is difficult because of the delicacy of the items. Rags can get caught on fragile objects.

• Cloth mini-blinds—another time-consuming chore.

• In between piano keys.

• Drapes, lamp covers and shelves that contain books and other objects.

In the garage and shop

Cars have lots of nooks and crannies. Dust isn't the only culprit that builds up in a car. A light coat of dirt is common in warm climates, and food crumbs are inevitable.

A rag often can't get to hard-to-reach areas in the car, including dashboards, dashboard vents (spray sideways, not directly), radio control panels, areas around the steering column, the center console and the seat rails.

Before using a compressed-gas cleaner in a vehicle, make sure to open your car windows or doors for sufficient ventilation. After spraying, vacuum the car to remove the materials that were dislodged.

Compressed gas is also a great way to clean tools, such as saws with accumulations of sawdust.

Whatever you use a compressed-gas cleaner for, be careful not to tilt the duster at too extreme an angle; in doing so you run the risk of dispensing the product in liquid form. It is best to keep the can in the most upright position as you spray. △

NORCOM

Tools For Knowledge
Griffin, GA 30224
www.norcominc.com

IN DEFENSE OF WRITING PADS

THESE DAYS MANY people use computers to take notes. But there are several good reasons to stay with the standard: writing pads. Here are a few:

- No batteries are involved, so they never run out of power.

- They're extremely portable and versatile, and they come in a variety of sizes.

- You don't have to worry about losing the information due to a data crash.

- They allow for a personal touch.

- They are easily disposable and can be recycled. Plus, they can be shredded for safety. △

ACCO BRANDS

ORGANIZING WITH THREE-RING BINDERS

GET YOUR PAPERWORK under control, make your office space more manageable and upgrade your presentations with these simple binder tips.

PRESENTATION: Customize the front cover and spine of a binder for professional-looking presentations. Find templates to help create a unique look at *www.wilsonjones.com.*

ORGANIZATION: Don't let regular communications, monthly reports or annual tax documents take over your office space. Consider using indexes and sheet protectors for further organization to help you find what you need—when it's needed.

STORAGE: If space is tight, consider binders as an alternative to file cabinets for storing documents. They're also an easy way to store financial, legal or marketing documents that need to be shared among departments. △

■■DIXON®
DIXON TICONDEROGA COMPANY

LOOK FOR SAFE PENCILS

RECENTLY, CONCERNS HAVE arisen about the safety of lead and paint. During the Middle Ages, lead was used to make a mark on paper. Today, the black cores in pencils are a combination of graphite and clay, not lead. The coating on the outside of pencils is lacquer, not paint.

Look for the Pencil Makers Association (PMA) seal of approval on packages of pencils. This seal is a guarantee

from the PMA that all materials used in the production of the pencils are totally safe for consumers. The PMA certification program guarantees that only pencils manufactured from materials that are free from toxins receive this endorsement. △

Home Project Primer

WE'RE DOING EVERYTHING on our own these days, from having babies at home without medical intervention ("Do-It-Yourself Delivery," *Washington Post*, July 31, 2007) to "Do It Yourself Funerals" (NPR's *Morning Edition*, December 8, 1997). Of course, most do-it-yourself projects are less dramatic. We're painting our houses, installing hot tubs, landscaping our yards, recaulking bathtubs, adding crown molding and restoring old cars.

Some projects will eventually require a redo. According to the National Association of Home Builders, toilets, wood floors, insulation, and steel and wood exterior doors should last the lifetime of your house. Wood decks should go about 20 years, depending on climate, kitchen faucets should last about 15 years, linoleum floors have a life expectancy of about 25 years and furnaces can be expected to last 15 to 20 years. ▲

Using software for your home remodeling project

IN THE NOT TOO DISTANT PAST, designing a major remodel at home required endless drawing and erasing, moving around heavy furniture to try things out and doing a lot of guesswork. Today, computers and special software enable pros and do-it-yourselfers alike to conceive and execute major remodeling projects—all with a few clicks of the mouse.

These programs use sophisticated drawing technology to show things such as a kitchen or a backyard, then enable you to place new objects in those areas. In essence, you're able to try out a lot of different looks and concepts without lifting a finger. And many of these programs are easy enough for nontechnical people (that is, most of us) to use.

Starting from scratch

The nature of your project dictates which step to take first. If you're starting from scratch, the software program can show a blank room or an empty backyard, based on the dimensions that you enter. From there, you can create a floor plan, add objects, test various window and door designs, create custom trim, etc. The detail available goes as deep as electrical and plumbing systems.

If you're remodeling rather than starting from scratch, your camera is an essential tool. With some programs, you can take photos of your yard or room, import the image into your computer and make changes.

Here's a step-by-step example to show how easily this works for a landscape project.

1. Take a digital picture of the front of your house. Be sure the lighting is bright for the best effect. Sunsets and sunrises produce the best light, but taking the photo on a sunny day works too.

2. Save the photo in a folder on your computer.

3. Using the photo tool in your home-design software, import your photo directly into the project. Find the picture of your house that you saved on your computer and select it. The software will import the 2-D image into the 3-D program and you will be able to navigate around the image.

4. Now you can easily add plants, trees, shrubs, outdoor fireplaces and so on to your project by simply dragging and dropping them from the landscaping objects libraries that are part of the software.

Your finished project will give you a realistic view of what your house will look like after all of the changes.

The software even knows what plants are indigenous to your geographic location, so you will be picking plants that will actually grow. And you can use the automatic-growth feature in the software to see what the plants will look like in five or even 10 years.

Choosing the right program

Home-design programs can tackle many other chores, such as estimating construction costs, thanks to databases built into the programs. And some have powerful architectural tools, based on the same sophisticated programs that professional architects use. Given the variety of programs available, and the unique nature of your project, it's smart to make sure you choose the right one for your needs.

Good advice on finding the right program is offered by *eHow.com*, a Web site offering tips on "How to do just about everything." The Web site recommends following these steps:

1. Decide what sort of software you want. There are different programs for decorating and furniture arranging, landscaping, painting and from-the-ground-up home design. Some are available in bundles that have it all.

2. Read the software's system requirements to make sure it'll work on your computer.

3. Take your time learning the software. The best design programs are complicated, and you won't be drawing plans the day you install them.

4. Think about the features that are most important to you. For example, do you want to see a 3-D view of your sketch, build a rough construction budget or add landscaping to your design? Different programs have different features.

5. Measure the lot you'll be building on, if you've already selected it. You'll need the contours of the land as well as its dimensions.

6. Ask paint dealers if they have paint-simulating software. These programs let you apply various color schemes to a digital photo of your house. ◭

Home and backyard before.

A dream home and backyard can be envisioned using design programs.

The right window coverings for a room

WHETHER YOU'RE REDECORATING a room, building a new home or noticing a cold draft coming through an old window, you may want to think about your window coverings. Window coverings dramatically affect the mood and ambience of a room, adding color and style and helping you control the incoming light.

Start by looking at how you use the room. Do you need extra privacy? Are you concerned about energy efficiency? Do you have hard-to-reach windows? What's your personal style? Here's a look at the popular options.

Wood blinds in rich stains and classic colors make homes warmer in winter and cooler in summer, keeping energy costs down. More economical than wood yet as substantial and durable, **composite** and **faux wood blinds** are made of synthetic materials and are suitable for bath or kitchen areas as they don't absorb moisture.

Cellular shades provide a soft look and the highest level of insulation of any window covering. Their construction forms pockets of air to keep out winter cold and summer heat. Fabrics are available in light-filtering or room-darkening opacities in a full color palette.

Sun screens and solar shades allow you to control light, heat and glare without losing your view. Also, these screens and shades protect your furnishings from fading because they block ultraviolet light.

DID YOU KNOW? Opening blinds and shades on south-facing windows during winter days helps to naturally heat your home

Top row, left to right: bottom-up/top-down cellular shade; faux wood blind; real wood blind; Roman shade.

Bottom row, left to right: sheer horizontal shade; vertical blind; sun screens.

HOW TO MEASURE A WINDOW

To measure a window for a covering, first determine whether you want an inside or outside mount. An inside mount is installed within the window casing, while an outside mount is installed outside the window casing, covering an area larger than the window itself.

Using a tape measure, follow these three simple steps:

WIDTH
Measure in three places, from left to right; use the smallest measurement.

HEIGHT
Measure in three places, from top to bottom; use the smallest measurement.

DIAGONAL
Measure in two places, from top left to bottom right and top right to bottom left. If diagonal measurements are not equal, the window opening is not square and you may want to consider an outside mount for optimal light control and aesthetics.

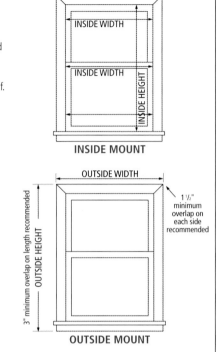

INSIDE MOUNT

OUTSIDE MOUNT

HOW TO ORDER WINDOW COVERINGS AT COSTCO

MAKE YOUR COLOR AND FABRIC SELECTION by viewing and feeling an actual swatch of the materials. You can check out a sample book at your local Costco warehouse, view the fabrics in the warehouse display or request fabric swatches on *www.memberblinds.com*. A checkout fee will be refunded to you when you return the sample book.

MEASURE YOUR WINDOWS following the how-to-measure instructions for the product you have selected. For convenience, the Web site listed above has a worksheet you can use. Print it out and fill in the measurements.

FILL OUT THE COSTCO WHOLESALE PURCHASE FORM at your local Costco, or you can take it home to complete. For step-by-step ordering assistance, call toll-free 1-800-538-9419 or send an e-mail to *member_blinds@sourcenw.com*.

PAY FOR YOUR ORDER at the warehouse by bringing the completed form to a cashier.

MAIL THE GREEN COPY using the postage-paid envelope provided on the purchase order form. (These can also be faxed.) Your order will not be manufactured until a confirming green copy of the order is received.

The blinds you have ordered will be shipped directly to the address specified on the purchase order form. Install and enjoy your new window coverings! △

Sheer horizontal window shades, which suspend soft fabric vanes between two sheer fabric facings, provide a filtered view and privacy.

Motorized blinds and shades operate with the push of a button to create instant privacy or light. They're especially helpful for hard-to-reach windows above a counter, above a bathtub or in a tall foyer.

Want even more choices? Consider sleek, contemporary vertical blinds. For more casual décor, choose natural shades in woven bamboos, jutes, reeds or straws. And don't forget about colorful and affordable 1-inch aluminum mini-blinds. △

Choosing the perfect laminate floor

WITH SO MANY THINGS TO CONSIDER, choosing the perfect laminate floor for your home can be a daunting task. But here are three easy steps to choosing the right floor for you.

Pick the color

Your new laminate floor will form the design foundation of your room, so decide what color will best create the look you want.

Do you want a light, medium or dark tone? Consider the wood tones in your room's cabinetry and furniture as well as the wall colors, fabrics, rugs and accessories. If you want your floor to create a strong contrast, pick one at the opposite end of the light-to-dark spectrum. If you want the floor to blend in with its surroundings, pick a tone that is similar to the other items in the room. Lighter floors will tend to make the room look brighter; darker floors will add more drama.

   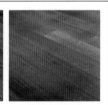

YELLOW/GOLD BROWNS
These colors work well in modern interiors where a clean, light look is desired. As these go darker, they become more dramatic and develop a time-worn patina.

AMBER BROWNS
These coordinate well with most of today's popular cabinet colors and are ideal choices if you want your floor to blend in.

CHOCOLATE BROWNS
These are the true browns that are not heavily influenced by other colors and tend to coordinate with virtually any other color in a room. If you want the floor to take a secondary role in the room, these colors would be ideal.

RED BROWNS
If you want drama, the red-influenced browns never fail to get noticed. Many of the products in this color family use exotic woods as their inspiration.

Choose the design

Each floor has a design that, along with its color, will make a big difference in your room's final effect.

Calm looks. If you want a floor that doesn't assert itself too strongly, focus on birch, maple, European oak and exotic wood designs with straight grain patterns and lighter colors.

Stronger looks. If you want your floor to make a statement, look at red oak, hickory, antique maple and walnut designs that have stronger grain patterns using medium to dark colors.

Flooring width. The plank or strip width will have an impact on the look of your floor. Don't worry so much about the actual size of the plank. Instead, focus on the size of the plank in the design.

- **Narrow strips.** Small strips range from 2 to 3 inches in width. Reminiscent of traditional strip wood flooring, these designs are perfect for rooms where the floor should be secondary to its surroundings. They tend to be calmer and more sedate than wide plank looks.
- **Wide planks.** Large planks range from 4 to 6 inches in width. Wide plank designs use everything from sophisticated exotic wood looks to rustic hand-scraped looks to traditional oak and cherry designs. They tend to be more dramatic and add character wherever they are used.

Choose a surface and edge treatment

Once you've narrowed down the color, design and strip width of the flooring, think about the surface and edge details.

Surface finishes. Choices include smooth finishes with light grain texture, medium grain texture and heavily textured hand-scraped and soft-scraped surfaces. Combined with the color and design, the surface finish will determine whether your floor plays a background role or is a starring player.

Edge treatments. There are three primary edge treatments:

- **Square edge.** This is the most traditional edge effect. With this treatment, the color and design create the biggest impact.
- **Micro-beveled edge.** These planks have a small amount of the edge removed, creating a more distinctive look and making the individual planks stand out more. These floors have a more sophisticated appearance than traditional square-edge looks.
- **Rustic edge.** This is the most dramatic edge. Its wide beveled edge is ideal for rustic hand-scraped designs and soft-scraped designs. These floors have the most character and are perfect for rooms meant to hearken back to earlier times.

Have fun and remember that the only rule you need to follow is this: Pick the floor that makes you happy! 🄰

Going green: new life for old carpet

WHAT DO YOU DO WITH OLD CARPET when it comes to upgrading your home or office? Unfortunately, the usual solution has been to send used carpet to a landfill.

But new technology and improved business practices by flooring manufacturers have created a new option. Carpet made from Type 6 nylon (N6) can be recycled.

Here's how it works. Specialized recycling facilities, such as the Shaw Evergreen Nylon Recycling Facility in Augusta, Georgia, can take carpet made from N6 and remake it into new nylon fiber over and over again—without the loss of beauty or durability.

A large percentage of carpet found in American households incorporates N6. The recycling process is known as "cradle to cradle"—breaking down a used product into its raw material and rebuilding the raw material back into the same product. So far, only N6 has this "cradle to cradle" capability. Many collection sites can "downcycle" other carpet fiber types into items such as automotive parts.

What kind of impact does this recycling effort have? Since the opening of its facility in February 2007, Shaw has recycled more than 75 million pounds of post-consumer N6 carpet. The facility will recycle more than 100 million pounds of nylon carpet each year, which would have otherwise gone to landfills.

There's an additional bonus to recycling carpet: Consumers, installers and retailers who recycle their carpet at designated carpet collection sites can avoid paying fees associated with the disposal of used carpet. This can help lower costs on remodeling projects.

To find out if a carpet is made from recyclable N6 nylon, look at the label on the back (certain brands, such as Shaw's Anso® nylon, use N6 exclusively). And don't think these carpets are in any way inferior to their nonrecyclable counterparts. These stylish products feature a wide variety of crisp, clean colors and cutting-edge designs—and they are extremely durable and inherently stain resistant.

A good resource for finding carpet collection sites is at *www.shawfloors. com/recycle*. Shaw maintains more than 50 carpet collection sites throughout the nation, and this network is growing. Another helpful resource is the Carpet America Recovery Effort at *www.carpetrecovery.org*. ◭

THIS&THAT

WHAT IS TYPE 6 NYLON (N6)?

There are two types of nylon fiber, Nylon 6,6 and Nylon 6, which differ according to their molecular structure. Currently only Nylon 6 can be completely recycled into dyeable carpet fiber. Nylon 6,6 is usually "downcycled" into other products, such as automotive parts.

Developing a floor plan

INSTALLING NEW FLOORING is one of the most dynamic ways to transform the look and feel of a home, but it's also one of the more costly home-decor decisions consumers make. According to the World Floor Covering Association (*www.wfca.org*), the type of flooring you choose will determine not only the mood of a room, but how practical it will be.

Because most types of flooring are relatively permanent, the flooring you install should be tailored to the people who use it. Here are some pros and cons of five popular flooring types.

Hardwood

Pros: Will usually last a lifetime. Easy to clean. Warm colors. Coordinates well with almost any décor. Usually easy to repair when necessary.

Cons: May scratch or dent. Easily damaged by moisture (not recommended for bathrooms); color can fade over time. May require professional installation.

Laminate

Pros: Realistically simulates wood and other natural materials. Extremely durable. Easy to clean. Can usually be installed throughout a home. Easier for homeowners to install, depending on general home-improvement skill level. One of the more affordable flooring options.

Cons: Quality varies greatly, depending on manufacturer. Though more durable than wood, may scratch or dent.

Ceramic tile

Pros: Wide variety of styles, patterns, colors, textures and sizes. Can achieve different looks and feels through installation techniques. Moisture resistant. Easy to clean. Extremely durable.

Cons: Grout lines can stain if not properly installed. Costly to change design or color scheme. May require professional installation. Should be resealed regularly. Cost varies greatly, depending on the type of tile.

Vinyl

Pros: Wide variety of styles, patterns, colors and sizes. Water resistant. Tends to be quiet and comfortable. Easy to clean; affordable.

Cons: Not terribly durable, depending on manufacturer and grade. Usually requires professional installation.

Carpet

Pros: Many colors and textures available. Warm, extremely comfortable and quiet. Easy to replace.

Cons: Requires frequent vacuuming and should be professionally cleaned every 12 to 18 months. Cleaning may require restretching. ▲

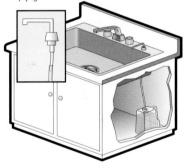

Romancing your stone tabletop

NATURAL STONE TABLETOPS are popular because of their beauty. Marble, granite, travertine, quartzite limestone and many other popular natural stone surfaces are sought after because of their beauty and durability. All of these popular natural materials are created through eons of geological activity and are not easily or accurately replicated by synthetics.

You'd think these surfaces, being stone, are impervious to damage. However, all natural stone is absorbent to some degree. This is why all quality stone furniture is protected with a specially formulated sealer to minimize stains that can result from accidental spills and exposure to other potentially harmful substances.

Most manufacturers of stone furniture use high-quality sealers that protect stone surfaces from nearly all stains and acidic liquids. These sealers do not normally break down over time or with normal outdoor (or indoor) use.

To help protect the sealer, most manufacturers recommend using coasters and place mats when dining. Coasters help absorb moisture from "sweaty" drinking glasses and prevent mugs from leaving rings. Place mats help catch spills and prevent dishes, platters and flatware from scratching tabletops during meals. If your stone tabletop is outdoors, cover it with a quality furniture cover when it's not in use.

While high-quality stone tabletops should not require frequent reapplications of sealer to maintain protection, they still require frequent cleaning. Nearly all manufacturers recommend using clean water and mild dish soap. Clean the tabletop with a soft white cloth or sponge, and don't use scouring creams or other abrasive cleansers, or acid- or petroleum-based products, including cleaners that contain lemon or vinegar.

After applying mild dish soap with a soft cloth or sponge, rinse the tabletop with plenty of clean water and dry it thoroughly to prevent buildup of any residue from minerals that might be in your water supply—even if you have softened water.

Accidental spills need to be cleaned up immediately. The aforementioned sealer is a protective barrier that minimizes potential damage, allowing you more cleanup time, but addressing spills quickly will increase the longevity of the sealer. A

Ten steps to a perfect paint job

IF YOU ARE A DO-IT-YOURSELFER, you can spruce up your house by re-painting parts of it or even the whole structure. The right tools and techniques will help to ensure a professional look. Here are some pro painting tips to use with a spray painter.

1. Remove peeling paint and dirt by sanding, scraping or pressure-washing the surface. Patch small cracks and seams with caulk and add primer to any bare wood. Remove shutters and cover windows, doors, the ground around the house, bushes, flowers, trees, deck, etc.

2. When selecting primer, choose a breathable oil primer to allow moisture buildup from inside the house to escape.

3. Choose a color that will complement existing features such as the roof, doors, railings, brick or other surfaces that will not be painted.

4. Dark colors require more maintenance because they fade quicker and are more difficult to touch up. Remember that light colors make objects seem larger; dark colors make them seem smaller, but can be used to draw attention to details.

5. Glossy surfaces are easier to clean; however, the glossier the surface, the more likely it is to show imperfections.

6. Don't forget to test your color in a small area before you paint—colors almost always look different on the surface than you imagine they will.

7. Cover the primer with two coats of 100 percent acrylic latex paint to resist mildew and hold color best. Avoid painting if rain or very high humidity is predicted within 24 hours, and be sure to finish early enough for the surface to dry before evening dew sets in.

8. Practice on a piece of scrap wood or cardboard before you spray to test your spray pattern. Start painting from top to bottom in back-and-forth or up-and-down motions that are slightly overlapping.

9. Keep your arm moving at a constant speed and keep the sprayer at a constant distance from the surface—between 10 and 14 inches is recommended. Be sure to stop the flow of paint at the end of each stroke before moving to the next stroke. This will help you avoid an uneven finish.

10. If you are going to be painting a surface with details, spray the base (or dominant) coat first and paint the details with a brush.

Remember to allow proper time for the paint to dry, and enjoy a home that is protected from winter's harsh elements. ◮

Installing a water-saving toilet

YOU MIGHT NOT REALIZE IT, but the biggest water user in the home is the toilet. Research finds that the average household uses 185 to 291 gallons of water per day, with 60 percent of a family's water bill going down the drain in the toilet and shower, 20 percent in the laundry and the remaining 20 percent in the kitchen.

Older toilets are particularly big water guzzlers, using 3 or more gallons per flush (gpf)—or more than 20 gallons per person per day. New toilets can reduce that consumption significantly. Replacing an older 3.5 gpf toilet from the 1980s with a 1.6 gpf toilet could save more than 2 gallons per flush, for a total household savings of 12,000 gallons of water per year.

Even more water savings can be earned by installing the new dual-flush toilets. Dual-flush technology features two buttons: one for liquid waste, which uses a partial flush (0.8 gallon) and the other for solid waste, using a full flush (1.6 gallons). In most cases the partial flush is sufficient for all waste. Depending on the number of users in a home, a dual-flush toilet can save thousands of gallons of water while reducing the load on sewers and septic systems.

Installing a new water-saving toilet isn't very difficult for do-it-yourselfers. You'll need a putty knife, a small wrench, a socket set, a flat-head screwdriver and a level. Having a scraper and a few old towels at the ready is a good idea. See the directions on the opposite page.

By the way, some municipalities offer rebates of up to $50 for purchasing a qualifying water-saving toilet. Toilets listed under "MaP" and "HET" are typically eligible. Check your local government for details. ◮

THIS&THAT

A LOOK AT THE NUMBERS

While most toilets appear much the same on the outside, their water consumption can vary greatly, as can their effect on your water bill. Before the 1950s toilets used a whopping 7 gallons per flush (gpf). By the 1960s toilets flushed with 5.5 gallons, and by the 1980s it was down to 3.5 gpf. Due in large part to the water conservation movement and the National Energy Policy Act, by 1994 toilets could not exceed 1.6 gallons per flush.

Despite the new regulations, it's estimated there are more than 100 million outdated toilets still in use in the United States alone, consuming 3.5 to 7 gallons of water each time they are flushed. It all adds up to a lot of wasted water.

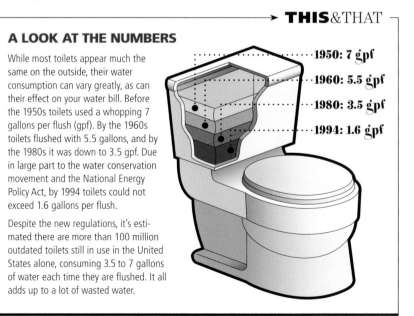

1950: 7 gpf
1960: 5.5 gpf
1980: 3.5 gpf
1994: 1.6 gpf

HELPFUL **HOW TO'S** ←

1. REMOVE EXISTING TOILET (IF NECESSARY).
- Turn off and disconnect the water supply.
- Dismount floor bolts and remove the old toilet.
- Remove the old wax ring with a putty knife.

2. PLACE THE NEW WAX RING ON THE TOILET.
- Invert the toilet on the floor (cushion it to prevent damage).
- Install the new wax ring over the horn on the bottom of the toilet, with the tapered end of the ring facing up.
- Apply a thin bead of tub and tile sealant around the toilet base.

3. SET THE TOILET ON THE FLANGE.
- Set the floor bolts into the flange channel. Turn 90 degrees, and slide into place 6 inches (152 mm) apart and parallel to the wall.
- Place the toilet over the flange, with the bolts projecting through the mounting holes of the toilet.
- Press down firmly, while gently twisting and rocking the toilet.

4. MOUNT THE NUTS.
- Hand-tighten the washers and nuts onto the bolts.
- Alternately tighten the nuts with a wrench until they are snug.
- Don't overtighten the nuts, or the base may become damaged.

5. INSTALL BOLT CAPS.
- Cut screws to size before installing caps (if needed).
- Install caps on washers and nuts.

6. CONNECT THE WATER SUPPLY.
- Install the braided hose onto the threads of the tank fill valve.
- Connect the braided hose and the water supply pipe with the angle supply valve.
- If needed, wrap plumber's tape around the threads of the connections to avoid leakage.

7. SET TANK COVER.
- Carefully position the tank cover on the tank.
- Be sure to position the push button and the flush valve so they are facing in the right direction.
- The large push button should be in line with the yellow button on the flush valve, and the small one in line with the blue button.

8. INSTALL THE TOILET SEAT.
- Put the toilet seat on the toilet. Put bolts through the holes of the toilet seat and the bowl. Tighten the nuts on the bolts with a screwdriver until they are snug.
- Snap the caps covering the screws on the seat into place.

9. FINAL CHECK.
- Turn on the water supply to the toilet.
- Flush the tank and check for leakage.
- Carefully tighten any connections that are leaking.

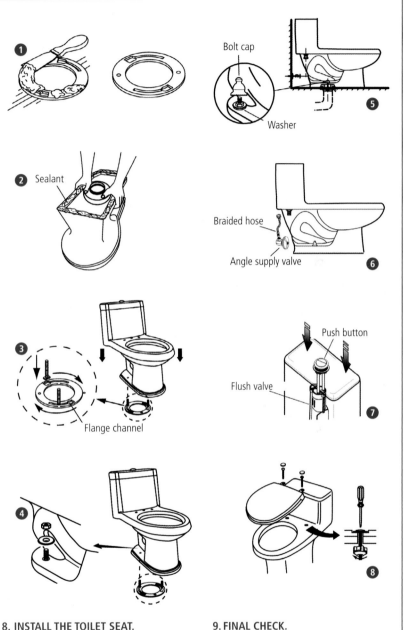

①

② Sealant

③ Flange channel

④

⑤ Bolt cap / Washer

⑥ Braided hose / Angle supply valve

⑦ Push button / Flush valve

⑧

Diagnose and treat those pool problems

By Donald Lapa

IT WOULD BE NICE if every pool water problem could be prevented. But even the most diligent adherence to routine maintenance programs can't eliminate every algae bloom, stain or odor. If you're a pool owner, you're undoubtedly all too familiar with these problems and the products available to treat them. Here is a guide to some of the most common obstacles to pool owner happiness, and some solutions.

Before any problem can be treated, however, the water chemistry must be checked, preferably by an experienced person who can diagnose, solve and, hopefully, prevent future pool water problems.

Cloudy water

The culprit is either water chemistry imbalance or insufficient filter operation. Factors include algae, high levels of total dissolved solids, body oils, insufficient sanitizer levels, high pH or hardness levels, channeling sand (torn or damaged grids) or poor water circulation due to debris in a skimmer, pump basket or elsewhere.

Solutions: One of the simplest ways to treat cloudiness is to drain about a foot of water from the pool and replace it with fresh water.

Many clarifiers on the market remove particulate matter when a properly operating filter just can't catch it. These products—chelating agents, flocculants or sequestering agents—generally coagulate particles. Then the filter can catch the larger clusters, or the clusters become heavy enough to fall to the bottom of the pool, where they can easily be vacuumed.

"Shocking" the pool also helps clear water by oxidizing organics such as algae and bacteria. When cloudiness is caused by algae blooms, there are other factors to consider (see below).

Algae

Floating green algae is the most common, followed by yellow or mustard algae and black algae. All forms of algae can eventually root in pool walls, but the more common types generally don't do so as quickly, or as stubbornly, as black algae. Algae blooms can usually be blamed on inadequate sanitization and too often greet pool owners at the beginning of the season.

Solutions: Different types of algae can be treated with particular specialty products. Some algae treatments remove essential nutrients from the water, thus starving the algae, and are called chlorine enhancers, not algaecides. Chlorine also kills algae; therefore, chlorine shocks are usual algae remedies.

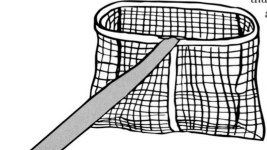

One aspect of algae treatment is brushing. Some say algae should always be brushed to expose as many cells as possible. Others say only black algae requires brushing, and then with a wire brush. Whatever brushing regimen and algae-control product you choose, it's important to make sure the product is well circulated.

Stains

Stains are either organic or metallic. Organic stains develop when leaves, for example, sit on the pool floor and transfer tannins to the surface. Metallic stains can occur when pH fluctuates. When pH drops, the corrosive water can attack a copper heat exchanger, drawing copper ions into the flow and then depositing the copper in another form as the pH comes back up.

Solutions: Identify what you're dealing with—color can be a good indicator. Greenish blue, blue or black stains indicate copper. Reddish or brown spots are usually iron. Tan or purple point to manganese. Grays, however, can be caused by a litany of things.

Most common are copper and iron. Low pH and high chlorine levels and copper are the conditions that lead to most stains. Once you've identified the culprit, the cure can probably be found in the right bottle.

There are two ways to approach a stain—gradually or aggressively. Some preventive products can be added weekly or biweekly as part of routine chemistry maintenance and can eventually remove existing stains. It may seem expensive, but it's less expensive than an acid wash, an aggressive approach in which chemicals are applied directly to the stain.

Discolored water

This category of pool water problem is perhaps the most mysterious. Manganese can appear brown or black. Copper and iron may give the water a greenish cast, although brown hues have also been identified as iron. Algae blooms and cloudiness, discussed earlier, can also be the root of discolored water.

Solutions: There are two families of products that help remove metal from pool water. Sequestrates tie up metals so they can't come out of solution. Some consider this a temporary fix because metals aren't removed from the pool system. Instead, they recommend flocculants, which collect unwanted particles into clusters that can then be filtered or vacuumed.

Eye/skin irritations

This condition is usually caused by insufficient sanitizer levels or pH outside recommended ranges, although swimmers often think there's too much chlorine in the pool.

Solutions: First, test to see what's out of whack: It could be pH, alkalinity, sanitizer levels, some other factor or any combination of these. Then adjust the water chemistry balance and shock the pool to convert unwanted, irritating chloramines back into the acceptable form of chlorine. It is generally accepted in the pool industry that chlorine is most effective at pH levels between 7.2 and 7.8. After shocking the pool, keep swimmers out until the chlorine residual drops below 3 ppm.

Scum

A combination of soaps and oils from skin, detergents from swimsuits, cosmetics and lotions, and even gritty air pollution can accumulate on the water surface—or in skimmers, filters, etc.—and cause general unpleasantness. Scum is rarely harmful, however.

Solutions: Tile cleaners will remove scum lines. Also, most enzyme products break down scum effectively. Besides simply keeping the pool free from scum-causing culprits, try one of the numerous scum-absorbing products on the market. ◮

Costco member Donald J. Lapa has owned and operated Mister Poolman *(www.misterpoolman.com)* in the Los Angeles area for more than 20 years.

Purchasing your next family heirloom

THE HISTORY OF FURNITURE making goes back centuries, but many of the techniques that distinguished the best furniture then are still found in high-quality furniture today. If chosen carefully, new furniture will provide years of service and be in your family for years to come.

The right materials and techniques

Hardwoods such as cherry, maple, ash and mahogany are strong and dent resistant. High-quality furniture is generally constructed of hardwoods, sometimes solid, sometimes mixed with veneers. Avoid paper laminates. Furniture made with paper laminates and softwood is inexpensive but generally will quickly show signs of wear.

A sure sign of superior construction is evident in the joinery. Dovetailing, a technique that uses a series of interlocking pins and tails cut from the wood, keeps drawer joints from pulling apart.

A well-applied finish can add years of service to wood furniture and enhance its natural beauty. A proper finish will also provide resistance to temperature changes and moisture. Look for uniform color and shine across the finish, and consider choosing a distressed or rough-hewn finish for furniture in high-traffic areas to hide nicks and scratches.

Dovetailing

Smart and functional touches

High-quality furniture should withstand the rigors of daily use. European hinges are durable and easy to adjust, and add value to any armoire or desk. Full-extension metal ball-bearing drawer slides will endure the strenuous test of everyday use. Felt or rubber stops add a nice cushion to closing doors and seated shelves, and prevent wear or rattle from shock or vibration.

European hinges

Consider ergonomics as well. A properly designed desk or chair should allow you to sit in a relaxed, natural position, looking straight ahead at your work, with all of your peripherals within easy reach.

Also, assess your technical needs for built-in options such as keyboard trays, power centers and plug-ins or routers for electronic devices. And don't forget about the time-tested benefits of organized storage, adequate task space, ease of use and comfort.

Consider the present and the future

When making a furniture purchase, you will most likely be trying to solve an immediate need, but keep future considerations in mind. Sketch a simple floor plan or use an online room planner. Consider dimensions, color, other pieces in the room and the short- and long-term use of the room or space. Buy furniture for the way you want the room to be, not the way it is.

If you do your homework and look for these lasting furniture features, your next furniture purchase could become your next family heirloom. △

All Costco tire technicians are Michelin Certified. That means they've received some of the most intensive training available on tire sizes, types, installation, maintenance, and more. They are qualified to answer all of your questions, and will make sure that you get the right tire for your vehicle. It's just one of the many ways that Michelin and Costco are dedicated to going the extra mile for members like you.

High Definition. It's in our DNA.

Whether it's the Sony® professional HD cameras used in sports and entertainment or the Sony® HD products you use at home, they all share the same genetic code. We call it HDNA. Our passion and knowledge for all things High Definition extend through every HD product we make. HDNA is what allows Sony to bring you truly unmatched HD experiences.

Cyber-shot® Camera — DSC-W150

DVDirect Multi-function
DVD Recorder — VRD-MC5

HD Handycam
Camcorder — HDR-SR11

SONY

BRAVIA LCD HDTV — KDL-135

Blu-ray Disc™ Player — BDP-S301

BRAVIA Home Theatre — DAV-HDX274

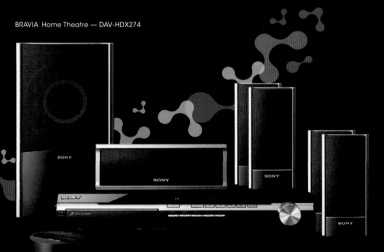

Sony® BRAVIA® LCD HDTV

The ultimate in picture performance. 120Hz Motionflow™ technology is engineered for fast-action sports, movies and games, while the BRAVIA Engine™ technology creates images with amazing detail and improved contrast. Available models: KDL-52WL135, KDL-46WL135, KDL-40WL135.

Sony Blu-ray Disc™ player[1]

See the crystalline clarity of 1080p Blu-ray Disc movies and DVD upscaling that brings your DVDs to the highest possible quality, meaning your favorite movies have never looked or sounded so good. (HDMI Cable included)

Sony BRAVIA® Home Theatre System

Complete your HD home theater with amazing surround sound. Experience Digital Cinema Sound™ processing that offers optimal audio settings from the experts who make the movie sound.

Sony Handycam® camcorder

Capture faces clearly with Face Detection technology[2] and record your life's stories beautifully in Full HD 1920 x 1080 resolution video.

Sony DVDirect® recorder

Transfer your home movies and digital pictures to DVD (sold separately), quickly and easily — without a PC.

Sony Cyber-shot® camera

Capture smiles automatically as they happen with Smile Shutter™ technology[2] and share them in High Definition with the HD Output.[3]

Store your world in ours®

Your pictures, your music, your work, your world.

2GB microSD 2-Pack + Adapter
Using the latest advances in flash memory technology, SanDisk co-developed the microSD format. Approximately one-quarter the size of a standard SD card, microSD is the smallest memory-card format in the world. MicroSD is predominantly used in mobile phones because of its small size—these cards provide expanded memory capacity for the majority of late-model cellphones. Costco's microSD 2-pack includes a microSD-to-SD adapter for use with any device that uses standard-size SD cards. Item #281576

2GB Cruzer Micro 3-Pack/ 8GB Cruzer Micro
SanDisk's Cruzer Micro is an incredibly small, compact and portable USB 2.0 flash drive. This tiny drive fits easily on a keychain, and the retractable USB connector eliminates the need for caps, while protecting the connector contacts. Costco sells the SanDisk 2GB Cruzer Micro in a 3-pack or the single 8GB flash drive. Each drive includes password protection and is compatible with Windows Vista, 2000 and XP, and Mac OS X and OS 10.1.1+. An amber LED glows when it is in use. Item #199305, 278600

2GB SD Ultra II 2-Pack
SanDisk co-developed SD flash memory. Each Ultra II memory card delivers high performance and incredible speed (15Mbps read/write). The result is a superb image, and less of a wait when transferring data from camera to PC. SanDisk Ultra II cards are manufactured to help you get the most out of your digital SLR, SD camcorder or advanced, feature-rich compact digital camera. Item #218821

4GB SD Ultra II High-Capacity
To support the demands of high-quality A/V recording, higher-capacity SD cards required a new design. The result was SD High Capacity, or SDHC. A new industry standard—2.0— now applies to all SD cards with capacities of 4GB or more. The 2.0 standard rating on each SanDisk SDHC memory card guarantees that card will deliver the speed and capacity to record high-quality A/V. SDHC is compatible with SDHC devices only. Item #199285

4GB CF Ultra II
SanDisk pioneered the flash media technology with the invention of CompactFlash. Our newest Ultra II product is the fastest yet (15Mbps read/write speed) and is covered by a lifetime warranty. Ultra II CompactFlash is rugged and reliable, with the speed capabilities required by professional photographers. SanDisk Ultra II CompactFlash—the card to use when every shot counts. Item #220324

2GB MSPD 2-Pack
Costco offers members the SanDisk 2GB Memory Stick Pro Duo in a 2-pack. SanDisk's unique memory technology led to their co-developing the MSPD format with Sony. That means each SanDisk MSPD card is guaranteed for optimal performance and compatibility when used in any MSPD-compliant devices. SanDisk MSPD cards all include embedded MagicGate technology for the safe transfer of copyrighted content. Item #277456

Dust-Off® Doesn't Play Favorites.

We Clean it All! From computers and printers to phones, TVs, DVD players, stereos and cameras, our products get rid of harmful dust and dirt that could put at risk the valuable assets stored within the workings of your equipment. Your time is valuable… divided between work and family, you don't have time for electronic equipment failure. Simple preventive maintenance means no worries or lost time. Dust-Off has a complete line of cleaning products to keep all your home and office equipment at peak performance. Trust our products to deliver optimum care without damaging your sophisticated high-tech investments.

For More Cleaning Tips and Products,
Visit us online at:
www.dust-off.com

Cleans dust and dirt from:

- CPUs
- Scanners
- Mouse
- Keyboards
- Fax Machines
- Filing Cabinets
- Disk Drives
- Monitors
- Laptops
- Desktops
- Phones and Cell Phones
- Copiers
- CDs/DVDs
- PDA's

Contains a Bitterant to help discourage inhalant abuse.

Support you trust.
Comfort you'll love.™

WHY PURCHASE A SEALY MATTRESS AT COSTCO?

VALUE: Costco Wholesale is committed to maintaining the tradition of the highest-quality products at the best possible price.

SELECTION: A complete range of comfort choices to meet your individual requirements.

QUALITY: Comfort, support and durability. Only Sealy Posturepedic can provide the comfort and suppo for a truly restful and healthy night sleep. Sealy uses only the finest materials and the best workmanshi so that the Sealy Posturepedic mattress will provide years of comfor

CONVENIENCE: You'll never have to "flip" your mattress again. In addition to comfort and durability, Sealy's Unicased Edge Design technology offers the convenience of a one-sided non-flip mattress. Now you can have both durability and the convenience of a non-flip Sealy Posturepedic.

SEALY COMFORT STORY

Since the average person spends nearly one-third of a lifetime sleeping, a restful night's sleep may depend on the mattress that is selected. Choose your mattress set based on which mattress feels the most comfortable for you.

SUPPORT VS. FIRMNESS

Support and firmness do not mean the same thing. Support is determined by the overall sleep system, primarily the innerspring unit and the box springs. Regardless of which firmness you select, you will get the maximum support you require from Sealy's new Comfort Support System (CSS). Firmness describes the comfort or feel of the top quilt system of the mattress. One of the Sealy choices available at Costco will be the right one for you and will give you the Support you trust. Comfort you'll love.™

MEMORY-FOAM BENEFITS

The technical name for memory foam is visco-elastic. It's called memory foam because the foam slowly returns to its original shape when weight is removed.

This feature allows memory foam to conform to your body's contour, providing individualized support an pressure-point relief. This is especia useful in promoting a comfortable, restful night's sleep.

Most Sealy Posturepedic mattresses offered through Costco have strategically placed memory-foam components of various types. By varying the location and type of memory foam in different models, Sealy is able to maximize memory foam's advantages while maintaining a wide variety of comfort levels to satisfy your personal preference of firmness.

Check each individual mattress specifications sold by Costco to determine which mattress will be right for you.

MADE IN U.S.A.

Sealy FlameGuard Protection™

C S S
comfort   support   system

exclusively by Posturepedic

Designed for your life

At Philips, we believe that innovation is more than just technology. That's why Philips lifestyle products are designed to enhance the health, appearance, living spaces and experiences of the people that use them. And these are just a few of the inspired Philips products that you'll find at Costco.

Raise the bar
Home cinema will never be the same, thanks to the ability of **Ambisound** to deliver multi-channel surround sound from a sleek 1-piece integrated system with built-in upscaling DVD player.

Immerse yourself
Be impressed with this Philips **DVD player** with 1080p high definition upscaling. HDMI digital video and audio connection bring you into a whole new home entertainment arena.

Entertainment harmony
Eliminate irritating background noise and enjoy your music or movie in peace with Philips premium **Noise Canceling Headphones**.

Brilliant design, powerful performance
Philips **Flat TVs** combine a full HD 1080p display with fantastic invisible sound for an inspired style that takes your space to new heights, 120Hz available in some sets.

Redefine clean
Sonicare Flexcare with Pro Results Brush Head provides superior plaque removal. In just 10 minutes, UV Sanitizer sanitizes your brush head.

A closer, faster shave
Patented Reflex Action and 50% larger shaving surface help the Norelco **Speed XL** give a faster, smoother, closer shave.

PHILIPS
sense and simplicity

SHARP

Sharp's goal is to minimize the environmental impact of our products by continually implementing and improving product technologies, designs and programs aimed at environmental conservation, from the materials used in the manufacturing and packaging of our products, to their transportation, use and safe disposal at the end of their product life.

SHARP – A PASSION FOR QUALITY AND CONSERVATION.

SOLAR

Sharp has been the world leader* in solar cell production for the past seven years.

ENVIRONMENTALLY CONSCIOUS FACTORIES

AQUOS® LCD panels are manufactured in an over three million square foot environmentally friendly complex in Kameyama, Japan. Sharp's Kameyama plant number two is the most environmentally conscious LCD factory in the world. All of the water used in LCD production is recycled, purified and reused. Cogeneration and the world's largest roof-mounted solar electric system supply approximately one-third of the plant's energy and help to reduce the overall CO_2 emissions by 40%.

ENVIRONMENTAL ACTIVITIES

Sharp's industry leadership extends to a number of affiliations and organizations which encourage our company to go above and beyond their legal environmental obligations.

*According to the March 2007 issue of PV News, a US publication

Print and archive your digital pictures

Fast:
- High-quality prints from digital and film cameras in as little as one hour

Convenient:
- Order at the 1-Hour Photo lab OR from home at costco.com (click on "Photo") and pick up while you're shopping at Costco

Preserve:
- High-quality long-lasting prints: 4" x 6", 5" x 7", 8" x 10" and larger
- Archive your photos on a Costco Gold CD designed to protect your photos for 300 years. Includes viewing and organizing software

Custom:
- Choice of glossy or luster prints
- Border or borderless
- Color or black & white

Create:
- Greeting cards for all occasions

More services from Costco's online Photo Center:
- Create calendars, photo books, gifts and more
- Enhanced editing options such as cropping, red-eye removal, decorative borders and more
- Share your photos with friends and family
- Go to costco.com and click on "Photo"

Did you know that Costco 1-Hour Photo offers passport and ID photos for $4.99?

THE BEST ADVICE FOR YOUR FAMILY IS NATURE MADE.

For more than 35 years Nature Made has offered high-quality vitamins, minerals and herbal and other supplements for nutritional needs. That's why so many health-conscious people trust Nature Made. Each Nature Made product is specially formulated with the most beneficial ingredients to enhance health and well-being. Now many Nature Made products are formulated for easy absorption, and we guarantee that Nature Made vitamins, minerals and supplements contain no artificial flavors or preservatives. So when you're looking for the best prices and the best selection of Nature Made supplements, the best place to look is Costco.

FUEL YOUR GREATNESS.℠

warehouse/costco.com

naturemade.com

Samsung Series 5 LCD HDTV
with Ultra Clear Panel

| Conventional | Ultra Clear Panel |

Ultra Clear Panel
Samsung's Ultra Clear Panel offers brilliant
viewing under any conditions. Thanks to its
high-contrast picture with bold, bright colors
and deep, dark black tones, you can enjoy
all your HD programs and movies to the full-
est in any type of light, day or night.

Introducing 46" LCD HDTV with Ultra Clear Panel

Series 5 LCD with 1080p Resolution

Experience the next generation of HD television in all its glory. Full 1080p HD resolution and 35,000:1 dynamic contrast ratio offer amazing image detail and color clarity.

- Full 1080p HD: Delivers lifelike picture and color

- Watch your favorite photos in a slide show (including MPEG) and listen to your MP3s with WiseLink™ (USB 2.0)

- 3 HDMI™ inputs to quickly and simply connect your cable box, DVD or Blu-ray Disc™ player, computer and more

SAMSUNG

Home Essentials

"HOME" IS ONE OF THE MOST ingrained concepts in our lives. For starters, it's where the heart is. When we're nearing the end of a project, we're on the home stretch. Baseball players hit home runs.

Perhaps most resonant is the phrase "home, sweet home!" It comes from a song that was adapted from the 1823 opera *Clari, the Maid of Milan*. Its opening lines are still famous:

Mid pleasures and palaces though we may roam,
Be it ever so humble, there's no place like home.

And, of course, there *is* no place like home. That's what Dorothy said as she clicked her heels at the end of the 1939 film *The Wizard of Oz*. Sharp ears will recognize the melody that's playing in the background: "Home! Sweet Home!"

Keeping your home safe from fire and carbon monoxide

FIRE AND CARBON MONOXIDE can be deadly threats in any household or business. Fortunately, there are steps you can take to avoid these dangers.

What to know about fire

Fire can strike anywhere, at any time. The frightening truth is that the nearly 381,000 home fires in the United States in 2005 resulted in some 16,000 injuries and deaths combined, according to the National Fire Protection Association. You can be prepared by using the tools for fire protection.

Smoke alarms provide a warning of fire. They are the easiest, most cost-efficient way to alert your family of a developing fire. The more smoke alarms you have installed in your home, the more your chances increase that you will be alerted to a fire.

Fire extinguishers provide a tool to fight small fires. Having a fire extinguisher in your home can increase your chances of keeping a small fire from getting out of control and becoming deadly.

Using both smoke alarms and fire extinguishers in your home, along with knowing what to do in case of fire, can help save your life.

The facts about fire

Fire is darker, smokier, hotter and faster than you can imagine. Here are four important facts to increase the chances of a safe escape.

1. Smoke is dark. Most people expect fire to be light. For this reason, people have been trapped in their homes because they could not find their way out in the dark—they didn't have a flashlight and didn't practice an escape plan.

2. Smoke can be deadly. Because most fire fatalities occur between 2 a.m. and 6 a.m., when most people are sleeping, the only thing standing between the deadly fumes of fire and a safe escape may be the piercing sound of a smoke alarm.

3. Fire has intense heat. Fire can cause the temperature to rise several hundred degrees in just seconds. One breath in the heat can cause severe lung damage and even unconsciousness. Escape time can be valuable.

4. Time is critical. A home fire can double in size in just 30 seconds. You must know what to do to help get you and your family out safely. A closed door is often the best way to stall a fire; it could give you valuable seconds to use an alternate escape route.

DID YOU KNOW?

Fires and burns are the third leading cause of home injury

→ HELPFUL **HOW TO'S**

WHAT TYPES OF FIRE EXTINGUISHERS ARE THERE?

FIRE EXTINGUISHERS are categorized by ratings. These ratings determine the size and type of fire that the extinguisher can successfully put out. Fire can be divided into three categories: A, B or C. A-type fires are primarily wood, paper and fabric. B-type fires are primarily flammable liquids such as gasoline and oil. C-type fires are electrical.

The number preceding the A, B or C rating determines how big of a professionally set

fire the extinguisher can put out. For example, a fire extinguisher rated 1-A:10-B:C can handle a 64-square-foot wood panel or a 25-square-foot fire of flammable liquid (such as gasoline) or electrical origin. In contrast, a fire extinguisher rated 3-A:40-B:C can handle a 144-square-foot wood panel or a 100-square-foot fire of flammable liquid or electrical origin.

It's another easy and convenient way to add fire protection to a home.

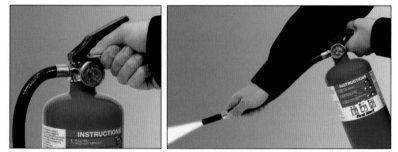

When using a fire extinguisher, think "PASS": pull, aim, squeeze and sweep.

Smoke alarms

The National Fire Protection Association recommends installing smoke alarms on every level of a home and in every bedroom. Smoke alarms should also be installed in the main hallway outside each bedroom area. Check local building codes for specific requirements. Fire extinguishers should be installed on each living level, as well as in rooms that pose potential fire hazards (e.g., kitchen, garage).

Take the following steps to maintain smoke alarms and fire extinguishers once they are installed.

• Test your smoke alarms weekly and test your fire extinguisher by checking the pressure gauge.
• Replace the battery in each smoke alarm at least once a year.
• Never remove the battery except when replacing it with a fresh battery.
• Clean the smoke alarm at least once a year.
• Follow the instructions in the product's owner's manual for specific instructions on how to install and maintain smoke alarms and fire extinguishers.

What to know about carbon monoxide

Carbon monoxide (CO) is an invisible, odorless gas. It is a common byproduct of incomplete combustion, produced when fossil fuels (such as oil,

TIPS &TRICKS

WAYS TO LOWER FIRE RISK

THE FOLLOWING FIRE safety checklist will help you to lower the chances that a fire may start in your home.

• Keep the furnace in working order.
• Use a fireplace screen.
• Have proper ventilation for heaters and other small appliances.
• Do not smoke in bed.
• Use fuses that are the correct size.
• Don't use worn-out electrical wiring or run it under rugs or out windows or doors.
• Clear away refuse—the less clutter, the less fuel a fire has to feed on.

By properly equipping your home with smoke alarms and fire extinguishers, you'll be taking an important first step in improving total fire protection for your family. ▲

TIPS&TRICKS •··············

WHAT TO DO IF AN ALARM SOUNDS

NEVER IGNORE THE SOUND of an alarm. If the smoke or carbon monoxide alarm is sounding its alarm, there is a reason. Here are several steps your family can learn and rehearse for an emergency.

SMOKE ALARM

1. Have an escape plan and practice it. Know two exits from every room in the house.

2. Feel if the door is hot. If the doorknob or door is hot, use an alternate exit to escape.

3. Crawl on the floor—smoke and heat rise.

4. Meet at a prearranged spot outside the home.

5. Call the fire department from a neighbor's home.

6. Never go inside a burning building. Never return inside the house for any reason.

CARBON MONOXIDE ALARM

You may not experience symptoms of CO poisoning when the alarm sounds. The alarm is designed to go off before you may feel sick, so you have time to react and take action.

1. Press the mute button to temporarily quiet the alarm.

2. Call 911 or the fire department.

3. Immediately move everyone to a source of fresh air.

4. Leave the CO alarm where it is.

5. Do not reenter your home until the emergency responder has arrived, your home is aired out and your CO alarm returns to normal operation. ▲

gas or coal) burn. Because you can't see, taste or smell it, carbon monoxide can kill you before you know it's there. Exposure to lower levels over time can make you sick.

CO can be produced by the combustion that occurs from fossil-fuel-burning appliances such as a furnace, clothes dryer, range, oven, water heater or space heater. When appliances and vents work properly and there is enough fresh air in your home to allow complete combustion, the trace amounts of CO produced are typically not dangerous. And normally, CO is safely vented outside your home.

Problems may arise when something goes wrong. An appliance can malfunction, a furnace heat exchanger can crack, vents can clog or debris may block a chimney or flue. Fireplaces, wood-burning stoves, gas heaters, charcoal grills and gas logs can produce unsafe levels of CO if they are unvented or not properly vented. Exhaust can seep into a home from vehicles left running in an attached garage.

Why is carbon monoxide so dangerous?

CO robs you of what you need most: oxygen. This brings flu-like symptoms, such as headaches, fatigue, nausea, dizzy spells, confusion and irritability. Because these symptoms are similar to those caused by flu, carbon monoxide poisoning can be misdiagnosed. As the problem worsens, victims suffer vomiting, loss of consciousness and eventually brain damage or death.

Early warning is important: Install one or more alarms. The Consumer Product Safety Commission recommends that every home have at least one carbon monoxide alarm with an audible warning signal installed near the sleeping area. Choose a CO alarm that is tested and listed by a nationally accredited lab such as ETL (ETL Testing Laboratories) or UL (Underwriters Laboratories).

Have your appliances checked regularly. Have a qualified appliance technician check all fossil-fuel-burning appliances and venting and chimney systems at least once a year, or as recommended by the manufacturers.

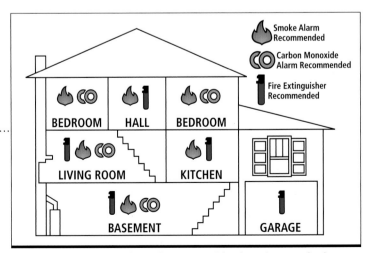

Place a smoke alarm and a carbon monoxide alarm in every bedroom and at least one on every level of the house. Have a fire extinguisher on every level of the house as well as in the kitchen and garage.

Where to look for potential sources

Forced-air furnaces are frequently the source of leaks and should be carefully inspected by a professional. Have a professional perform the following tasks.

• Check furnace connections to the flue pipes and venting systems, as well as furnace filters and filtering systems.

• Check forced-air fans for proper installation and to assure correct airflow of flue gases.

• Inspect the combustion chamber and internal heat exchanger for cracks, holes, corrosion or dirt and debris, along with burners, ignition systems and pilot lights.

• Check fireplaces for closed, blocked or bent flues, soot and debris, along with all venting systems to the outside of your home.

You should take several additional steps on your own to ensure safety. Do the following procedures at least once a year.

• Check all other appliances in the home that use fossil fuels such as natural gas, oil, propane, wood and kerosene. Appliances include water heaters, clothes dryers, kitchen ranges, gas heaters, ovens or cooktops, wood-burning stoves, gas refrigerators and alternative power sources such as generators.

• Be sure that space heaters are vented properly. Unvented space heaters that use a fossil fuel such as kerosene or propane can release carbon monoxide into the home.

• Check the clothes dryer vent opening. Lint may block proper venting outside the house.

Other considerations to keep in mind

Barbecue grills should never be operated indoors under any circumstances. Also, cooktops and ovens that operate on fossil fuels should never be used to heat a residence.

A broken thermostat can keep the furnace running continuously, depleting the oxygen supply inside the house. This may lead to back-drafting. Check to make sure your thermostat is working properly.

Be aware that in multiple-family dwellings such as apartments and town-houses, where living spaces share walls and pipes, carbon monoxide from one unit may go into a neighboring space through floorboards and cracks or underneath doors. ◮

Easy energy-saving tips

IF YOU THINK SAVING ENERGY in your home or office is going to require investments in new equipment and so on, you're wrong. You can save energy—and money—with some simple no-cost steps.

Flip the switch ... on your ceiling fan, that is

A ceiling fan is naturally energy efficient—it circulates air while using very little electricity. Most people don't realize a ceiling fan can help warm you up in the winter as easily as it can cool you down in the summer.

Most ceiling fans have a switch that controls the direction of the blades. When the fan runs counterclockwise, it blows air down, providing the cooling effect desired during warmer months. Running the fan clockwise during colder months circulates the warm air near the ceiling. This makes the room warmer, which decreases demands on the heating system and allows you to comfortably turn down your thermostat to save on energy costs. Operated correctly, a ceiling fan that's sized appropriately for the room can save you up to 10 percent on your heating bills.

Get with the program

According to Energy Star,™ while many homes have a programmable thermostat, approximately 70 percent of consumers find it too difficult to operate and, as a result, lose out on energy savings. Forgetting to turn down your thermostat just one time before you leave for work can mean several dollars in lost energy savings. That's why a programmable thermostat is so useful: It doesn't forget.

Programmable thermostats save energy by offering convenient, preprogrammed temperature settings that allow you to scale temperatures back as you leave and warm things up upon your return. When used properly, a programmable thermostat can save you as much as $150 annually in energy costs.

Go unplugged

Up to 75 percent of the electricity used to power home electronics is consumed while the products are turned off. According to the Department of Energy, power continues to run through your home electronics even when you have them turned off—yes, even the coffee maker. If 60 percent of your energy bill is electricity—15 percent of that from electrical devices—it's easy to imagine how much you can save as a result of some simple unplugging.

Among the most common household devices that consume electricity while not in operation are computers, TVs, cable boxes, cell-phone chargers and other power adapters, and anything else with a microchip that requires at least some juice to keep its inner clock ticking. So, while you might think it's a nice convenience to have a clock around every corner, if you want to save money, don't rely on your VCR or microwave to display the time.

Creating a daily unplugging routine is easy. Go around the house and unplug devices that do not need to be plugged in, especially those that operate in standby mode, such as computers and home entertainment systems. According to the National Resources Defense Fund, cable and satellite setup boxes, and digital video recorders such as TiVo,® are among the worst offenders for using energy when not in use.

For those often-used devices that are found in groups, such as the TV, cable and surround-sound system or the computer, printer and scanner, use a power strip. It allows you to run a number of devices from one power source and operates via one convenient switch.

Assess your saving potential

If you are interested in energy savings but don't know where to start, performing a home energy audit is a good first step. It will help you prioritize your energy upgrade needs and give you a better understanding of how you and your home consume energy. A good energy auditor will uncover any air leaks or insulation problems and recommend energy-saving products. The Department of Energy provides a free do-it-yourself plan at *www.eere. energy.gov.*

Check with your local energy company to see if it offers free professional audits. If it does not, they should be able to recommend an agency that will. A professional audit will give you a more accurate assessment than one you do on your own. △

→ HELPFUL **HOW TO'S**

HOW TO SELECT A CEILING FAN

Simply follow these steps:

1. SELECT YOUR PRODUCT.
Choose the appropriate-size fan for the proper combination of comfort and efficiency. (If you're unsure about the room

ROOM	BLADE SIZE	MAXIMUM SQ. FT.
GREAT ROOM/LIVING ROOM	60"+	625
MASTER BEDROOM/DEN/LIVING ROOM	50"–56"	485
BEDROOM/OFFICE/KITCHEN	42"–48"	225
LAUNDRY ROOM/BATHROOM	32"–36"	100

size, choose a larger fan to maximize your comfort at low/medium speed.)

2. WHAT STYLE AND COLOR DO YOUR PREFER?
For a coordinated look, match the blade finish to furniture or molding. Or select a fan body finish that matches door or cabinet hardware. Many fans feature reversible SwitchBlades.® A different finish on each side of the blade permits styling flexibility.

3. HOW HIGH IS YOUR CEILING?
The height and orientation of your ceiling are key considerations. For low ceilings, the motor housing of the fan fits flush to the ceiling. If your ceiling is 9 feet or higher, you'll need an extension downrod. Such extensions are also needed for angled ceilings.

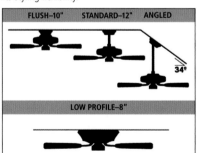

4. DO YOU NEED A LIGHT?
Choose a fan with a coordinated light fixture included or customize the fan with an accessory light fixture.

5. SELECT A FAN CONTROL.
To operate your fan and light separately from a single switch without additional rewiring, choose a wall control. For convenient, easy operation in bedrooms and rooms with high ceilings, consider a wireless remote control.

ENERGY-SAVING LIGHTS

THERE ARE MANY good reasons to consider using energy-efficient compact fluorescent light bulbs (CFLs) in your home and work.

- CFLs use up to 75 percent less energy than incandescent light bulbs. Since lighting accounts for nearly 20 percent of the average homeowner's electric bill, these savings can really add up.
- According to Department of Energy estimates, each CFL saves at least $30 over its life compared to incandescent bulbs. CFLs save money in two ways: the overall cost of the light bulbs and the savings in energy they deliver.
- If every home in America replaced just one incandescent light bulb with an Energy Star–qualified CFL, enough energy would be saved to light more than 3 million homes and the equivalent of some 800,000 cars' worth of greenhouse-gas emissions would be eliminated annually. △

Smart advances in lighting

THE INCANDESCENT LIGHT BULB has been the standard for lighting homes and businesses since the time of Thomas Edison. But new lighting technologies are emerging that are more energy efficient. In particular, light-emitting diodes—commonly known as LEDs—are growing in popularity for numerous uses.

LED light bulbs have been around for 45 years, but until recently were too expensive and difficult to produce in mass quantities. The need for energy independence from oil, concern over global warming and environmental issues are providing the investment incentive for manufacturers to find solutions. Also, federal legislation calls for a phase-out of regular incandescent light bulbs in 2012, with all such bulbs banned by 2020.

LEDs promise several advantages over other types of lights. Incandescent and halogen bulbs use only 10 percent of the energy they consume to create visible light—meaning that 90 percent of the energy is wasted through heat. LED products are up to 90 percent more efficient than these lights. Also, LEDs are up to 40 percent more energy efficient and last five to seven times longer than compact fluorescent light bulbs.

➤ **THIS**&THAT

ENERGY COST SAVINGS

Replace your neon sign and save significantly on your utility costs per year.

COST PER KILOWATT HOUR (kWh), varies by region	8¢	10¢	12¢	16¢
ANNUAL ENERGY COST SAVINGS ("OPEN" SIGN)	$47	$59	$70	$94

Neon signs waste 80 percent of the energy they consume through heat output. LED technology eliminates this waste to provide the same high-quality light at a fraction of the cost.

Other advantages of LEDs include:

- They last up to 50,000 hours (that's 35 years operating four hours per day).
- They're mercury-free, which means no recycling issues.
- They are heat-free. Incandescent and halogen light bulbs, on the other hand, generate excessive heat.
- They are available in any color, including bright white, soft warm white, red, green and blue.

Take a look at the possibility of using LEDs in your home or business. The energy savings and other advantages are worth considering. ◪

DID YOU KNOW? The first light bulb marketed by Thomas Edison was a 16-watt bulb that could last for 1,500 hours

NEW USES FOR LEDS

Manufacturers are designing LEDs into many products that formerly used incandescent, halogen, fluorescent or neon lights. Products available today include:

OPEN/CLOSED SIGNS
These signs can be operated manually or with remote control and use only 8 watts of energy, compared to 140 watts used by neon signs.

LIGHT BULBS
These range from decorative flame-tip bulbs for outdoor coach lanterns and chandeliers to reflector floodlights for indoor and outdoor use to MR-16 mini-spotlights for track and recessed lighting. They use up to 4.5 watts of energy, compared to 45 watts used by incandescent and halogen bulbs.

DESK LAMPS
LED desk lamps, with small and fashionable lamp head designs, consume 6 watts of energy or less, compared to 60 watts used by incandescent and halogen bulbs.

OUTDOOR COACH LANTERNS
LEDs can be operated with motion and dusk-to-dawn controls and provide a beautiful decorative light effect. These use only 6 watts of energy, compared to 120 watts used by incandescent and halogen flame-tip bulbs.

PUCK LIGHTS
These small lights can be mounted under kitchen cabinets, over workbenches and inside curio cabinets and entertainment centers. They can be powered through an outlet or by batteries.

OUTDOOR SOLAR LIGHTS
These low-voltage lights are used in landscape pathways and in gardens. They use only 5 watts of energy.

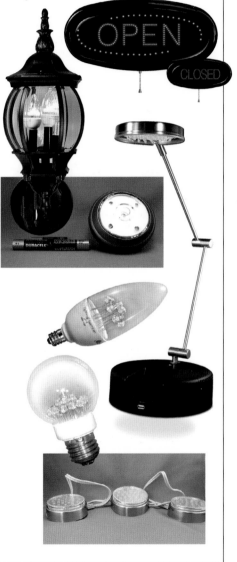

TIPS & TRICKS

SPONSORED BY

SEVILLE CLASSICS ™

USING A FAN TO COOL OFF

AIR CONDITIONING IS a lifesaver when the humidity and the temperature climb. But running an AC unit consumes considerable energy.

Once the air conditioner has done its job and a room's air environment is at a humane level—72 to 78 degrees F and 35 to 60 percent humidity, according to the American Society of Heating, Refrigerating and Air-Conditioning Engineers (ASHRAE)—consider switching off the AC and turning on a fan.

With moderate air movement, the comfort range of a room can be extended to 82 degrees, ASHRAE says. And each degree you are able to raise the thermostat will save 3 to 5 percent on air-conditioning costs.

Set an oscillating fan near the corner of a room so that it can easily sweep side to side, but not so close that it picks up and circulates dust from the walls or corners. Variable speeds allow you to adjust the amount of air movement preferred, with lower speeds using less energy. A timer will let you set the fan to run in a bedroom at night and shut off in the morning.

A handy remote control will also save energy—yours—as you won't need to get up to turn on the fan.

The importance of purifying the air

THERE'S LITTLE DOUBT THAT the air inside houses and offices can contain allergens, pollutants and irritants. Fortunately, modern air purifiers can help. But you must make sure to get the right one to effectively remedy the problem. Consider the following information to help you make the right choice for your health.

One of the most popular purification techniques involves circulating air through a special filter that traps allergens, pollutants and irritants. These filters, known as HEPA (high efficiency particle arresting) and HEPA-type filters, can remove 99 percent of all particles as small as 2 microns (a micron is one-millionth of a meter). HEPA-type units now have permanent filters that can be vacuumed or cleaned. These are highly effective for cleaning the air of dander, pollen and even the smell of smoke on curtains, carpets and furniture.

If you want to get rid of airborne germs, viruses and bacteria, an air purifier equipped with a lamp that emits ultraviolet (UV) light will kill up to 99.9 percent of these germs. However, a UV light by itself will not remove particles or pollution. Look for an air purifier that combines the technology of a UV light and a HEPA filter.

Many people do not know that indoor pollution also includes household chemicals, toxic paint fumes and chemical emissions from carpet, paint and particleboard. An effective way of removing volatile organic compounds from the air is a photo catalyst filter, which can be found on some air purifiers that include a UV light.

The size of the room is another factor. Make sure the air purifier is powerful enough to purify the desired space. You may need multiple air purifiers to clean the air in your entire home.

An investment in an air purifier is an investment in your health and the health of your family. You don't drink polluted water; why would you breathe polluted air? Consider ways to improve the quality of the air in your home and office. ◢

➤ HELPFUL **HOW TO'S**

DETERMINING THE SIZE YOU NEED

Most air purifiers are designed for individual room use rather than for the whole home.

To determine what size you need, look for the CADR number. This number indicates the Clean Air Delivery Rate, which should always equal at least two-thirds of the total square footage of the room. For example, a 10-by-12-foot room with a normal ceiling (not cathedral) has 120 square feet and needs a purifier with a CADR of at least 80.

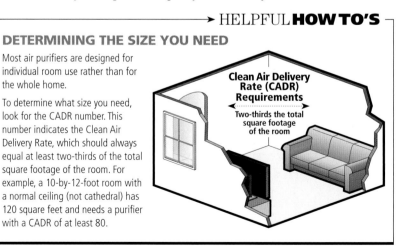

Clean Air Delivery Rate (CADR) Requirements

Two-thirds the total square footage of the room

Leather: stylish, versatile

FINDING THE right furniture for your home is tricky. It involves balancing factors such as décor, compatibility, function, comfort, quality and price.

Incorporating leather furniture can help simplify the process, because it works well in a variety of settings. And leather furniture is versatile: It lends an air of formality to a casual room, yet brings a touch of relaxation to a formal room.

Because leather lasts four to five times longer than fabric upholstery and requires very little maintenance, it's ideal for furniture. And because leather is a natural product, individual hides vary due to wrinkles and other anomalies, lending each piece its own unique personality.

Here are some things to look for when selecting leather furniture.

The real deal. Top-grain leather is the most expensive grade, but comfort, quality and durability are the returns on your investment. During the tanning process, hides are selected and sent to a splitting machine. The top three-sixty-fourths of an inch of the original hide is called the top grain.

Many manufacturers use leather on the panels that can be seen and touched, but use synthetic material to cover the back and other, less visible areas. This is common for furnishings such as theater chairs. It's an option that can keep furniture costs down.

Color to dye for. Aniline is a process in which the leather is dyed all the way through so that as it ages it retains a uniform color and appearance. An additional pigmented top coating is applied to the surface of the leather to offer greater longevity to the overall appearance.

Built to last. Look for frames made of hardwood. All stress joints should be reinforced with additional corner blocks for strength and stability. The best cushions are made from dense, pure foam that has been double-wrapped in Dacron polyester to ensure that they retain their shape.

A final note. Because leather has been preserved during tanning, cleansers such as saddle soap and ammonia water are unnecessary and harmful. If you dust your leather furniture weekly and occasionally wipe it down with lukewarm water, it will look great for years.—*Will Fifield*

TIPS&TRICKS

TO FIX A WOBBLY chair or table leg, slice off a thin piece of a wine cork and slip it under the shorter leg. When the table or chair stays steady, attach the cork with a dab of glue.

Paste shoe polish can help mask gouges and knicks in wood tables and chairs. Choose a shoe polish color that closely matches the shade of the wood. Take a small dab and carefully work it into the ding, then wipe gently with a soft cloth.

Choosing the best foldable table

A FOLDABLE TABLE is an incredibly useful piece of furniture. You can pull it out for projects at work and home, as an extra table for a holiday meal, as a food station for an outdoor gathering and much, much more.

But not all foldable tables are made the same. Buy one of inferior quality and you might be sorry at an inopportune time. Here's a primer of what to look for in table construction.

The right materials

Top-quality tables begin with the right materials. The three important factors are:

High-impact polyethylene. This makes tables stronger, lighter and more durable than wood. Polyethylene will not crack, chip or peel and is formulated to withstand extended wear and tear and the harshest elements. These tabletops are stain resistant and easy to clean.

High-impact polyethylene can include UV inhibitors that make the table resistant to heat and extended exposure to the harmful UV rays of the sun.

Powder-coated steel. Powder coating makes steel parts more resistant to chips, scratches and regular wear and tear. It also makes parts resistant to corrosion and protects them from UV damage brought on by exposure to the sun, making it a great all-weather finish.

Mar-proof leg caps. High-impact plastic leg caps give tables a stable and balanced foundation, preventing the steel tubing from leaving marks on the floor or scraping the ground.

Advanced design features

A look at design and construction can help you determine a table's quality. Consider these factors:

Leg design. Is the steel tubing strong enough to handle the load? Also, good leg design gives the user more leg clearance at each end of the table, providing more comfortable sitting area while maintaining strength and stability.

Double-wall construction. Dual-wall construction improves rigidity and keeps the table panel flat so there are no sags or soft spots.

Parting-line design. The bond at the parting line (the blow-molding seam) is important. The seam should be thicker than the rest of the plastic wall, providing a strong seal.

Corner design. Corners should be impact resistant to keep the top from crushing if the table is dropped inadvertently on its corner.

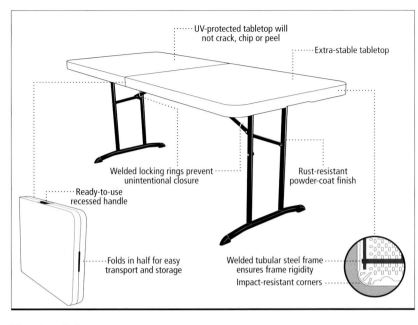

UV-protected tabletop will not crack, chip or peel

Extra-stable tabletop

Welded locking rings prevent unintentional closure

Rust-resistant powder-coat finish

Ready-to-use recessed handle

Folds in half for easy transport and storage

Welded tubular steel frame ensures frame rigidity

Impact-resistant corners

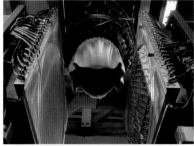

A high-quality plastic tabletop starts with the blown-molding process.

After initial molding, excess plastic is trimmed to meet size specifications.

Table legs are precision welded for strength during the assembly process.

Raw steel coil is converted into table legs and other metal parts.

Testing is key

Top-quality tables are classified as commercial grade. To earn this classification, they must meet or exceed safety and performance standards established by the American National Standards Institute (ANSI) and the Business and Institutional Furniture Manufacturer's Association (BIFMA). The standards, developed by the BIFMA Engineering Committee, involve seven tests that ensure table strength and functionality.

These standards are intended to provide manufacturers, specifiers and users with a common basis for evaluating safety, durability and the structural adequacy of the specified furniture, independent of construction materials. The standards define specific tests, laboratory equipment to be used, the test conditions and the minimum acceptance levels to be used in evaluating these products.

Examples of the tests include applying a 300-pound concentrated load to the center of the table span for 15 minutes, applying a 200-pound concentrated load to the center of the table span for one hour and applying a 200-pound load for a few seconds—repeated through 20,000 cycles.

To test operational safety, leading manufacturers subject their furniture to tests established by the American Society for Testing and Materials. These tests look at pinch points and exposed sharp edges.

Some manufacturers have developed their own tests to ensure real-world durability. These include dropping heavy weights (200 pounds or more) onto the tables and dropping the desks onto their corners from certain heights to ensure against table damage during transport.

As you can see, there is more to a table than just four legs and a tabletop. Look closely and you'll be happy with your purchase for years to come. ◢

FOR IDEAS ON HOW TO USE A FOLDABLE TABLE WHEN ENTERTAINING, SEE PAGES 102-103.

How to plan the perfect party

By Deborah Fabricant

CATERING FOR COMPANY

- Have a good invitation; this sets the stage for your party.

- Plan the menu two weeks in advance. Prepare easy do-ahead dishes, thinking about the freshest ingredients, balance of flavors and how it will all look on the plate.

- Make as much as you can ahead of time, and freeze or refrigerate items that will keep well (breads, rolls, sauces, etc.).

- Find out guests' dietary restrictions ahead of time and try to accommodate.

- Ask someone to help you in the kitchen and with cleanup.

- Remember to have good lighting (lots of candles!) and good music.

- Plan food and decorations to go with the season.

- Buffet food should be easy to eat.

- Have plenty of silverware and glassware. ◪

ENTERTAINING FOR LARGE GROUPS, be it family affairs or for friends, can be stressful. The logistics alone can be daunting. Where do you seat everyone? Do you have enough chairs? What to do with the food: Do you need a buffet? How about a beverage station?

When you need extra seating, another table or a serving buffet, it can be as easy as unfolding some tables and chairs. Tables are available in a variety of sizes, so you can combine several sizes or shapes to create a unique arrangement for the extra space you need. For large parties of 20, try using two tables in a T pattern—great for lively conversation. Extra seating is a snap with folding chairs.

With this in mind, here are some party pointers and easy entertaining ideas to ensure that your next event will be an organized and successful affair.

Be prepared for easy summer fun

When summer is here entertaining should be easy! As you jump into the pool, enjoy the endless sun-filled days and gather with friends and family, your goal should be simplicity. The easiest way to entertain in summer is to focus on fresh, simple and uncomplicated ideas.

Invariably, friends and their kids drop in for a visit, it gets to be late in the afternoon, everyone is hungry and you invite the whole gang to stay for dinner. What to serve? Here are some tips and ideas for easy, stress-free entertaining during the summer.

Extra service and extra seating are imperative. Get a couple of folding tables: one for serving, one for extra seating. Have a cupboard devoted to your summer entertaining accessories, be they paper goods or plastic ware. Keep everything in one place so it is readily available for impromptu parties. Make sure it is stocked with napkins, plates, flatware, glassware, votive candles and a tablecloth. Invest in two glass hurricane vases—they are perfect for big, fat candles, flowers or a collection of shells and can be used throughout the year. Now, set up your table, top it with a colorful cloth or place mats and you are ready to go!

Impromptu entertaining is fun when you are well prepared. Keep these items on hand for quick meals during the summer:

- A couple of good bottled marinades for chicken, beef or fish
- Individually wrapped, frozen boneless chicken breasts, small steaks, seasoned hamburger patties
- Frozen hamburger buns
- Packaged pasta or rice
- Packaged salads
- Toasted pine nuts, made ahead and frozen
- Good bottled salad dressings
- A loaf of garlic bread, frozen
- Parmesan cheese
- Two quarts of your favorite ice cream
- Graham cracker or chocolate cookie pie shell
- Chocolate and caramel sauce
- Frozen whipped topping
- Emergency munchies: peanuts, chili-lime chips, salsa, pretzels, etc.

For the kids, thaw the hamburgers and buns. Toss the burgers on the grill. Serve with chips and salsa, fresh fruit and cookies.

For the adults, marinate chicken breasts, small steaks or fish (thawed in the microwave) for about 15 minutes. Grill. Serve with a salad made from prepackaged greens, adding pine nuts, Parmesan and veggies. Toss with your favorite dressing. Pop the garlic bread under the broiler.

For dessert, fill a pie shell with softened ice cream and freeze. Serve with a choice of toppings. Hint: Make a couple of pies ahead of time and freeze them. Instant dessert!

Now, sit back, take in that fresh summer air, linger around the table with family and friends, and enjoy!

Costco member Deborah Fabricant owns The Art of Entertaining, a Los Angeles–based business that brings the easy elegance of entertaining to today's busy people. She is also the author of Stacks: The Art of Vertical Food *(Ten Speed Press, 1999).*

TIPS&TRICKS

EASY ENTERTAINING IDEAS

- Pick a theme and colors to carry throughout your party. Purchase fabrics from outlets, and design your invitations on your computer, then print them on colored paper.

- Build a beautiful buffet with different heights. Use metal risers, upturned bowls or terra-cotta pots, covered with cloths, to create different levels.

- For larger tables, think big for decoration: big bowls of lemons; tall vases with branches towering over the buffet; big pots of fresh herbs, fruits and flowers; breads tumbling out of wicker baskets laid on their sides.

- To create a centerpiece for a sit-down affair, bring the outdoors in. Arrange branches and leaves (magnolias work great!) down the center of the table, creating a garland effect, then nestle fruits, vegetables and herbs in and around the leaves. Place votives or tea light candles in juice glasses and tuck them into the garland. It's a great solution if you are on a budget.

- Try dressing up folding chairs by wrapping the backs with a complementing fabric and tie the back with a nosegay of leaves and herbs.

- Be realistic about what you can and can't do. If you are on a tight budget, look around you—what is seasonal and accessible? Don't be afraid to use your imagination. (A bucket of paint and some old sheets can create a wonderful table covering. Or use giant philodendron leaves to decorate.) Decorations don't have to be expensive, but rather a reflection of you having fun entertaining.

Being prepared for an emergency

EVERY TIME THERE'S a major fire, earthquake or tornado—or the electricity goes out for a couple of days—do you say to your family, "We need to get organized for an emergency"? Maybe the reason it's so hard to make progress on this goal is that it reaches into so many areas:

- Reviewing insurance policies and preparing a household inventory
- Backing up important files, papers and photos
- Gathering necessary supplies
- Putting together a communication plan
- Plotting escape routes from within your home
- Locating nearby emergency shelters
- Planning evacuation routes from your community
- Determining what to do about pets
- Educating yourself about how to respond to potential disasters in your area
- Creating emergency kits for your home, car and office
- Getting the whole family to practice the plan

Here, with the help of Costco members Marty Kuritz of Active Insights (*www.active-insights.com*) and Sam Brown of Your Survival (*www.your survival.com*), is a guide to preparing for an emergency. Kuritz, who himself needed to evacuate his family during recent fires in Southern California, swears by the checklist approach. It's easy to get rattled when faced with danger, and a checklist helps keep everyone focused.

Involving the whole family in this planning project, with regular deadlines, could be a real lifesaving effort.

Devise a communication plan

Keeping in touch with loved ones or with emergency personnel is crucial during a disaster. Here are some things to consider.

Designate an out-of-town contact person

Often, during a disaster, it's easier to call long distance than it is to call locally. Choose a friend or relative who lives out of town who can be your family's point person in case you're not together when disaster strikes. Be sure that each family member has the telephone number and e-mail address of the contact person and the resources to make contact (cell phone, coins, prepaid calling card). In the case of young children who might be at school or with a child-care provider, be sure that the school and child-care provider know to call the central contact in the event you cannot be reached.

Have several ways to communicate

- Transistor radio. You'll need to get news, information and advisories from authorities. For this, there is no better alternative than a simple transistor radio or a NOAA weather radio with built-in AM receiver.

- Text messaging. To alert others to your location and condition, you'll want to have a cell phone with text-messaging capabilities. Because of the narrower bandwidth required for text messaging, it's more likely texts will get through (use a simple "I am OK" or "Need help"), even when phone calls can't be completed.
- Basic corded telephone. You should always keep at least one old-fashioned corded telephone around the house. That's because it runs on the phone company's power source. So while the circuits can still jam, a corded phone has a better chance of operating during a power outage—which will immediately knock out cordless sets.
- Two-way radios. Today's basic units work within six miles on standard batteries. They can be an effective means of communicating during short forays for additional supplies or if family members evacuate in separate cars.

Pick a physical meeting place
Plan a rendezvous point where your family will meet both inside and outside your immediate area. Practice ahead of time getting to that rendezvous point from different locations at different times, just to get a feel for how it will go in an emergency.

Create in-case-of-emergency (ICE) contacts
Should paramedics or police officers need to contact designated next of kin during a crisis, have everyone in the family enter the acronym ICE (for "in

TIPS&TRICKS

BATTERY USE AND CARE TIPS

- Use the correct size and type of battery specified by the manufacturer of your device.
- Keep battery contact surfaces and battery compartment contacts clean by rubbing them with a clean pencil eraser or a rough cloth each time you replace batteries.
- Remove batteries from a device when it is not expected to be in use for several months.
- Remove batteries from equipment while it is being powered by household (AC) current.
- Make sure that you insert batteries into your device properly, with the (+) and (–) terminals aligned correctly. Caution: Some equipment using more than three batteries may appear to work properly even if one battery is inserted incorrectly.
- Store batteries in a dry place at normal room temperature. Do not refrigerate Duracell batteries. This will not make them last longer. Most Duracell batteries will provide dependable long life even after five years of storage in these conditions.
- Extreme temperatures reduce battery performance. Avoid putting battery-powered devices in very warm places.
- To prevent battery shorting, leakage or rupture, never dispose of batteries in a fire, as they could explode. And do not attempt to recharge a battery unless the battery specifically is marked "rechargeable." △

TIPS & TRICKS •

THE "BUG-OUT" BAG

- Change of clothes (seasonal)
- Socks/underwear
- Sturdy shoes
- Extra set of car and house keys
- Lighter (adults only)
- Pocket knife (adults only)
- Permanent marker
- Notebook
- Flash drive with important financial documents
- ID tag on backpack
- Stuffed animal
- Deck of cards
- AM/FM/NOAA radio
- Batteries
- Quart of water
- Toothbrush
- Toothpaste
- Extra pair of contacts/glasses
- Tissues
- Deodorant

"BUG-OUT" CAR

- Flashlight
- Extra batteries
- Water
- Hearty snacks (such as granola bars)
- Blankets
- Additional jackets and spare items of clothing
- Jack
- Tire-patch kit
- Signal flares
- Metal lockbox or metal/plastic container to store items Ⓐ

case of emergency") into their cell phones along with the number of the person you'd want contacted if they were injured and couldn't respond.

Grab-and-go supplies

Experts suggest that after a disaster every household should be prepared to manage at least 72 hours on its own. That means putting together comprehensive survival kits for each member of the family as well as kits for your office and cars. Several sources give suggestions as to what to include in these kits, depending on your family's needs. The following helpful information and lists are excerpted from *Your Survival*, by Dr. Bob Arnot (Hatherleigh Press, 2008).

There may come a time in a disaster when, no matter how much care you've dedicated to fortifying your home and stockpiling supplies, you may need to leave it all behind and just get the heck out—or "bug out" in disaster parlance. In that case, you'll want to grab whatever few essentials you'll need on the road, and fast. Which is where the bug-out bag comes into play.

To create bug-out bags simply stuff a backpack for each family member with the items on the list at left, and store them with the rest of your supplies. Also get in the habit of storing your family's sleeping bags nearby, along with a handful of other items that could be useful on the road, such as a couple of small tube tents, a leash and a small bag of pet food. That way, the entire family can sling their bug-out bags over their shoulders, help grab the med kit, vital financial records box, tents and sleeping bags, and just go.

Think of your car bug-out kit as a very mini, car-based version of your usual basement stockpile, for those times when your family is stranded on the road. (See "bug-out" car sidebar at left.) If you own a pickup, a metal lockbox would be the perfect place to store it; if not, any sort of metal or plastic container will do.

Gadgets to have on hand

There are a handful of other gadgets that every family should have on hand to ease the burden of an extended utilities outage.

Water filter. A great backup to a bottled water supply, it will remove toxins and bacteria in the event tap water becomes contaminated or you have to rely on external sources such as rain or stream water.

Gas grill. An outdoor portable propane-powered grill with at least one full tank of propane in reserve as a disaster spare can cook your meals.

Metal coffeepot. Caffeine withdrawal can be unpleasant, with symptoms mimicking the flu. Invest in a metal coffeepot that can withstand the extreme temperatures of a grill.

Kids' entertainment devices. Buy yourself some much-needed peace with portable Game Boy systems or their equivalent.

Battery-operated lights. Spend the money for a powerful flashlight that can withstand hours of use and abuse during an emergency. You'll also want to pick up a couple of battery-powered headlamps, so you don't have to juggle a flashlight. Also stock up on some battery-operated LED hurricane lamps for ambient lighting to read and cook by.

Batteries. Even LED lights need to have their batteries replaced occasionally. Count on at least three refills of batteries per battery-operated gadget. Be sure to double-check which kind (D, C, AA, etc.) goes in each. And remember to replace all of the batteries in your disaster supplies once a year before they lose their juice.

Weather radio. This lifesaver is a great addition to any household in the possible path of severe weather. You keep it on 24 hours a day, and normally it remains silent, but the instant the National Weather Service issues a warning the radio emits a piercing beeping sound. In the meantime, pick up a NOAA radio. Look for a brand with "S.A.M.E." technology, which enables you to focus the alert on your immediate vicinity. It'll cut down on annoying false alarms.

Protecting the stuff you can't live without

In the aftermath of any disaster, the reports of victims who have lost all of their family mementos and treasures tug at the heartstrings. These items that insurance can't replace are often what people hold most dear. To help assure that these items are protected, here are some steps to take.

- Open a safe deposit box at a bank. Even with a watertight, fireproof home safe, it's a good idea to keep items that cannot be insured or replaced in a bank vault. Keep a current inventory of the contents of the safe deposit box and appoint a trusted person who can access the box in your absence.

- Obtain and copy all important papers, letters and documents; copy, scan or preferably digitize one-of-a-kind photographs, slides, home movies and videos; and store them on DVDs. Items that cannot be scanned or photocopied (e.g., coin and stamp collections) should be kept in the safe deposit box.

- Duplicate your computer program files and a complete and current backup of your computer data. While it might not be feasible to store duplicate copies of all receipts, tax records, photo negatives and miscellaneous other papers in your safe deposit box, it's a good idea to store the originals or copies at a safe off-premises location, such as your office or the home of a friend or relative.

The process of keeping valuables in a safe deposit box and storing copies and originals in two places will help protect that which you hold dear, regardless of whether you are at home or away if disaster strikes. △

FUN WITH CRAYONS

MAKING HEART SUNCATCHERS

Crayola® crayons
Pencil sharpener
Wax paper
Recycled newspaper
Iron (adult use only)
Crayola blunt-tip scissors
Hole punch
Ribbon

1. Peel the crayon labels if necessary. With a pencil sharpener, make crayon shavings in several colors. Arrange the shavings in a thin layer between wax-paper sheets on newspaper. Cover with a newspaper sheet and lightly iron the newspaper to melt the shavings.

2. When cool, cut out heart shapes. Punch a hole in each and thread with ribbon.

3. Hang hearts in a sunny window!

(The craft is appropriate for children 4 years and older. Adult assistance is required. Be sure to melt crayons in a well-ventilated area: Melting or ironing crayons may release irritating fumes. Ironing should be done by an adult.) 🅰

Litter Purrfect™

PURRFECT SOLUTIONS

WHEN IT COMES TO keeping your feline friends happy, it's not possible to designate a personal litter box for each cat in the household, as cats will use any litter box that's available. Try these suggestions.

● Have at least as many litter boxes as you have cats. That way, none of them will ever be prevented from eliminating in a litter box because it's already occupied.

● Place litter boxes in several locations around the house, so that no one cat can "guard" the litter box area and prevent the other cats from gaining access.

● Place at least one litter box on each level of the house.

Occasionally, a cat may refuse to use a litter box after another cat has used it. In this case, you will need to keep all of the litter boxes extremely clean and you may require additional boxes. 🅰

Ziploc®

ZIPLOC BAGS FOR EVERYDAY USE

ZIPPER FREEZER AND storage bags are essentials for preparing and storing food. For example, you can use one as a handy marinade tool—just mix all of the ingredients inside, add your favorite main ingredient, zip it up and freeze until you're ready to make the meal, letting your food marinate as it defrosts.

But zipper bags are also handy for countless other uses. Here are some examples.

● Use a zipper bag as an on-the-go first-aid kit for a purse, backpack or glove compartment. Include bandages, alcohol wipes, cotton balls, safety pins and an index card with emergency phone numbers.

● Use larger bags to keep sweaty workout clothes separate from other items in a gym bag or suitcase. Simply seal the dirty clothes in a bag for the laundry, keeping everything else clean and dry.

● For cameras, camcorders, computers and other electronics, keep all of the cables, chargers, manuals, CDs and receipts for each organized in separate bags. Mark the bags to avoid confusion.

● Zipper bags are also great for storing and organizing toys with many parts or pieces, such as Legos™ or board games. 🅰

Bed, Bath and Laundry

WE ALL ENJOY an occasional soothing bath, but the ancient Romans really knew how to do it right. Aside from conquering unruly tribes throughout Europe, these people were incredibly devoted to building elaborate baths. At one time, there were almost 900 baths in Rome alone.

These baths were much more than just a place to wash. They were huge complexes that served as a community center, restaurant, fitness center, bar and performance center. Roman baths were beloved by everyone. According to one story, a foreigner asked one Roman emperor why he took the trouble to bathe once a day.

His reply: "Because I do not have the time to bathe twice a day."

Smart ways to store things at home

AS YOU ORGANIZE all the things in your house, it's clear that items such as blankets, toys, seasonal products and so on take up lots of room. A very clever storage solution is the vacuum-seal storage bag. These bags have airtight and watertight zippers and a one-way air valve so that, using an ordinary vacuum, you can suck out all the air in the bag. The result is a smaller package to store, saving space and keeping the items clean and safe.

There are dozens of smart applications for these vacuum-seal storage bags. Here are a few.

In the closet

When it comes to our wardrobes, most of us wear 20 percent of our clothes 80 percent of the time. That leaves a lot of clothes just hanging around the closet. And if you're working with a small closet, those garments are taking up some prime real estate!

The first step to any closet overhaul is remove everything. Then, separate everything by season, or winter and summer wear.

Store all your winter items, such as sweaters, ski coats, pants and bulky comforters, in vacuum-seal bags. Once the seasons change, your winter clothing comes out fresh and clean. Do the same for your summer wardrobe when the time comes.

Kids' stuff

Infant and toddler gear expands exponentially. You can store a child's precious baby clothes safely and securely; compress and protect extra bedding, pillows and blankets; and provide a dirt- and allergen-free storage place for the stuffed animal overflow.

Around the house

For belongings you want by your front door, use a bag in the nearest closet. It's a handy way to store mittens, scarves, hats and the like. The front-door closet is also a great place for storing winter coats and foul-weather gear.

For the dining room, seal your good silver in airtight and watertight vacuum-seal bags to put the brakes on the tarnishing process. Silver will tarnish when exposed to air and moisture.

In your attic, take advantage of empty suitcases by compressing seasonal clothing or bedding in bags, then place them inside the luggage. Stored items will be safe from moisture, pests, mildew, dirt and odors, and take up zero additional space. ◭

Conforms to the shape of your moving boxes.

Adds extra capacity to your storage bins.

TYPES	STANDARD SIZES	NUMBER OF CUBES
Plastic bin	40 qt. (38 L)	1 extra-large
Plastic bin	30 gal. (11.4 L)	1 jumbo + 1 large
Medium moving box	18" x 18" x 16"	2 large + 1 extra-large
Large moving box	18" x 18" x 24"	1 jumbo + 1 extra-large

TIPS FOR TRAVEL

ON THE ROAD

Vacuum-seal bags can be very handy on the road. In larger suitcases, they can be used to compress and organize the contents. Fill and compress one with just underwear, another with socks and scarves. Another can hold soft items such as T-shirts and nightclothes.

If you're traveling with kids, these bags can hold complete outfits so that the kids can find their own items and dress themselves.

Take along extra bags to hold dirty laundry and keep the rest of the contents in the suitcase fresh and clean. Also, use a bag to hold film, extra batteries and other items you want to keep waterproof and easy to find.

IN THE RV

Here are four road-tested ways to improve your RV experience with vacuum-seal bags.

- Store clean towels, linens and extra pillows for protection against dirt, bugs, moisture and odors, while freeing up vital space.
- Protect maps, road atlases and other important documents such as vehicle registrations, extended-service agreements, manuals and campground permits.

VACUUM OUT THE AIR

- Trade your onboard laundry hamper for a large bag to keep the interior of your RV odor-free and dry.
- Be prepared with foul-weather gear, but keep it compressed in a storage bag and stowed out of the way.

ON THE BOAT

Every boater shares two common challenges: how to stow the most items in limited space and how to protect them from the ravages of moisture, mildew and water. Use vacuum-seal bags to keep clothing, charts, matches, flares and other important items clean, dry and ready to use. These bags can shrink the volume of clothing, bedding and blankets in half, making room for more stowage in tight spaces.

Before   After

TIPS & TRICKS

SPONSORED BY

KIRKLAND Signature

CARING FOR CASHMERE

CASHMERE SWEATERS are the ultimate luxury. They are soft, lightweight and can be worn throughout the seasons. Sweaters made with two-ply cashmere yarns are dense and will not excessively stretch or pill, even with repeated wear.

To keep cashmere sweaters looking their best year after year, just handle them with a little TLC.

- Let garments rest for at least 24 hours between wearings; any wrinkles will vanish.
- Store sweaters folded, with a sachet or cedar block tucked inside. Never hang a cashmere sweater or store it in plastic.
- Treat stains as quickly as possible. Rinse immediately with cold water; hot water may set the stain. If garments get wet, allow to dry away from direct heat.
- Dry cleaning is recommended because it will help maintain the shape of the garment. Knits can be carefully hand-washed in cold water, using a fine-washables soap, then rolled in a bath towel to remove excess water and dried flat.
- Moths are attracted to stains and soil left on the garment, not to the material itself. At season's end, clean and store cashmere garments in a chest or drawer. ▲

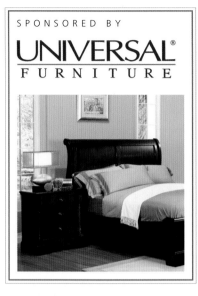

Buying the best bedroom furniture

HAVE YOU SHOPPED for furniture lately? In today's market, the options seem limitless. As this market has become more global, more people are making and selling furniture than ever before. With good photography, advertising can make two vastly different pieces of furniture look almost the same.

Many times, consumers are bombarded with beautiful pictures, lots of options to make the purchase as easy as a phone call (such as zero percent interest for extended periods of time, in-home delivery or even "free" stuff) and prices that just seem to have no bottom. All of this can be quite confusing.

Here are a few things to consider when you make your next bedroom furniture purchase.

Storage and other considerations

Storage space in bedrooms is still a major consideration. As our household inventories grow with things that are supposed to make our lives easier, finding places to store them is becoming more and more difficult. So, when selecting your next bedroom furniture, consider how much and what kind of storage space you need.

Many smart options are being offered, such as:

• Hidden jewelry storage
• Built-in storage units under the bed
• Pull-out trays in nightstands (some with capacity to hold beverages)
• Cell phone outlets in nightstands
• Cedar-lined drawers
• Velvet-lined drawers (for delicates)
• Fully finished drawers (again for delicates)
• Sweater storage
• Mirrors

Another important factor to consider is whether you'll have a television in your bedroom. What are the space requirements? Will weight be a factor? And do you have other components to consider (for example, a DVD player or cable box)?

Televisions have undergone huge changes in the past few years. Furniture that accommodates these changes has followed. Now, TV consoles come as an alternative to traditional armoires, offering additional drawer storage space as well as a platform for a flat-screen TV. Some include electrical components built into the case to help with wire management for your TV, cable box and other components.

Good-quality drawer construction is a hallmark of heirloom furniture.

Built to last

It's amazing how dressing items up makes them look better. But, when you look a little closer, you can often see many differences that can help ensure you are getting the best value for your money. Here are a few details to consider.

Drawer construction. Drawers should be made with solid wood or unidirectional plywood drawer sides and backs. Unidirectional plywood is sawn or sliced lumber that has been glued back together with the grain running in the same direction.

All joints on the drawers should be English dovetail or French dovetail construction. The bottoms of the drawers should be glued on all sides

English dovetail joinery is strong and results in a large-capacity drawer.

with corner blocks in each corner. Drawer slides should be made of hardwood. Paraffin waxes are used to help the drawers operate more smoothly. Tension stops are used on the bottoms of the drawers to help keep them from pulling out of the cases. Some drawers have "kicker" cleats added to the case above the inside of the drawer so that when they are fully open the drawer's deflection downward is minimized.

Ball bearing glides are also used as an alternative to hardwood slides. Ball bearing glides often allow you to open the drawer farther than hardwood slides and perform better in harsher climates.

Case construction. Dustproof panels between each drawer add value and strength to the case. Solid wood edges, especially where there is a profiled shape on the edge, increase performance.

Avoid exposed medium-density fiberboard or particleboard edges. If glass is used, make sure it is tempered. If glass shelves are used, 3/8-inch (8 mm) thicknesses are preferred.

Look for levelers built into the case, usually underneath the feet. On heavy cases, levelers may be adjusted from inside. Levelers are usually used

TIPS&TRICKS

TIPS ON SPACE

IN THE LAST DECADE, furniture seems to have put on some weight. The pieces just get bigger and bigger. Many of the collections offered today will not fit in an average-size bedroom.

Measure your bedroom space before shopping. Make a small sketch of your bedroom and mark the location of windows, doors, and phone and cable connections. Knowing the size of your bedroom and where doors, windows and phone and cable connections are located will help simplify your decision. **A**

to properly align doors or drawers (or the gaps made up by them) when the floor isn't level.

Along with being decorative, hardware should be functional and strong. It should be solid (not hollow) whenever possible. This is often difficult to determine on a piece of furniture, but the hardware's weight is usually a good determining factor.

Another common question is whether solid wood is better than veneer. Veneer is not necessarily a cheaper alternative and can last as long as and possibly longer than solid wood. One advantage of veneer is that the manufacturer can create fancy faces that can't be made with solid wood.

Several different types of core materials can be used with veneer, including particleboard, medium-density fiberboard and solid wood. Each has advantages and disadvantages, depending on the application within the product or in the manufacturing process.

Climate is another important issue to consider when choosing between solid wood and veneer. Veneer applications (with medium-density fiberboard or particleboard cores) are more stable than solid wood applications. Wood, in any state, is a living product. Even after assembly and finishing, wood parts can gain and lose moisture based on outside conditions. Very cold, dry climates will cause wood to dry and shrink (both solid and veneer). Warm, moist climates will cause wood to gain moisture and swell.

Changes in seasons from the cold of winter to the heat of summer will cause this movement. The more solid wood there is in a product, the higher the chance of movement. ⬛

FURNITURE STYLES EXPLAINED

Furniture, and home décor, can represent various styles. Here's a look at the most common styles, courtesy of the American Home Furnishings Alliance.

TRADITIONAL FURNITURE is formal in every sense, with symmetrical designs, graceful carved curves, rich and mellow colors, dark polished wood and elegant upholstery. The style includes reproductions of antiques made before 1900, such as Biedermeier, Chippendale, French Empire and Sheraton. Wingback chairs, damask and chintz fabric covers, cherry and mahogany woods, indoor topiaries and Oriental carpets are classic examples of the time-honored traditional style.

COUNTRY-STYLE décors exude welcoming, heartwarming coziness. Timeworn furnishings, distressed and painted woods, plump sofas and ruffled skirts are reminiscent of the style pioneered by the settlers of North America. Country's hallmarks include pine and oak, rounded and soft cushions, floral prints, bold stripes, gingham and plain fabric covers. Accent pieces include quilts, braided rugs and folk art.

CASUAL FURNITURE caters to today's easy-living lifestyles. Think overstuffed sofas, care-free fabric covers, matte finishes and a range of wood, including oak, pine, ash and maple. Combined with earthy neutral colors, textured upholstery and personal keepsakes, casual interiors are spaces with warmth, friendliness and lived-in ease.

CONTEMPORARY FURNITURE encompasses all things simple, streamlined and sleek. Evolving since 1900, the look is modern. Bold colors. Sharp lines. Minimalist patterns. Larger-scale accessories and art pieces are often used to complement metal and glass—setting the stage for refreshing, uncomplicated contemporary interiors.

ECLECTIC INTERIORS are highly individualistic and feature a mix of many styles. Collected objects from around the world and ethnic or artisan pieces may be highlighted accents. Furniture and textured fabric covers cross styles and periods, while color is often the common denominator. True eclectic style reflects a unique eye and personal interests.

To find out your style, take the style profile quiz at *www.findyourfurniture.com.*

• HELPFUL **HOW TO'S**

PROTECTING YOUR INVESTMENT

YOU SHOULD ALWAYS protect finished surfaces. Most common furniture finishes will not resist severe and, in some cases, even moderate scratching. To take care of your furniture, follow these easy steps:

- Use a soft, clean cloth that will not scratch the surface when dusting.

- Using furniture polish is not necessary. If you choose to use a furniture polish, test it in a hidden area.

- Using solvents of any kind may damage the finish.

- Never use water to clean your furniture.

- Always use coasters or protective pads under beverage glasses, flower pots and lamps.

- Liquid spills should be removed immediately. Use a soft clean cloth and blot the spill gently. Avoid rubbing.

- Direct sunlight may damage wood finishes.

- Extreme temperature and humidity changes can cause warping, shrinking and splitting of wood furniture. It is best to keep furniture in a climate-controlled environment.

- Always use protective pads under hot or cold dishes and plates. Extreme temperatures can cause chemical changes that may create spotting within the finish.

- Stains or marks from crayons or markers will be difficult to remove. Use a professional to do so. ▲

Know your sheets

REMEMBER WHEN A SHEET was just a sheet? Nowadays, it's all about thread count, or so it seems. But that's just one of several factors to consider when purchasing sheets.

Thread count. This refers to the number of vertical (warp) and horizontal (weft) threads in a square inch of fabric. Typically, the higher the thread count, the softer and more lustrous the fabric.

Most people prefer a higher-thread-count cotton sheet. Years ago, 180 to 200 thread counts were considered the standard for a quality sheet. Now, with advanced weaving techniques, sheets are produced in higher thread counts ranging from 400 to 600 thread counts using single-ply cotton yarns.

However, if you see sheets with very high thread counts, the manufacturer may be weaving two-ply yarns and counting the plys, or individual strands, that are twisted together to make the thread. Don't expect the same performance and durability from a sheet made with two-ply (twisted) yarns as those made with single-ply yarns.

Fiber length. The longer the fiber, or staple, the stronger and softer the resulting fabric. Both Egyptian and Pima or Supima cottons have long staples and are usually identified as such.

Combed or carded cotton. A good bet is combed cotton. Combing removes fibers that are short or dead (which appear as specks on finished sheets). Combed yarn is stronger, softer, more lustrous and has a more even appearance.

Subtle patterns lend a touch of class to bedroom décor.

Solid-color sheets and pillowcases have a calming effect in the bedroom.

Bold, yarn-dyed plaid patterns in the pillows and sheets draw attention to the bed.

Mercerized. The mercerization process removes irregularities from the woven fabric, leaving it extremely smooth and soft. Mercerization also increases the yarn's luster, strength and affinity for dye pickup, resulting in improved shade brilliancy and evenness.

Anti-crease finish. This finish gives easy-care ironing properties to sheets and also improves the softness and handling after every wash without substantially affecting the sheen of the fabric.

Yarn-dyed. Dyeing yarn before it is woven or knitted results in a more uniform color.

→ HELPFUL **HOW TO'S**

YOU GOTTA KNOW HOW TO FOLD 'EM

IS THERE ANY household task more challenging than folding a fitted sheet? For most people, the answer is a resounding no. Here is the process made simple.

1. Slip your hand into two top corners of the sheet.

2. With one hand inside each of the top two corners, fold the sheet in half horizontally (right sides together). Slip each of the top corners into one of the bottom corners.

3. Lay the sheet on a bed or table. Arrange and fold the corners neatly. Turn in the selvage edges enough to make four straight sides.

4. Fold in half, then in half again. (All four corners will be stacked together, and the sheet will be in a long strip.)

5. Fold the long strip in half, then in half (or thirds, depending on the size of the sheet) again to make a square.

6. Smooth sheet and place on shelf.

TIPS

1. Learn how to fold sheets consistently so that they remain neat each time.

2. Store sheets in sets (flat, fitted and cases) if that is how you use them.

3. Mark shelves with sheet sizes, or use different shelves for different-size sheets.

4. For patterned sheets, fold the bottom sheet inside out and the top sheet right side out, and you'll be able to easily tell the difference.

• **TIPS**&TRICKS

MATTRESS MATTERS

TO GET THE BEST from your sheets, it's important to know a little bit about your mattress. Before buying a sheet set, make sure you know the size of your mattress. Keep the following factors in mind:

- The new pillow-top styles may be 18 to 21 inches deep. Measure the thickness of your mattress to see if you need "deep-pocket" sheets.

- What is a California king versus an Eastern king? A California king-size mattress is 84 inches long by 72 inches wide. It is longer but slightly narrower than an Eastern king. California kings are usually found only in homes in California, homes of former Californians who have taken their mattresses with them elsewhere and homes of basketball players. An Eastern king-size mattress is 80 inches long by 78 inches wide. This size is usually found everywhere else in the country and usually just takes on the designation king-size without the word "Eastern" preceding it.

Bed, Bath and Laundry ● **117**

How to pick a perfect pillow

ONE-THIRD OF YOUR LIFE is spent in bed. Shouldn't the pillows you use help you enjoy that time instead of leaving you achy and restless? Here are some tips for finding the perfect pillow—which can lead to a healthy, restful and comfortable night of sleep.

Determine your pillow style. The position you sleep in says a lot about the type of support you need in a pillow. Stomach sleepers need a soft pillow with little elevation, back sleepers need a medium pillow with moderate elevation and side sleepers need a firmer pillow with maximum elevation. When purchasing a pillow, keep in mind how you sleep to determine what type of pillow to sleep with.

Keep it fresh. Pillows should be replaced every one to two years to ensure proper health and support. Lumpy or flat pillows are a good indication that a pillow has reached the end of its life span.

Beware of a pillow past its prime. Even if your pillow is not flat or lumpy, do not wait more than two years to replace it. A pillow past its prime could contain a high level of dust mites, which increase breathing disorders, asthma and allergies. The older the pillow, the more it can contribute to sleep deprivation and body aches as well.

Take the test. One good way to determine if your pillow might need replacing is the following test. Take your pillow and fold it in half. Place a tennis shoe on the pillow. If the pillow throws the shoe off, it still has some life. If the pillow just sits there with the shoe on top, it's time to purchase a new pillow. ◬

➤ **THIS**&THAT

SLEEP FACTS

1. The American Sleep Disorders Association recognizes 85 sleep disorders.

2. Losing 1 1/2 hours of sleep per night reduces alertness by 32 percent.

3. Fifteen hundred deaths a year result from drivers falling asleep at the wheel.

4. Women report more sleep problems than men.

SLEEPING SOUNDLY

HOW CAN YOU TELL IF YOU HAVE A SLEEP PROBLEM?

It isn't so much about how long it takes you to get to sleep or how often you wake during the night as it is about feeling good and productive during the day. If you feel tired every day, then you probably have some kind of a sleep problem. If you do not feel alert and with-it during the day, you probably have a problem getting quality sleep. If the problem persists over a period of weeks, consult your doctor.

WHAT ARE SOME OF THE REASONS PEOPLE HAVE A HARD TIME GOING TO SLEEP?

Stress is one of the biggest reasons for having trouble getting to sleep. Many people have an overactive mind that takes over when they lie down to sleep. They review lists of things that they forgot to do during the day, worry about bills and external events, and generally have a hard time winding down from the stress of their day.

Also, eating too close to bedtime can cause you to have trouble falling asleep. And room temperature is important. To get quality sleep you need to be comfortable, not too cold or too hot.

IF YOU HAVE A GENUINE MEDICAL REASON FOR LOSING SLEEP, WHAT CAN YOU DO FOR IT SHORT OF TAKING SLEEPING PILLS?

Make sure your sleep environment is supportive of a great night's sleep by making it comfortable, dark and quiet. Move computers, TVs and other electronic distractions into another room. Stick to a routine and try to go to bed at the same time every night. Soon your body will learn that that time is a cue to sleep. Eliminate caffeine, stop smoking and don't drink alcohol before bed. Give yourself time to wind down; perhaps take a soothing bath, stretch or read a book. Don't engage in stimulating or stressful activities (such as paying bills or watching late-night news).

—*Mary Kelley, Sleep expert*

LAUNDRY TIPS

YOU CAN KEEP your clothes looking newer longer by following a few simple steps.

PROPER SORTING

Sort garments according to like colors, fabric types and soil content to help prevent laundry problems such as dye transfer and garment shrinkage.

STAIN TREATMENT

In addition to your regular detergent, add a scoop of oxygen-based stain remover to every wash load. These stain removers contain natural oxygen-generating ingredients that work to remove a variety of stains. Adding it to every load means it will attack and remove stains you didn't even know you had. Extra-stubborn stains can be pretreated following package directions.

THE RIGHT TEMPERATURE

Following garment-label care instructions, wash garments in the hottest water the fabric will allow.

PREVENT FADING

Chlorine can be disastrous to some garments. Oxygen-based stain removers contain natural ingredients that help to neutralize chlorine found in municipal water systems. Adding them to your wash along with your regular detergent can help protect clothes from fading. ▲

The lowdown on down

IMAGINE YOURSELF SNUGGLING beneath a fluffy comforter filled with the
cozy lightness and warmth of down or resting your head on a pillow that gently
cradles your neck in a natural, healthy alignment with your back.

Many people aspire to this kind of sleep experience but find themselves
confused when it comes time to make a purchase decision. Cleanliness and
fill power are the best indicators of quality. Here are answers to some of the
most commonly asked questions.

Why buy a down comforter?

Down provides light, breathable comfort. Ounce for ounce, it's the best
insulator on earth. It insulates by trapping warm air and it wicks away moisture, making it extraordinarily comfortable in a wide range of temperatures.
There's nothing like the luxurious feel of a down comforter.

Why buy a down pillow?

Health experts agree that diet,
exercise and sleep are the three foun-
dations for good health. Most people
spend a considerable amount of time
and money trying to improve their
diet and exercise programs, but a
good pillow is also essential to long-
term good health.

Down pillows provide wonderful, luxurious comfort and automatically
put your body in a healthy sleeping posture. Poor-quality or worn-out pillows
can twist your spine and create neck tension.

What are down and feathers?

Down and feathers are nature's fluffiest and lightest sleeping materials.
A down puff is a small three-dimensional cluster of many filaments that
expand to trap air. When used in comforters, down allows air to circulate
around you, leaving you to sleep more comfortably and soundly. When used
in pillows, down provides soft adjustable comfort that conforms to your
changing sleep positions.

Feathers are naturally fluffy and have a resilient quill structure. This spring-
like quality provides resilience and support in pillows and feather beds.

What about allergies?

Most sleepers who experience allergy symptoms are actually reacting to
poorly cleaned down. If down is properly and thoroughly cleaned, the dust,
dirt and allergens are removed, eliminating the cause of allergy symptoms and
other problems. What remains are the lighter-than-air down puffs.

Is down too hot?

Down maintains a comfort level in a wide range of temperatures, thus
providing year-round comfort. ◭

THE DOWN BUYING GUIDE

Not all down bedding is created equal. When comparing products, here's what to look for.

ADFC CERTIFICATION

The American Down and Feather Council (ADFC) is an association of manufacturers of natural-fill bedding products as well as dealers, buyers, sellers and processors of down and feathers. Their goal is to maintain and improve product quality and labeling accuracy.

FILL POWER

A fill power of 525 or more is considered excellent.

CLEANLINESS

Look for Hyperclean down or other indications of cleanliness levels.

WARRANTY/GUARANTEE

Look for products that carry guarantees against defects in materials and workmanship. The best products have the longest warranties, making them the best value. Also, look for warranties that a product is allergen-free.

FABRIC

The best fabrics are the lightest possible 100 percent cotton. The tighter the weave (thread count), the lighter the fabric, which maximizes down loft.

LEAKPROOF COVER

Higher-thread-count, tightly woven fabrics help keep down from escaping from bedding. However, thread count in itself does not guarantee downproofness. Shoppers should look for product information that tells them the item can meet a "downproof" claim.

CONSTRUCTION (STITCHING)

The best comforter stitching allows the down to loft the most, providing maximum insulation, breathability and durability. At the same time, the stitching should minimize shifting. Baffles and sewn-through designs are best.

SIZE

Oversize comforters tend to drape better and accommodate larger mattresses. (Queen = 90" x 98", King = 108" x 98".)

FOR INFORMATION ON CARING FOR DOWN, SEE PAGE 122.

• **TIPS** &TRICKS

DOWN TERMINOLOGY

BAFFLES are small interior walls of fabric that are sewn between the top and bottom layer of the outer fabric, forming enclosed three-dimensional boxes. These chambers keep down in place while allowing maximum lofting for the fluffiest of looks.

FILL POWER indicates the loft or insulation ability of down products in cubic inches per ounce. The higher the number, the greater the fill power. High fill power means a loftier and more durable product.

THREAD COUNT is defined as the number of threads per square inch of fabric. Two-ply yarns are counted as one thread and may not be used to double the thread count per the American Society of Testing and Materials. It is important to note that even within a single thread count there can be many quality levels—much of it depends on the weaving and finishing techniques. ▲

Caring for down

WHEN YOU DECIDE to purchase a down comforter you are selecting the coziest, most luxurious and comfortable way to sleep. Possibly you want to be warmer in bed or just sleep better. Since you spend one-third of your life in bed, you should invest in a high-quality down comforter, and you will enjoy it year-round for many years to come.

Energy experts say that for every degree the thermostat is lowered, your heating bill can drop by about 2 percent. Because down's insulating power is so efficient, it will keep you warm and cozy all through the chilliest nights. So cuddling up under a down comforter can benefit your pocketbook as well as enhance your sleeping comfort.

Down comforters

Cleaning. Always follow the instructions on the care label. Using a duvet cover is recommended. If used with a duvet cover, your comforter will need to be cleaned only every three to five years. Comforters should be professionally dry cleaned or laundered. Nonprofessional laundering is not recommended because home washers and dryers are too small to accommodate the size and dimensions of down comforters. Also, most household washing machines have an agitator in the center, which places unnecessary stress on comforters.

Down pillows

Down pillows are easy to revitalize. To refluff your pillows, pop them in your dryer on low heat along with a damp washcloth. The warmth and humidity will make your pillow like new.

Washing. Always follow the instructions on the care label. Pillows can be laundered in a home washing machine one to two times a year or as needed. Professional laundering is an alternative. Pillow protectors are also recommended to further extend the life of the product and reduce the amount of washing needed.

Drying. Place the pillow, along with one to two tennis balls, into your dryer. Use low heat. The drying process may take several hours to completely dry your pillows. As with all down/feather-filled products, drying times may vary, but it is important that the products be thoroughly dried before they are put back in use. ▲

HEALTHY SLEEPING TIPS

- Sleep on your back to keep your spine in alignment.

- If you sleep on your side, place a second pillow between your knees to prevent your legs from separating and twisting your lower back.

- Don't sleep on your stomach. It puts the most stress on your spine, forcing your neck severely out of natural alignment.

- Orthopedic doctors and chiropractors agree that nearly all neck and back problems are worsened, if not caused, by improper sleeping habits.

- Minimize light and make your bedroom sleep-friendly—dark, quiet and uncluttered.

- Control the temperature. The ideal room temperature for sleeping is 65 degrees, with 65 percent humidity.

- Maintain a screen-free zone in the bedroom. Watching TV or working on the computer stimulates the brain.

- Listen to calming music or a relaxation CD before bed.

- Indulge in caffeine in the morning only. It can stay in your system for as long as 20 hours.

- Make sure your medications aren't interfering with sleep.

TIPS & TRICKS

FINDING THE PERFECT COMFORTER

THE EMBRACING, INSULATING warmth of a down comforter can vary depending on how much down is used.

To find the perfect comfort level for you, follow these guidelines:

- If you sleep in a cold climate or cooler environment and like to sleep warm, look for an Extra Warmth rating.

- If you sleep in a warmer environment and like to sleep cool, look for a Light Warmth rating.

- If your sleep environment is moderate and does not change during the year, look for a Year Round Warmth rating.

How memory foam works

AFTER A LONG DAY, few things are more inviting than the thought of falling into bed. To help ensure a good night's sleep, the fatigued across North America are discovering the comfort and support of memory-foam pillows, mattress toppers and mattresses.

History of memory foam

Memory foam was originally developed by the U.S. National Aeronautics and Space Administration (NASA) in the 1970s to provide astronauts with relief from the tremendous G-force involved in space travel. NASA scientists added chemicals to polyurethane foam, the same material used by upholsterers, to increase its weight and density. The result was padding that conformed to an individual's body yet resumed its original shape after use.

Unfortunately, T-foam, NASA's version of memory foam, was never used on a space mission because it released gases, making it unusable in sealed, confined environments. However, because it effectively eliminates incorrect pressure points and prevents the spread of bacteria and microbes, hospitals began using memory-foam mattresses for patients, especially for those confined to bed for extended periods.

The memory-foam mattresses used in the medical industry were, and still are, very expensive. That's what led innovators to develop a more affordable line of high-quality memory-foam products. Today, memory foam is the fastest-growing line of products in the sleep industry.

How memory foam works

Memory foam has two characteristics that make it ideal for a good night's sleep. First, it consists of millions of pockets that compress and spread their air pressure to adjoining pockets. Second, it is temperature sensitive: At lower temperatures it is firmer, while at higher temperatures it is softer and more conforming. Therefore, it becomes softer where your body makes contact and remains firmer in areas where there is less body contact.

The difference between the traditional spring-coil mattress—the most popular mattress option

Lie down on a memory-foam mattress and the heaviest parts of your body, usually your hips, sink in farther than lighter parts such as your feet.

If you want the benefits of a memory-foam sleeping surface without replacing your current mattress, a memory-foam topper (a pad ranging from 2 to 4 inches thick that sits on top of your mattress) offers an excellent alternative.

for decades—and a memory-foam mattress is that memory foam conforms to a person's body, evenly distributing a person's weight across the entire surface. That means that pressure points are reduced or eliminated, which promotes orthopedic wellness and comfort. With pressure points eliminated, people are less likely to toss and turn, which often occurs while trying to find a comfortable spot.

On the other hand, spring-coil mattresses offer support by using varying degrees of pressure, known as "push-back" pressure. With this pressure eliminated, the chance of a stiff neck or back is reduced.

The science of memory foam

Scientists measure pressure by mmHg, which stand for millimeters of mercury. One mmHg is a unit of atmospheric pressure. Sleep experts have found that when it comes to people sleeping, at 32 mmHg the capillaries in the body become stressed and force the sleeper to turn.

Memory foam distributes the body's weight, which results in a pressure reading of 22 mmHg, 33 percent less than conventional mattresses. Less pressure on the body results in a better night's sleep. Ⓐ

Choose a memory-foam pillow for the finishing touch to a perfect night's rest. Available in a wide range of shapes and levels of support, a memory foam pillow conforms to the natural shape of your head and gently cradles your neck.

➤ THIS&THAT ⌐

MEMORY FOAM HAS MANY BENEFITS

FEWER PROBLEMS WITH MORNING SORENESS. Since memory foam effectively reduces push-back pressure, it can help minimize waking up with a stiff neck or sore back.

LESS TOSSING AND TURNING. Memory foam provides even support to your whole body, eliminating the need to toss and turn.

REDUCES PRESSURE POINTS. Memory foam reduces and eliminates pressure points because it conforms to the shape of your body.

BETTER QUALITY OF SLEEP. Because memory foam lets you make the most of your sleeping hours, you wake up refreshed and rejuvenated.

LONG-LASTING SUPPORT. Memory-foam toppers not only extend the life of your mattress but give continued comfort and support.

• THIS&THAT

THE LAST WORD ON SLEEP

The best bridge between despair and hope is a good night's sleep.
—E. Joseph Cossman

People who say they sleep like a baby usually don't have one.
—Leo J. Burke

Sleep is like the unicorn; it is rumored to exist, but I doubt I will see any.—Anonymous

A good laugh and a long sleep are the best cures in the doctor's book.
—Irish Proverb

Early to bed and early to rise makes a man healthy, wealthy, and wise—Benjamin Franklin

Laugh and the world laughs with you. Snore and you sleep alone.
—Anthony Burgess

Beautify your bath on a budget

BATHROOMS IN TODAY'S HOMES have moved beyond a utilitarian water closet to large and luxurious spaces evoking a spa experience. If your bathroom doesn't measure up, you might want to look at several low-cost improvements that can quickly transform the space.

Color. If you're stuck with ceramic tile that screams 1950, try camouflaging it with new towels, bath rug, shower curtain and other accessories that will make the room feel more contemporary. For example, try deep brown with pink tile, or bright blue with light green tile. Because most bathrooms are small, painting the walls a bold color can breathe new life into the space. For a more restful feel, stay with muted pastels. A slightly darker color on the ceiling will help overcome the towering feeling in small bathrooms.

Fixtures. Switch from shiny chrome to pewter or brushed stainless steel fixtures for the tub, shower and sinks. It's an updated look and easier to clean, because it doesn't show water marks.

Lighting. Look at lighting not just for illumination but for creating ambience. Sconces on either side of a mirror are much more pleasing than overhead lights.

Mirrors. A new mirror can also add a decorative element. Consider a collection of mirrors to visually expand the space.

Furniture. If you have room, consider an étagère. The open shelves will provide room for extra storage or accessories— the perfect place for extra towels, a stack of magazines, an MP3 player or plants.

Accessories. Get creative with decorative items: tissue boxes, soap dishes, scented candles. Don't limit yourself to bathroom items—a lovely serving bowl could hold potpourri, a clear vase can display bath salts or cotton balls, and baskets could hold rolled-up towels.

Once you've completed your bathroom makeover, keep it fresh by changing the look from season to season with new towels, bath rug and other accessories. △

Smart uses of bleach

BLEACH HAS PROVEN to be a very effective cleaner, possibly for thousands of years. Early history records people mixing wood ashes with water to create a lye solution that could be used to clean clothes, with the sun serving as a dryer.

Scientists, of course, refined those early processes to create today's bleach. There are actually different types of bleach, but the most common for households is chlorine beach, which contains sodium hypochlorite. Bleach works by breaking down the chemical bonds that allow soils and stains to attach to fabrics, making it easier for detergents to wash them away.

Bleach has numerous uses, but it's most effective when used in the right amounts and methods. Here's a look around the house.

Kitchen

- Sanitize sponges and dishcloths every day by soaking them in a solution of ¾ cup of bleach per gallon of water.
- Clean sinks with the same solution, then pour in a cup of full-strength bleach to flush the drain. Flush again with hot water.

Bath

- Use the bleach solution to clean and disinfect porcelain, tile, counters, sinks, fiberglass, tubs and showers.
- To clean and disinfect toilet bowls, pour in a cup of bleach, brush thoroughly and let stand for 10 minutes, then flush.

Nursery

- Use bleach solution to clean and disinfect nonporous toys, changing tables, painted cribs, high chairs, plastic mattress covers, bumpers and diaper pails.

Note: It's important to never use bleach at full strength for cleaning surfaces. Also, wear gloves when cleaning for prolonged periods of time. △

MEMBER**TIP**

COURTESY OF
CARALYN HOUSE
RALEIGH, NC

I AM A PASTRY chef, and chocolate stains are the worst. Here is my "stain recipe" for cleaner clothes: Pour 1 cup Cascade dish detergent and 1 cup Clorox 2 for Colors into washing machine. Add clothes, and fill with hot water. Let agitate for a few minutes, then let soak overnight. In the morning, finish the cycle. This process will remove the majority of stains! △

MEMBER**TIP**

A stain solution cheat sheet

A STAIN DOESN'T HAVE TO ruin a garment. With the right steps, even the toughest stains can be removed.

The best defense in removing stains is to treat them immediately. Make sure you blot up liquid spills or scrape off solid buildup with the edge of a dull knife. Work from the outer edge to the center of the stain—and don't rub.

Always check the care label first, and pretest stain-removal products. If the item is dry-clean only, blot the excess and take the item to the cleaners within 24 to 48 hours of the stain.

Most stains fall in one of the following categories. With all stains, rinse and inspect the washed (or treated) garment before drying.

Protein: Baby food or formula, body soils (feces, urine, vomit), blood, dairy, dirt/clay/mud, egg, gelatin dessert.

The solution: Soak fresh stains in cold water. Rub fabric against itself gently to dislodge stains. If stains are old, scrape off the crusted material and soak in cold water with a good liquid detergent. Launder in warm water.

Do not use hot water to soak or wash items with protein stains; hot water may set these types of stains.

Oil-based: Grease or oil from cars, makeup and food (including butter and mayonnaise), collar/cuff soil, deodorant/perspiration, gasoline.

The solution: Pretreat with a good liquid detergent. Make sure to work detergent into the stain and let set for 10 to 15 minutes, then wash in the hottest water safe for the fabric.

Tannin: Beer, coffee, tea, soft drinks, fruit and juice (including red berries), perfume, wine.

The solution: First rinse in cool water, then wash fresh stains in the hottest water safe for the fabric, with a good laundry detergent. Use a detergent with bleach or bleach alternative for old stains. Do not use bar soap on tannin stains—it makes them harder to remove.

Dye: Dye transfer, fruit (blueberry and cherry), grass, Kool-Aid,® mustard.

The solution: Pretreat with a good liquid detergent and rinse thoroughly. Soak in a diluted solution of water and a detergent with bleach or bleach alternative, then wash in the hottest water safe for the fabric.

Others: Ballpoint ink, candle wax, chewing gum, crayon, lipstick, shoe polish, chocolate, gravy, ketchup, tomato-based sauces.

The solution: These stains generally involve two components: oil/wax and dye/pigment. Remove the oily portion first and then the dye portion.

For most other combination stains, rub a good liquid detergent into the stain, then wash in the hottest water possible for the fabric with a detergent with bleach or bleach alternative.

For more information on removing specific stains, see *www.tide.com* and visit the Fabric Advisor. △

Travel and Recreation

BAD NEWS FOR MODERN cubicle-farm dwellers: According to Wikipedia, the typical adult male peasant in the UK in the 13th century put in some 1,620 hours each year on the job. Today, the average worker in the United States logs some 2,000 hours each year on the job. This means that despite all our computers, phones, PDAs and other devices meant to save time, those cow-milking peasants had more leisure hours than we do today.

No figures are available on what they actually did with all that extra time, but one thing is clear: They weren't watching TV. According to AC Nielsen, the average American watches more than four hours of TV each day—28 hours per week. That means that a 65-year-old has spent nine years glued to the tube. Our point: Get out and do something leisurely! △

Travel with an open mind and think globally

By Rick Steves

FOR MANY PEOPLE, the critical question nowadays is "How can we make ourselves safer in the world?" I think we'd be safer by better understanding our world. A great first step is to travel—thoughtfully.

Thoughtful travel—becoming a "temporary local" to really get a break from our cultural norms—shows us how the world sees us. My travels have taught me that people around the world are inclined to like citizens from other countries, even though they often disagree with their governments.

Though many people travel, millions more don't venture out to see or experience the world. Many do not hold a passport. Many of them have world-views based on little more than TV news. Travel gives us a firsthand look at the complexity and struggles of the rest of the world, enabling us to digest news coverage more smartly.

Travel helps us celebrate, rather than fear, diversity. On a trip through Afghanistan, I was eating lunch in a Kabul cafeteria. An older man joined me with his lunch, intent on making one strong point. He said, "I am a professor here in Afghanistan. In this world, one-third of the people use a spoon and fork like you, one-third use chopsticks and one-third use fingers, like me. And we are all civilized."

Whether seeing the sights in Spain, sampling cheese in London or cycling through Amsterdam, gaining a better understanding of the world can help create better, stronger and safer societies for us all, says travel expert Rick Steves.

Travel helps us appreciate the challenges other societies face. Stepping into a high school stadium in Turkey, I saw 500 teenagers punch the sky with their fists and shout, "We are a secular nation!" I asked my friend, "What's the deal? Don't they like God?" She said, "Sure, they love God. But here in Turkey, we treasure the separation of mosque and state as much as you value the separation of church and state. And, with Iran just to our east, we're concerned about the rising tide of Islamic fundamentalism."

Travel shows us how few of us are the haves in a have-not world. In contrast, nearly half of this world's people live on $2 a day. And travel teaches you that, if you know what's good for you, you don't want to be filthy rich in a desperately poor world. It's just not a pretty picture.

Travel combats ethnocentrism. For instance, I was raised thinking the world is a pyramid with America on top and everyone else trying to get there. But as I traveled, I met intelligent people—living in countries nowhere near as rich, free or full of opportunity as my country—who wouldn't trade passports with me. Rather than the American dream, they have the Nepalese, Bulgarian, Turkish or Nicaraguan dream.

Such cultural snapshots—the essential joy of travel—have made me an enthusiastic citizen of the planet.

I have some Slovenian friends who muse that the world would be smart to establish a scholarship giving each person a free trip abroad as a high school graduation present. While they know that's unrealistic, they're convinced that if more people traveled before they voted, they would elect a government with policies that don't put their country at odds with the rest of the world.

Travel gives us a perspective that can translate into policies that will not alienate us from the family of nations. And when that happens, I believe we'll all be truly stronger, safer and better off. ◣

Costco member Rick Steves, owner of Seattle-based Europe Through the Back Door, spends four months a year in Europe, writing guidebooks, leading tours and producing a popular public television series on travel.

How to travel light and smart

PACKING LIGHTER IS ONE solution to the problems and challenges of air travel. Here are five easy ways to pack less and pack light.

Take versatile clothes

Take clothes that can be worn several times, such as a blazer worn on the plane that can also go casual with jeans or be dressed up for dinner. Another practical piece is a denim shirt that can be worn as a shirt or light jacket, or over sleepwear as a robe. A different outfit for every day is a travel luxury; it's best to mix and match a few versatile pieces.

Pack around laundry stops

Plan a mid-vacation break at a coin-operated laundry. That halfway stop will double your clothes options. Invest in underclothes made of comfortable wicking fibers that can be washed in your hotel room and dried overnight. Pack only three pairs: one to wear, one to wash and a spare, and plan to do hand laundry.

Choose thin items over thick

A light turtleneck combined with a light sweater is a warmer, more versatile option and packs smaller than a sweatshirt or a bulky sweater.

Pack only the cosmetics needed

Cosmetics often represent half the weight of a fully packed suitcase. Buy sample-size cosmetics or transfer the amount needed to a small container.

Take only three pairs of shoes

Shoes are a very bulky item. Wear one pair and pack two. ▲

TIPS &TRICKS •

WHAT YOU CAN'T CARRY ON

CERTAIN ITEMS are deemed dangerous and can't be carried on an airliner. Instead, they are allowed only in checked luggage. These items include:

- Knives and scissors of any length
- All sporting bats, sticks, clubs, cues, poles and spears
- Ammunition
- Compressed-air guns, stun guns and shocking devices
- Martial-arts and self-defense items ▲

➤ HELPFUL HOW TO'S

WHEN IT'S GOOD TO CHECK LUGGAGE

Sometimes you've got no choice. Here are some situations when it's OK to resign yourself to checking luggage.

- You need to carry lots of equipment, beyond the carry-on limit.
- Your luggage is being handled for you by a tour company.
- You are traveling with small children and don't want to (or can't) deal with luggage, too.
- You are unable to handle your own luggage due to your or your traveling companion's physical condition.
- You require bulky cold-weather clothing or gear.
- You are planning to shop and need lots of room for souvenirs.
- You are going on a formal business trip and need several suits and dresses.

Six easy tips to the right luggage

YOUR LUGGAGE CAN HELP ensure that your clothes and other critical items will get safely to their destination. Here are six considerations to help you buy the right luggage that will meet your needs for years to come.

1. Lightweight luggage can be too light

Don't let the luggage's weight affect your purchasing decision. Most pieces of luggage weigh within 2 pounds of each other, and when it comes down to it 48 pounds feels just as heavy as 50, unless your arms have built-in scales.

Luggage with wheels and telescoping handles requires a reliable frame and construction. Some lightweight or partial frames are failure prone and compromise on durability and reliability. The stronger the frame, the more likely your new luggage will survive years of rough handling. Premium luggage utilizes space-age composites that combine light weight with strength and rigidity.

2. Look for organization features

A fully removable garment carrier is useful to pack your hanging garments. This will help to reduce their wrinkling during your travels. Laundry bags are great for separating wet or soiled garments from clean ones. Shoe pockets will keep shoes in a secure location away from your clothing. And probably most useful these days is a removable 1-quart clear zippered pocket—perfect for those 3-ounce travel-size liquids. No more sandwich bags!

3. Wheels and handles are key

Are the wheels equipped with lifetime sealed, rust-resistant ball bearings? Are the handles and wheels mounted to the case with screws through solid framing? Most manufacturers only partially mount the handles and wheels to the frame, and the balance of the mounting is simply through the fabric.

4. Luggage needs to be "thick-skinned" to resist abrasion, water, stains and tearing

A common description for luggage material is "ballistic" nylon. Don't be misled by this term. Ballistic is simply a weave, not a specification. Quality luggage should always come with a product information tag that includes the results of material strength and abrasion testing. These two factors affect a fabric's long-term durability. Compare resistance factors before you buy.

5. Poorly sewn seams are guaranteed to fail

Tighter stitching makes for stronger seams; only the highest-level manufacturers stitch more than five stitches per inch. Double-stitching makes even stronger seams. Nylon thread is substantially stronger than polyester thread. Very few luggage manufacturers use nylon thread and even fewer double-stitch their seams.

6. Make sure the zippers will stay zipped

What good is luggage if it doesn't stay closed or if the zipper breaks? One of the quickest ways to judge luggage quality is to check the brand of the zipper. Look for the YKK brand, the best-made zippers in the world. ◿

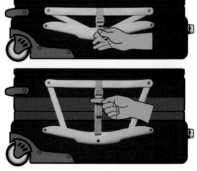

Most luggage expands, but not all luggage also adjusts. An expansion system that will adjust to meet your individual travel needs increases the usefulness of your luggage.

The benefits of GPS

YOU'RE DRIVING HOME FROM work, and you remember that you are out of toilet paper and AA batteries. Certain items, such as toilet paper and batteries, you always buy in bulk. You turn your car around to head to the nearest Costco. You're not exactly sure how to get there from the exit you just took off the freeway, but you've got a pretty good sense of direction so you wing it. Twenty minutes later—after having driven in circles—your exasperation leads you to give up and decide to head home. One problem: You don't know where you are.

"Why didn't I get a GPS?"

Sitting in your car, you remember having told yourself to invest in a Global Positioning System, or GPS, device "one of these days." Aside from pride in knowing all the back roads, perhaps the main reason for not purchasing a portable GPS is cost. According to a 2006 Consumer Electronics Association survey, 49 percent of nearly 3,000 consumers stated that a high price tag was the top reason for non-ownership.

DID YOU KNOW

One of the first commercial handheld receivers introduced in 1988 was 7.5" x 3.5" x 21" and weighed nearly 2 pounds

GPS manufacturers, aware of consumers' hesitations about spending more than $500 on a navigation system, are developing new product lines at lower price points to make GPS units more affordable to the mass market. Subsequently, the current market for GPS systems is substantial and rapidly growing. Industry research company IDC expects the worldwide personal navigation device (aka PND) market to reach $10.6 billion by 2011, which translates into about 38.9 million units.

GPS manufacturers are also enticing consumers by packing additional "luxury" features into their systems. Simply typing in an address is a thing of the past. Nowadays, devices come with wide screens or touch screens, and can help you do everything from calling your mom via Bluetooth to locating the nearest five-star Indian restaurant.

Some units get a leg up on the competition by offering exclusive content, such as AAA TourBook,® to provide consumers with travel information and roadside assistance. Other devices feature voice recognition, up-to-the-minute traffic reports and millions of searchable points of interest (POIs—the more, the merrier) to help get you to the nearest Starbucks for your morning cup of joe.

How GPS works

When people talk about a GPS, they are usually referring to a GPS receiver. The Global Positioning System is, in fact, a network of 24 orbiting satellites that send information to a receiver to calculate the vehicle's exact location anywhere on the planet.

In 1978, the U.S. Department of Defense launched NAVSTAR (Navigation System with Timing and Ranging) with 11 satellites in orbit for military navigation purposes. In 1983, President Reagan declassified the GPS satellites and made them accessible for public use under one condition: The system would work under Selective Availability, or SA, which meant civilian units were accurate only up to a 100-meter radius.

Today's units take advantage of that technology. However, it's important to note that, at times, satellite reception may not be picked up instantly or constantly by the GPS unit. Some new units have location approximation for times when reception is lost, such as in tunnels.

Choosing the right one

With so many brands and models to choose from, going to the store to purchase a GPS can be quite daunting. Don't fret. All you need to figure out is what you really need. Here are some suggestions.

Determine your budget. If you have a set amount of money to spend on a GPS unit, look for systems around that price range. Today's entry-level units process information and update maps faster than the high-end models from earlier this decade, so you can find good quality at value prices.

Choose a unit with the most up-to-date maps. Consider units that can be upgraded (sometimes requires a fee). GPS units are miniature computers—adding new software and additional maps can increase your device's power.

Find the right size. You can choose a standard unit (3.5- to 4.2-inch screen) or go for a larger screen, such as 5 inches.

Other features to consider are:
- Bluetooth capabilities for hands-free calling
- Text-to-speech to hear street names, etc.
- Sound quality and volume

The safety element

Whether you decide to buy a fully loaded high-end GPS model or your average "get me from point A to point B" unit, you will always know where you are, where you came from and how much longer it'll take to get to where you want to go. Sure, it's convenient to be able to type in your friend's new address and drive there without having to print out directions from your computer. However, if you're in the middle of nowhere late at night, the information provided by your GPS could literally save your life. △

→ **THIS**&THAT

HOW GPS WORKS

Twenty-four Global Positioning System (GPS) satellites orbit the Earth. Each satellite continuously sends a signal that contains its position in space and the precise time the signal was sent. A GPS receiver calculates the difference between the time the signal was sent and the time it was received. Because the speed of the signal is constant, this tells your receiver how far away it is from the satellite. At least three satellite signals are combined to triangulate the receiver's exact position on Earth. A GPS is accurate to within 3 meters. It can receive up to 12 GPS satellite signals, plus two additional signals from the U.S. Wide Area Augmentation System (WAAS) and the European Geostationary Navigation Overlay System (EGNOS). These systems provide GPS correction data from a

series of ground stations with known coordinates. The more signals received, the more accurate your positioning. A GPS offers maximum accuracy by taking advantage of the most signals possible.

Three steps to a better golf game

By Art Sellinger

I RECOMMEND A SIMPLE method for improving your golf game and shooting lower scores. It involves focusing your time and energy on what I call the "Three P's": power, precision and performance. Let's examine the Three P's and how you can incorporate them into your golf game to become the kind of player you've always dreamed of being.

Power in your swing

To add power and distance, follow these proven steps.

A. Lighten your grip pressure, which relieves tension in the hands, arms and shoulders. Tension is a tremendous power stealer, so make a conscious effort to eliminate it from the mix.

B. Build a solid power base for your golf swing by checking to see that your feet are spread at least as wide as your shoulders (measuring the distance from the inside of your feet, that is). Too many golfers get too narrow in the address position, which inhibits their ability to make a full shoulder turn and create maximum turn.

C. Concentrate on a low takeaway at the beginning of the backswing. This one move will widen your swing arc significantly and store power for later in the swing. Many golfers have a tendency to "lift" the golf club during the takeaway. This all-too-common mistake actually narrows the swing arc, producing a dramatic reduction in distance with each club.

D. Finish your backswing. One fault you will see at every level of the game, even among tour players now and again, is the tendency to get "quick." By that, I mean they transition to the forward swing before completing the backswing. One way to avoid this tendency is to take practice swings with a slight pause at the top. Many top players employ a 1-2-3 swing tempo, making sure they don't begin the downswing until they finish the count of 2.

E. Maintain the angle between your arms and the golf shaft for as long as possible in the downswing and deliver a late hit into the ball. This move is common among professional long drivers and other big hitters on tour. In other words, do not allow the club head to catch up with your hands until you reach the hitting area. This means the club is still accelerating at impact and "whips" through the ball. By contrast, short hitters allow the club head to race ahead of their hands on the downswing; they release early and the club head is decelerating at impact.

F. Extend the club down the target line, then swing up and around the body to a full, high finish. This particular sequence of motion ensures that maximum speed in the swing is achieved at (or beyond) the ball. To ingrain the feel of this move, take practice swings starting from the finish position.

Incorporate these proven power steps into your game and you'll feel like a

A LIGHTEN YOUR GRIP

B BUILD A SOLID POWER BASE

C LOW TAKEAWAY AT BACKSWING

D FINISH YOUR BACKSWING

E MAINTAIN ANGLE ON DOWNSWING

F SWING UP AND AROUND BODY

Precision is the key

The essentials for precision are grip, alignment and posture. Let's break them down.

Putting your hands on the club properly and keeping them there is essential to hitting crisp shots with metal woods, hybrids or irons. Too strong a grip, with your hands rotated to the right, can promote hooks and pulls. Too weak a grip, with the hands rotated to the left, can promote slices

and misdirected shots. And, as I mentioned earlier, holding the club too tightly, or putting a death grip on the club, creates tension in the hands, arms and shoulders that constricts the body and prevents a fluid motion.

Alignment is another element that separates accomplished players from average ones. The former set up to the ball with their shoulders, hips, knees and feet pointing down the same line, parallel to the target. The latter generally tend to aim directly at the intended target or to the right of the target. This setup promotes an over-the-top swing in which players attempt to steer the ball back to the target.

Posture speaks for itself. Good players look poised, balanced, relaxed and ready to make an athletic motion. Less accomplished players tend to be slumped, stooped, hunched over or scrunched up and not in a position to make an athletic motion. Stand in front of a mirror, bend from the hips, let the arms fall naturally and keep your back straight, not rounded. Don't bury your chin in your chest, either.

The other essential for developing precision is to establish a pre-shot routine that incorporates picking a target and intended line of flight, then setting up to the ball with the same grip, alignment and posture on each shot. Adopting this habit will eliminate variables and produce a more consistent shot pattern.

Performance: the end result

You have added power and precision to the equation. Now, how do you play your best golf? Based on more than 30 years as a junior golfer, college golfer, professional golfer and now power golfer, I submit that several factors—physical and mental—promote optimal scoring.

On the physical side, common denominators for good play are stretching properly and warming up with a purpose. Every good player incorporates them into his or her pre-round preparation. Stretching properly (everything from rotator cuffs to quads and hamstrings) brings the body to a state of readiness so you can swing efficiently from the first shot to the last one of your round.

Warming up with a purpose, which implies not merely crushing drivers but finding a tempo and rhythm for the day, and establishing feel, makes the transition from the practice range to the first tee a smooth one.

On the mental side, common denominators for good play are strategy and visualization. The two are inseparable. Strategy means having a plan for how to play a particular hole—what side of the fairway to favor, for example, or what trouble around the green to avoid. Visualization refers to seeing yourself executing those particular shots before you do.

The final elements of performance that deserve a mention here are patience and positive self-talk. Patience reflects confidence, a deep-seated realization that you don't have to try to force things or attempt the spectacular shot outside your comfort zone. Positive self-talk is crucial because as golfers we tend to get down on ourselves.

In conclusion, I sincerely hope my thoughts on power, precision and performance help you become a better player. I already know that playing a Titleist Tour Prestige golf ball from Costco will. △

Art Sellinger is a two-time national long-drive champion and member of the Long Drivers of America (LDA) Hall of Fame.

The advantages of prepaid phone cards

WHEN YOU'RE ON THE ROAD, the ability to connect with family, co-workers, clients and friends is more important than ever. Prepaid phone cards are a smart solution in terms of cost and convenience. Here's a look.

Price savings

Making long-distance phone calls on the road can be extremely expensive. Prepaid phone cards can offer domestic long-distance calls for less than 3 cents per minute, while eliminating the need to keep coins in your pocket. They also offer huge savings on international calls: A 30-minute call from the United States to Germany could cost nearly $30, while the same call could cost less than $2 with an international prepaid phone card. (This rate is based on published AT&T Worldwide Occasional Calling Plan rates as of February 21, 2008.) And using a prepaid phone card at home can be cheaper than typical long-distance charges.

PIN-less dialing

This feature allows you to register a number of phone numbers that will not require a personal identification number (PIN) to be entered when using the card. When making a call from any of these registered numbers, the system automatically bypasses the PIN entry step. You merely dial the access number and the number you wish to call. This convenient feature is a big timesaver.

Speed dialing

You can store a large list of numbers with this feature. Simply assign a speed-dial code to the phone number you wish to speed dial. Then, when you wish to place a call to that phone number, use the shortcut. This feature is fast and enables you to safely store numbers in the system, rather than in a separate phone directory or PDA.

Auto recharge

This feature allows you to automatically add time to the prepaid phone card without going through the recharge process manually or through voice prompts. This eliminates worry about the balance on the card. By registering your credit-card information and selecting the amount you wish to add to your card, the system will be able to add that amount automatically when you reach a system-specified low balance amount. ▲

How to select the right bike

BUYING A BIKE CAN BE a confusing process. But it doesn't have to be. Taking the time to ask yourself a few questions before you buy can prevent you from bringing home a bike that doesn't fit your size, your budget or your lifestyle. Use this handy bike-buying category guide and detailed sizing information to steer you in the right direction and pedal your way to fun, fitness and family time!

Choosing your style

YOUTH

A child's first bike. 12-, 16- and 20-inch wheels are great for beginning riders.

BMX FREESTYLE

Smaller, single-speed bikes made for people of all ages who enjoy riding, jumping or racing on dirt or smooth surfaces. Freestyle bikes feature a brake-cable detangler for wheel spins and other tricks. 20-inch wheels.

ALL-TERRAIN DUAL SUSPENSION

Front-and-rear-suspension mountain bikes are perfect for more aggressive, off-road riding adventures. 24- and 26-inch wheels.

ALL-TERRAIN HARDTAIL

Front-suspension-only mountain bikes are ideal for general trail and path riding, thanks to their lightweight, simple construction. 24- and 26-inch wheels.

COMFORT

All-terrain bikes are versatile and comfortable, with ergonomically superior upright riding positions, suspension forks, soft grips, cushy saddles and wide-range gearing. 26-inch wheels.

CRUISER

Classic styling, fat tires and general simplicity set these bikes apart from others. Cruisers offer wide saddles, upright riding positions and wide swept-back handlebars. 26-inch wheels.

HYBRID

Great for paved trails and street riding, these lightweight bikes are a happy compromise between a road bike and a mountain bike, with narrow but rugged tires, multiple speeds and a shock-absorbing seat for a comfy, speedy ride. Perfect for the fitness-conscious rider. 700 cm wheels.

ROAD

Road bikes are designed for use on surface streets and have skinny tires, lightweight frames and wide gearing ranges, making them the most efficient bike for longer recreational rides. 700 cm wheels. ▲

TIPS&TRICKS

GETTING READY FOR BIKING

- Stay hydrated! Drink lots of water before and during your ride.
- Be safe—don't forget to wear your helmet!
- Use a pressure gauge to ensure that your tires are properly inflated (see manufacturer's instructions for correct pressure).
- Check the brakes—make sure the brake pads are coming in full contact with the rim for sure stopping power.
- Wear comfortable clothes and shoes to make your ride more enjoyable and relaxing.
- Enjoy a light pre-ride snack for an energetic way to start your ride.
- For more facts and information on biking, see *www.schwinnfamilybiking.com*. ▲

HELPFUL **HOW TO'S** ◀

ADULT SIZING

When purchasing a bicycle, sizing it correctly decreases the likelihood of an accident and improves a rider's overall comfort. However, sizing a bicycle for an adult requires different measurements than those required for a child. These tips will ensure that individuals purchasing a bicycle can size themselves properly.

Before you begin your search, make sure you consider the following:

- Wear the same shoes you would wear for biking, so your real height is represented.
- Define how the bike will be used (on streets or trails).
- Have a friend or family member come along to observe how a bike fits the intended rider.

The following guide can help you select the correct-size bicycle:

- Stand flat-footed on the floor.
- Straddle the bicycle.
- On a road bike, you should have about 1 inch of clearance between your inseam (A) and the top tube (B) of the frame. Clearance should be about 3 to 4 inches for a trail bike.

YOUTH SIZING

Kids use a different scale to size a bicycle, which takes growth into consideration. Since children change so quickly, bikes are designed to accommodate this seemingly overnight change. The wheel size serves as a good guide.

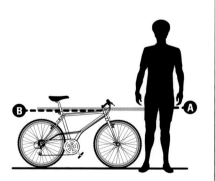

CHILD'S HEIGHT	BICYCLE SIZE
28–38 inches	12-inch wheels
38–48 inches	16-inch wheels
48–60 inches	20-inch wheels

Picnic planning made easy

WHEN WARM WEATHER beckons you to indulge in alfresco dining, what's more fun than a picnic? Whether you pick up a rotisserie chicken and a salad at your local Costco and head to the nearest park or bring burgers to grill at the beach, the casual environment lends itself to camaraderie. Here are some tips.

- When packing, use two coolers. Pre-chill the coolers, if you have time. Keep beverages and frequently used foods in one cooler and perishable foods, such as meats, in the other. The frequent opening of the beverage cooler can prevent foods from staying well chilled.

- On your way to the picnic site, put your cooler inside the air-conditioned car rather than in the hot trunk. Once you're there, place the cooler in the shade and keep the lid closed.

- Bring a first-aid kit, mosquito repellent, sunscreen and plenty of games and activities, such as Frisbees, decks of cards and so on, for family fun.

- Bring three trash bags to clean up after the picnic. Put recyclable cans and bottles in one bag. If your community recycles food waste, use the second bag for that, but remember: no meat or fish scraps; only vegetables, fruits, paper towels, napkins, etc. All other trash goes in the third bag.

- Keep your picnic supplies list on your computer, with a copy in your picnic basket, and you'll be ready to go at a moment's notice. Make sure to note anything you wish you'd brought along and add it to your list for the next time the picnic spirit moves you. ◭

→ **THIS**&THAT

WHEN FOAM PLATES MAKE SENSE

Today's busy lifestyles have everyone looking for ways to find more time to enjoy life. One way to make life a little easier is to use disposable foam plates, at home, business and on the road.

Strong, soakproof foam plates are perfect for the break room at work for snacks, bagels, doughnuts, parties, luncheons, desserts, etc. In your home, lunch or dinner compartment plates work very well for everyday meals and are particularly useful for special family events such as picnics, summer barbecues and holiday get-togethers. They also insulate better than other materials.

When you use disposable foam plates, little or no cleanup is required. Unlike thin paper plates, you don't need to use three or four

of them to make certain nothing leaks through. And you can feel comfortable that the plates won't fold under the weight of normal servings.

Whether it's a quick snack or a holiday lunch or dinner, foam plates will make your life a lot easier and give you more time to spend doing things you enjoy!

A drive with a view

THE WEATHER IS PERFECT. The car is running great. That new digital camera is just calling to be used. What better way to put all those elements together than to take a nice daylong scenic drive?

The Federal Highway Administration has made it easy to find the best routes with its National Scenic Byways Program Web site, *www.byways.org.* The site highlights 126 roads and highways in 44 states that have been designated by Congress as America's Byways. It offers customizable printing of the information and maps for your journey. You can even post an account of the trip to share with fellow adventurers.

Here's a sampling of some of the routes.

Chinook Scenic Byway *(Washington)*

Awe-inspiring views, lush vegetation and glacier-fed rivers are presided over by towering Mount Rainier.

Connecticut River Byway *(New Hampshire and Vermont)*

Historic landmarks, museums aplenty, lush scenery and dramatic vistas are enhanced by the beauty of the upper Connecticut River Valley.

Ebbetts Pass Scenic Byway *(California)*

Discover the Sierra Nevada and experience the serenity of pristine lakes, mountain vistas, massive sequoias and redwoods, and breathtaking panoramas on an exhilarating ride between Yosemite National Park and Lake Tahoe.

Indian River Lagoon Scenic Highway *(Florida)*

Beaches, wildlife refuges, state parks, museums, waterways and even the Kennedy Space Center provide plenty of exciting digital camera fodder.

Kaibab Plateau–North Rim Parkway *(Arizona)*

Spectacular views, natural pleasures and abundant wildlife are found throughout the geological wonders of the Grand Canyon.

Illinois River Road *(Illinois)*

Follow the route of early French explorers paralleling a chain of more than 100 nature sites, the Illinois River Country Nature Trail.

Wetlands and Wildlife Scenic Byway *(Kansas)*

Wildlife such as whooping cranes, pelicans, bald and golden eagles, shorebirds, ducks and geese fill prairie vistas under vast skies.—*Steve Fisher*

Chinook Scenic Byway, Washington

Kaibab Plateau–North Rim Parkway, Arizona

How an automatic watch keeps on ticking

WHILE WATCHES COME IN many styles, when it comes to function all watches generally fall into one of two categories: battery-run quartz watches and mechanical watches. Automatic timepieces are included in the latter group because of the fascinating and intricate mechanism that makes them tick.

An automatic watch is self-winding. The watch winds progressively with the motion of the wrist and body. This movement causes the small weight or rotor attached to the winding mechanism to pivot freely, thereby winding the timepiece.

Because these watches don't require batteries and are powered solely by the body's movement, they stop running if they are not worn for more than a day or two. When this happens, the wearer can turn the crown several times, thus creating some immediate reserve power. Once the watch has begun running, the date and time can be set.

A freely spinning rotator keeps an automatic watch wound while it's being worn.

It is recommended that automatic timepieces that are not worn daily be stored in a watch-winder box. A winder box can hold one or two watches and moves the timepieces in circles to approximate the motion of the body. Not only will the winding box keep an automatic watch always ready to wear, it will also prevent the lubricant within the gears from congealing, which, over time, can diminish the watch's accuracy.

Often appreciated for their craftsmanship, automatic watches are also built for longevity. In fact, these timepieces have traditionally enjoyed heirloom status with families throughout history. They are a wonderful example of how centuries-old, ingenious technology still very much has its place in our time. △

To keep an automatic watch wound when it is not being worn, store it in a watch winder.

Auto and Garage

THE NEXT TIME you take your favorite ride out for a Sunday spin or lie underneath it changing the oil, mull these quirky automotive facts, courtesy of skygaze.com (*www.skygaze.com*).

- Most American automobile horns beep in the key of F.
- The high roofs of London taxicabs were originally designed to keep gentlemen from knocking off their top hats as they entered and left.
- In 1906 the Autocar was manufactured in the United States with a new invention: headlights. They burned kerosene.

If you really want to delve into automobile trivia, find a copy of *The Essential Book of Car Facts and Trivia*, by Giles Chapman. It offers such tidbits as the cars mentioned most frequently in rap songs, the items most common left behind in London cabs, the 69 countries in which cars are driven on the left and much more.

Car battery basics

By Mike Bumbeck

AUTOMOBILE BATTERIES WILL USUALLY last as long as they're supposed
to—unless they are neglected. If your car came to you new off the lot, there is
no mystery involved in what kind of battery to choose when the time comes.

But the battery under the hood of that mint-condition 1991 Dodge Colt
Vista wagon you just picked up off eBay may be of more uncertain origin.
Worse, your car might not even have the right battery. New car or used, the
best time to buy a new battery is before the one presently under the hood
gives up altogether.

The battery will tell you when this is about to happen. Unless you left the
lights on or there is an electrical short, automotive batteries will not generally suffer from sudden death. The classic warning sign of impending battery
expiration is the starter laboring to turn over the engine in the morning. This
laboring will slowly sound more difficult until nothing but a few sad clicks
come from under the hood instead of the usual joyful cranking.

Battery blundering

A common and expensive "do-it-yourself" battery blunder is to assume
the battery has finally quit and replace it, only to discover a brand-new-but-
dead battery the following morning. If your vehicle seems to be laboring
to turn the starter in the morning, first check the charging system. Many
mechanics have portable diagnostic equipment they can roll out to help you
in this task.

If the charging system checks out, then it's time to run a battery load test
to determine if the battery needs maintenance or outright replacement. Also
check for electrical shorts. A frayed wire grounding out against the frame or
body of the car can create a short circuit and drain battery power. A spent
starter or starter solenoid can also mimic a dead battery.

If battery replacement proves the best option, making the best choice in
a new battery depends on several factors.

Determining the group size

The first consideration is choosing the correctly sized battery for your
vehicle. Automobile manufacturers divide batteries into what are called group
sizes. Fitment is an important concern. A perfect fit keeps the battery snug in
the battery tray and working with the factory battery hold-down system. This
prevents battery damage by keeping vibration to a minimum. A battery that is
too small can rattle around in the battery tray and suffer a short life.

It's cold cranking amps (CCA)

A battery must have enough power to turn over the engine. This cranking power is measured in cold cranking amps (CCA), and is the standardized
measured amount of cranking power that a given battery can deliver at zero
degrees Fahrenheit.

CCA is of particular concern for those who live where winter temperatures can dip below zero. Engine and transmission oil becomes thick at these
temperatures. Turning over the engine sometimes requires more CCA than
measured at zero degrees.

RECHARGING A BATTERY

Several different methods can be used to recharge a depleted battery. See your battery's owner's manual to decide which method may work best for your situation, or talk to your mechanic.

If your car has a manual transmission, you can push-start the vehicle. If the charging system (alternator and voltage regulator) are in proper working condition, simply push-start the car and kick it over, then drive long enough to let the charging system do its work. A good half-hour drive should give it a solid charge. Here are a few tips to quickly restore a battery using this method.

- Drive at a constant speed (highway driving) versus stop-and-go (city driving). This will allow the alternator to charge more evenly.

- Turn off all accessories (radio, air conditioner, etc.).

- If possible, drive during the day. Even headlights use power. Having them off increases the amount of electricity going to the battery.

Remember, this does not replace charging the battery. A car's alternator is not designed to fully restore a depleted battery, but rather to maintain a healthy one. As soon as possible, put your battery on a battery charger and give it a full charge for a day or two.

If you will be parking a car for long periods of time (weeks or months), it's best to disconnect the battery to prevent discharging. Use a crescent or open-ended wrench to loosen the strap from the negative terminal on the battery, then remove the connector. Make sure the connector is tucked away from the terminal, where it cannot come into contact with the post.

Select a battery with a higher-than-required CCA rating if the vehicle is operated in temperatures lower than zero degrees. Never select a battery that has less than the CCA required by your engine. A few extra amps are better than too few.

Notes on reserve capacity

The reserve capacity (RC) is the measure of battery strength when the going gets tough. RC is the amount of time the battery will deliver maximum amperage before discharging altogether.

A good example of RC in practice is trying to start a stubborn engine. A battery with a high RC rating will have enough power in reserve to get through tough situations, such as a stubborn engine or accidentally leaving the lights on while at the store. Because the RC is measured at warmer temperatures, it is of great importance to select a battery with a higher-than-required RC rating for a vehicle that is operated in colder climates.

Removing and replacing the battery

Hauling the battery out of the engine compartment and into the warehouse for a like-for-like comparison is one way to choose a battery, but not the most practical or reliable method. Compounding the confusion is that time and battery acid are usually not kind to any identifying labels on the battery.

When you buy a battery, choose one with the highest quality and CCA/RC rating your budget can afford. In general, selecting more battery power than you need is better in the long run than choosing just enough. △

Mike Bumbeck spends a great deal of his time in Los Angeles photographing, repairing and writing about cars and their odd effect on those obsessed with their powers. Copyright 2000–2008 autoMedia.com. All rights reserved, reprinted with permission.

FOR INFORMATION ON HOW TO JUMP-START A CAR, SEE PAGES 148–149.

TIPS & TRICKS

BATTERY MAINTENANCE

THE FOLLOWING TIPS apply to all batteries, including maintenance-free batteries.

- Make sure to wear safety glasses when working near or with car batteries.

- To ensure good connectivity, clean the terminals periodically with a wire brush.

- When removing a connector from a terminal, twist it from side to side and pull gently upward. Refrain from excessive tugging or prying.

- When reconnecting a connector to a terminal, seat it down firmly on the post. A few gentle whacks from a rubber mallet will do it. Don't overtighten and strip the nut.

- After securing the connector, coat the whole post with high-temperature grease. This will reduce corrosion and rust.

- If you keep having electrical problems (battery dies, car won't start, power is intermittent or weak), it's not necessarily the battery. It could be in the charging system, normally a bad alternator or voltage regulator. A mechanic can test the system to isolate the problem. △

Jump-starting a dead battery

By Tom Morr

WHEN THEIR CAR BATTERY DIES, many people would rather call for roadside assistance than lift their car's hood. However, jump-starting a car yourself can be more efficient than waiting for help. Here's how to do it.

Step 1: Select the right cables

Cables are a prerequisite for jump-starting a vehicle. The thicker the cable, the more electrical current can flow. Quality cables are available in thicknesses ranging from 10- to 2-gauge (the smaller the number, the larger the cable). Ten-gauge is usually sufficient for starting batteries in four-cylinder vehicles in warm weather. As the size of the engine increases and temperature decreases, fatter jumpers will do the job better.

Large motor homes or farm implements that need jumping in northern Minnesota in January are best served with 4- or possibly even 2-gauge cables. Thicker cables will also stay more flexible at colder temperatures.

A word of warning: If the cables get warm during use, it's a sign of too much resistance. Either the cables are too thin for the job or they're possibly frayed or have rusty clamps.

Cable storage is critical. During jump-starting, the cables' jaws often pick up battery acid from corroded terminals. This acid is highly corrosive, so cables should always be cleaned and stored in a bag.

Step 2: Prepare for the charge

First, inspect the dead battery. If it's leaking excessively or the case is visibly cracked, abort the jump-starting mission and replace the battery. A damaged battery won't hold a charge anyway. Besides, attempting to charge a battery that has a split case can eject acid, and your eyes or your skin could be seriously injured.

Inspect the battery terminals. Corroded studs and battery-cable ends will impede the flow of electricity from the jumper cables into the battery, so clean the posts and cable ends as well as possible. Remember to keep even dried battery acid away from skin, eyes and lungs. Wearing eye and skin protection is always advisable whenever dealing with batteries.

Park within jumper-cable distance of the dead car. Make sure that the cars aren't touching. Both vehicles should be put in "park" (automatics) or "neutral" (manuals) with the parking brakes set and all accessories such as headlights, dome lights and radios off. Turn both ignitions to the OFF position. Unplug any cigarette-lighter accessories such as radar detectors and cell phones: Jump-starting can send a voltage spike through the vehicle's electrical system and burn out these gadgets.

Identify the batteries' positive and negative posts. Then prepare the jumper cables by uncoiling them and separating the positive and negative clamps. Remember that red or orange is positive and black is negative.

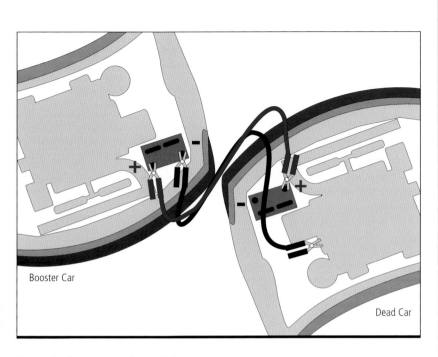

Booster Car

Dead Car

Step 3: Connect the cables

1. Connect a positive/red/orange (+) jumper-cable clamp to the positive (+) terminal of the dead battery.

2. Connect the other positive/red/orange (+) cable clamp to the positive (+) terminal of the charged battery.

3. Connect a negative/black (–) cable clamp to the negative (–) terminal of the charged battery.

4. Connect the other end of the negative/black (–) cable to non-painted metal that's away from the battery, such as the alternator mounting bracket. Do not connect the negative/black (–) cable to the negative (–) post on the discharged battery.

Step 4: Let 'er rip

Let the bad battery charge for at least a minute before attempting to start it. If the dead car's dome light comes on, then the cables are connected properly. Now try to start the car. If it cranks but won't fire, more charging time may be necessary. Revving the running engine will increase its alternator's output and send more juice through the jumper cables. Also check to ensure that the cable's clamps have a good bite, particularly on side-post batteries.

After the car starts, remove the cables in the reverse order of the connections, taking care to avoid moving parts such as fan blades. Also, make sure the cables' clamps don't touch until all four are disconnected.

If all of the above fails, you can always call AAA. ◭

Automotive journalist and editor Tom Morr has been repairing and writing about cars and the industry for about 20 years. Copyright 2000–2008 autoMedia.com. All rights reserved, reprinted with permission.

Everything you need to know about oil

MOST DRIVERS KNOW that motors need oil, but for many the understanding stops there. Here are some things you should know for a better appreciation.

How to check your oil

Checking your oil level is a fairly simple procedure. Experts generally agree that it's best to drive the car first before checking it. So take a little spin, then find a cool, shady spot to pop the hood.

Let the car sit for at least five minutes before checking, to give the oil time to settle into the sump, or reservoir, at the bottom of the engine.

With the hood open and securely propped, locate the dipstick. Its location varies, but you can find it by looking for a brightly colored handle—yellow, red or some other noticeable color.

Remove it and wipe it with a clean rag or towel. Reinsert it into the hole, then slowly remove it again. Check the level. The oil mark should fall between the two hash marks on the dipstick. If it's below the lower level, you need to add oil. Before you do so, though, wipe the dipstick again and check it a second time.

Still low? Add a quart and recheck it. (It's best to add the oil, then start the engine to circulate it, then let it sit for another five minutes before rechecking.) If it's still below the lower hash mark, you may need to add another quart, but be careful not to overfill it, as this can lead to other problems.

→ **THIS**&THAT

KNOWING YOUR ENGINE

1. Antifreeze reservoir
2. Belts and hoses
3. Transmission fluid dipstick
4. Oil dipstick
5. Air filter
6. Power steering fluid
7. Windshield wiper reservoir
8. Engine oil cap
9. Distributor cap
10. Battery

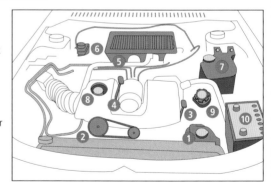

DECIPHERING OIL WEIGHT

Oil weight, or viscosity, refers to how thick the oil is. The temperature requirements for oil set by the Society of Automotive Engineers (SAE) is zero degrees F (low) and 210 degrees F (high).

Oils meeting the SAE's low-temperature requirements have a "W" (which stands for winter) after the viscosity rating (e.g., SAE 10W), and oils that meet the high-temperature ratings have no letter (e.g., SAE 30). Multi-weight oils (such as SAE 10W-30) are a new invention made possible by adding polymers to oil. The polymers allow the oil to have different weights at different temperatures. The first number indicates the viscosity of the oil at a cold temperature, while the second number indicates the viscosity at operating temperature. Engines need oil that is thin enough for cold starts and thick enough when the engine is hot.

The most popular motor oil weights and viscosity grades are:

- SAE 5W-30. Performs well in sub-zero temperatures. A relatively thin motor oil that provides excellent fuel economy and low-temperature performance. Used primarily in newer-model automobiles.

- SAE 10W-30. Performs well in temperatures above zero degrees F. A slightly thicker version of 5W-30 motor oil. Frequently recommended for most automobile engines, including high-performance multivalve and turbo-charged engines.

- SAE 10W-40. Performs well in temperatures above zero degrees F. A thicker oil that provides excellent viscosity. Works well for controlling engine wear and preventing oil breakdown from oxidation. This heavier-weight oil performs better in hotter climates and is typically recommended in vehicles and trucks with larger engines. Possibly a little too thick for wintertime in some cold climates.

- SAE 20W-50. Performs well in temperatures above 20 degrees F. Maximum protection for high-performance, high-rpm engines because of its high viscosity. An excellent oil for hot climates and towing at high speeds for long periods of time.

When choosing oil, always follow the manufacturer's recommendation for your vehicle.

How often should oil be changed?

If you change your oil and filter every 3,000 to 5,000 miles (or every three months, whichever comes first) and check its level regularly, chances are you'll never experience an oil-related problem. For drivers using synthetic oil, intervals as long as 5,000 miles or six months between changes are considered acceptable.

Some service centers will tell you that extreme driving conditions, such as stop-and-go traffic or extremely cold weather, require more frequent changes. The truth is that every three months or 3,000 miles is pretty extreme. If you aren't driving in stop-and-go traffic, through minus-20-degree blizzards or up mountain passes with a 5,000-pound trailer, you could

TIPS&TRICKS

FUEL INJECTOR CLEANER

TRAVELING THE OPEN ROAD can be enjoyable, especially if your engine is in top form. But clogged fuel injectors can adversely affect an engine's performance.

While all U.S. gasoline contains additives, some gasoline can cause performance problems related to deposits in the fuel intake system. If your car hesitates or stumbles during acceleration or experiences loss of power, a clogged fuel injector may be the culprit. These deposits can also lead to reduced fuel economy and increased emission of hydrocarbons and carbon monoxide.

A bottle of fuel injector cleaner added to a tankful of gasoline can help restore clogged fuel injectors to like-new cleanliness in one tankful, while you drive. In addition to removing deposits and helping to restore lost power and performance, fuel injector cleaner contains an inhibitor to protect the fuel system from rust and corrosion and helps remove water to fight gas-line freezing.

Look for a fuel injector cleaner that will not contribute to combustion chamber deposit-related engine knock, ping and run-on; is safe for catalytic converters and oxygen sensors; can be used with oxygenated fuels; and contains no alcohol.

Pour the entire contents of a bottle of fuel injector cleaner into a nearly empty fuel tank. Then refuel with up to 16 gallons of gasoline. Fuel injector cleaner is safe for use every 1,000 miles or as needed to keep fuel injectors clean. ▲

probably go longer between changes, and there's certainly almost no condition that would warrant even more frequent changes.

What about synthetic oil?

Synthetic motor oil is manufactured so chemicals that can lead to oil oxidation and sludge buildup, which may be present in conventional oil, are not present. They will not break down at high temperatures, unlike petroleum-based oils, and are not as affected by cold weather, which thickens regular oil and can add more wear and tear to an engine at start-up.

Synthetic oil costs three to four times as much as conventional oil and is mostly recommended for vehicles driven in extreme conditions and some high-performance vehicles. ⓐ

→ HELPFUL **HOW TO'S**

CHECKING THE AUTOMATIC TRANSMISSION FLUID

The automatic transmission fluid should be checked with the engine running. (Before you do, though, make sure to remove anything loose hanging from your neck, such as a scarf, sweater, necktie or long jewelry. These could get caught in a running fan belt and cause you to have a close encounter of the mechanical kind.) The transmission dipstick looks similar to the oil dipstick, but it doesn't stick up as high. If you have trouble locating it, consult your owner's manual. Oftentimes it will have the same colorful markings (yellow, red, etc.) as the oil dipstick.

Start the engine and locate and extract the transmission fluid dipstick. Wipe it clean and reinsert it, then extract it again. It will have

markings similar to those on the oil dipstick: one mark for too low, another for too high.

Transmission fluid will almost never be low. The automatic transmission/transaxle is a sealed system, requiring little maintenance. If the fluid is low, it most likely means you have a leak in the system, such as a worn seal or a crack somewhere. Have you noticed an oily red or reddish brown patch on your driveway where you park? If so, you may have a transmission leak and will need to see a mechanic.

Even if the level is OK, note the color and consistency of the fluid. If it is very dark or black, check your records and your owner's manual, and plan on getting it changed; it's probably overdue.

Recycling motor oil

ACCORDING TO THE AMERICAN Petroleum Institute, more than 600 million gallons of motor oil are purchased each year. More than half of this amount (345 million gallons) is purchased by "do-it-yourselfers"—those who change their car's motor oil themselves. One step that should never be left out of the process is the last one—recycling the used oil.

Used motor oil is a valuable energy resource. A large portion of recycled motor oil is reprocessed into fuel that is burned in furnaces, turbines, power plants and manufacturing facilities to provide heat and electricity. To put this into perspective, two gallons of used motor oil can generate enough electricity to:

• Power the average home for one day
• Cook 48 meals in a microwave oven
• Blow-dry a person's hair at least 216 times
• Vacuum a house for 15 months
• Watch television for 7.5 days (180 hours) straight!

Used motor oil may contain potentially toxic substances, such as lead, benzene, zinc and magnesium. Used motor oil can work its way to lakes, streams and waterways, polluting local water bodies and drinking-water supplies, as well as damaging aquatic environments and wildlife.

If you pour used motor oil on the ground or into a storm drain or throw it in a trash can (even in a sealed container), that is improper disposal. According to the U.S. Environmental Protection Agency, more than 40 percent of the nation's oil pollution comes from the improper disposal of used motor oil by do-it-yourselfers.

How to recycle used motor oil

1. Pour the drained oil into a leakproof container with a secure screw-on top. Use a clean container that has not held any type of household chemical. (Some auto supply stores sell dedicated containers for used oil.)

2. Label the container "used motor oil."

3. Find a collection center. Most service stations, repair facilities and quick lubes will accept used oil without charge. Check with your local government or recycling coordinator for procedures and collection services in your area. A good source for local collection center information is Earth 911 *(www.earth911.org)*. Just enter "motor oil" and your ZIP code under "Find a Recycling Center."

To recycle the oil filter and the bottle the oil came in, check the Filter Manufacturers Council's Web site *(www.filtercouncil.org)* to search for your state's regulations on the proper disposal of oil filters and a list of filter management companies that service your area.

DID YOU KNOW?

One gallon of used motor oil can contaminate 1 million gallons of water

Spruce-up plan for today's garages

By Ben Jacobs

THE NEXT TIME YOU DRIVE through your neighborhood, briefly look into any open garage as you pass by. You'll see that most of them have little or no room for a vehicle, let alone for organized storage or a work center for household projects. However, people are discovering just how valuable their garage can be.

Garages are becoming an extension of the home instead of just a place to store things. Modern and classic garage products as well as basic and creative home improvement ideas can help you get the most from your garage.

Take inventory

It's no secret that garages are the ultimate catch-all for seldom-used household items. Before you know it, you're overwhelmed with piles of garage clutter that continue to grow. When it comes to dealing with it, the thought alone is enough to make a lot of folks want to run and hide. An easy way to overcome this is to just go into your garage, look around for a few minutes and jot down the things you see.

The list doesn't have to be very detailed. For example, instead of listing nuts, bolts, washers, screws and nails, simply list it all together as hardware. Do the same with tools, auto parts, clothing, kids' toys, sports equipment, etc. Once you have the list, the next step is to make it as small as possible by getting rid of everything you can.

Making clutter go away requires decisions, and that's where reclaiming your garage begins. If you can't decide what to do with any particular item, put it in a pile with other undecided items and come back to it later. Getting rid of a few things makes it easier to get rid of a few more.

Here's a good rule of thumb: If you haven't used it in the last 12 months, say goodbye. Sell it, give it away, recycle it or trash it. Keep in mind that all remaining items need to be organized and stored, so the more you get rid of, the more garage you'll have. Once your list is reduced as much as possible, it's time to make a plan for your garage.

Zone in

The next step is to group related items. For instance, items you'll want to store as groups could include camping gear, blankets, books, automotive fluids, painting supplies, etc. When you're finished, you'll be able to designate zones in your garage for the different groups.

If you actually want to park in your garage, start with a designated parking zone. Another zone could be a work area; this is where the workbench goes and where household projects get done (or lie around for a while).

If you want lots of storage space, reserve several storage zones. Think about using hanging ceiling shelves and wall shelving for smaller, lighter items, as well as stand-alone shelving to get large, heavy items off the floor. Ceiling hoists are a nice way to store bicycles, wheelbarrows and other bulky items. Wall cabinets and rolling cabinets are great for storing car tools and parts, small hardware and other project pieces.

A garage can be a thing of beauty—not just a dirty place to keep your junk.

Trick it out

Give your garage some personality. Many builders do not finish attached garages. They do finish the walls and ceiling spaces shared with the house, but unless the buyer works out something ahead of time, there are usually two or three walls left unfinished. Adding drywall is an excellent do-it-yourself project.

Now add some color. Look at garage color schemes. Auto enthusiasts' garages often feature a theme such as racing, vintage cars or popular models such as Mustangs or Corvettes. Other garages may feature a favorite sports team.

Choose a floor covering. Whether you fancy a modern, sophisticated epoxy look or a classic checkerboard pattern, many options are available. Paint, epoxy, tile and parking mats are the most popular. Keep in mind that you get what you pay for when it comes to garage floor coverings. Paint typically requires continuous touch-up maintenance; epoxy doesn't. Floor tiles can be pricey, but they don't require any surface prep as paint and epoxy do.

Add some gizmos. There are all kinds of modern products for your garage. One of the most useful is an automatic garage door closer that attaches to the opener so you never have to worry about forgetting to close it. Parking gadgets are also quite useful. You can choose from laser pointers to guide you to the same spot every time, proximity sensors that work like stoplights, parking stops that are similar to car wash stops, as well as the classic tennis ball on a string guide. You can also add security devices such as motion detectors, glass-break detectors, open-door alarms and open-window alarms.

These days, more and more garage owners are taking advantage of their garage space by making it more useful for their particular needs. You can use it for piling clutter or as a multifunction extension of your home. You can shape it up on a shoestring budget or spruce it up with the best products money can buy. What really matters is to decide what you want your garage to do for you, and then put it to work. △

Ben Jacobs works in the facilities industry and is the father of five. While looking for ways to maximize his own garage space, he launched the Web site *www.home-garage-help.com* in 2005 to help other homeowners get more from their garages.

• MEMBER**TIPS**

COURTESY OF
KAREN CONNOLLY
TIGARD, OR

PUT A DRYER SHEET in the pocket of your car door. It is a cheap and very effective way to keep your car smelling fresh and beats hanging something ugly from your rear-view mirror. The trunk is another great place to keep a dryer sheet. △

COURTESY OF
PATRICK MINICK
JUNEAU, AK

THE PLASTIC JARS that Costco peanuts come in are great for storing screws and nails. In my basement I go one step further by hanging these jars from the ceiling by screwing the lids into the ceiling joists. They are in easy reach and you can see at a glance what's inside. You'll probably want to put two screws into the lids—with just one screw, the lids tend to spin around when you screw in the jars. △

Driving a road to simpler times

WALK THROUGH THE GLEAMING DOOR of a well-restored aluminum travel trailer from the 1950s and you'll feel as though you've entered a time portal. One second you're in the Information Age, the next you're still in the Atomic Age with Beaver Cleaver.

The nostalgia, charm and function of vintage trailers hold a curiously intense appeal for a growing number of enthusiasts. At rallies, such as those organized through the Southwest Vintage Camper Association (*www.swvca.com*), it's not uncommon to see young people with multiple body piercings and tattoos mingling with World War II veterans. Their common passion for vintage trailers brings them together.

According to Doug Keister, author of *Ready to Roll: A Celebration of the Classic American Travel Trailer* (Penguin Books, 2003), which profiles the rising popularity of vintage trailers, travel trailers built between the 1930s and the 1960s seem to mentally connect people with a simpler, more secure time.

"People in their 20s and 30s are into the retro aspect of these trailers," explains Keister. They want to experience a part of America's culture they've only seen in glimpses on old television shows. For older enthusiasts, the old trailers bring back fond memories.

Dax Downey, a Costco member who lives in Oroville, California, says he loves all things vintage. In 2003 he completely restored a 1953 travel trailer himself. "It was in rough shape, which is why I was able to buy it for only $700," he says. Using all his free time, Downey repaired and replaced everything from the tires and axles to the aluminum exterior and upgraded the wiring.

Not all vintage trailer fans are do-it-yourselfers, however. The rising popularity of vintage trailers keeps businesses such as Vintage Vacations (*www.vintage-vacations.com*), in Anaheim, California, and Iowa Boys (*www.iowaboys.com*), in North Hollywood, California, busy restoring them.

"Most of my clients aren't interested in 'correct restorations,' " says Vintage Vacations' Craig Dorsey. "They like the vintage look but also want a completely modernized inside." These touches may include flat-screen televisions with surround sound, modern appliances, freshwater and sewage tanks and solar-powered inverters that power everything.

Then there's the old-school trailer crowd. Many of Iowa Boys' customers get into vintage trailers through their love of old cars. They buy vintage trailers as an accessory for their hot rods. They take the car and trailer to shows because they match. And, on the practical side, a trailer is a perfect place to take a rest or get out of the summer's heat.

Whether they're old-school, modernized or a mix of the two, vintage trailers transport enthusiasts back to quieter, more easygoing days.—*Will Fifield*

Dax and Betsey Downey travel back to simpler times with Dixie, their restored 1953 travel trailer.

Taking care of tires

By Alex Markovich

TODAY'S TIRES ARE NOTHING LIKE those your grandfather used to buy. They last longer, resist flats and blowouts better and grip the road more securely. But they still need a little TLC. Here are some easy ways to keep them safe and make them last longer.

Give 'em air

Proper inflation is vital. Underinflated tires flex excessively, causing poor handling, increased tread wear and wasted fuel. Even worse, underinflated tires are more likely to overheat and blow out. Overinflated tires may also wear unevenly, harshen the ride and are more vulnerable to punctures from road hazards. To find out the recommended tire pressures for your car, look for a placard in the doorjamb, glove compartment or the fuel-filler door, or see your car owner's manual.

Tires lose pressure over time and from changes in the weather, so check them at least once a month—and don't forget the spare.

Watch for danger signs

Eyeball your tires periodically. A bulge or cut may be a sign of impending failure. Replace the tire right away. Also check the tread for wear. An inexpensive, easy-to-use gauge that measures the depth of the tread can help you spot a problem and remedy it before the tires are ruined.

Replace tires when the depth of the tread approaches two-thirty-seconds of an inch, the legal limit. Lacking a tread-depth gauge, insert a penny, Lincoln's head first, in each groove, and discard the tire if you can see the top of Lincoln's head.

Even out the wear

Front tires wear more quickly than the rear tires on most cars, especially on front-wheel-drive models. That's why most automakers recommend rotating the tires periodically—typically, every 6,000 or 7,000 miles—so the tires wear evenly front and rear.

Retire old tires

Many automakers recommend replacing tires after six years, even if the tread isn't worn and the tires lack obvious signs of damage. Over time, heat, ultraviolet light from the sun and electromagnetic waves from nearby electrical equipment can damage tires. The air used to inflate most tires—or, more precisely, the oxygen and moisture in the air—is also damaging. Under pressure, it rots the rubber compound and steel belts from the inside out. 🅰

Alex Markovich, the auto editor of Consumer Reports for 29 years, has been writing about cars for nearly 50 years. That's how he knows about your grandfather's tires.

• TIPS & TRICKS

HOW TO READ YOUR TIRE SIZE

WHEN YOU BUY new tires, you need to know the tire size. Your owner's manual may identify the proper size, or you can look on your current tire. The size is printed on the sidewall and looks something like this: P205-60-15, which means:

P = Passenger

205 = Width of tire in millimeters (section width)

60 = Ratio of sidewall height to width of tire (aspect ratio)

15 = Rim diameter in inches 🅰

HOW TO FIND THE TIRE'S DATE OF MANUFACTURE

TO DETERMINE a tire's date of manufacture, look for a code on the sidewall that begins with the letters DOT. The last four numbers indicate the week and year of manufacture. For example, 4906 would indicate that the tire was made during the 49th week of 2006. 🅰

A NOTE ABOUT NITROGEN

COSTCO TIRE CENTERS use nitrogen, a noncombustible, nonflammable, dry gas, to inflate tires instead of compressed air. Why? Because nitrogen is a better choice. Tires inflated with compressed air lose 1 to 2 pounds per square inch (psi) of inflation pressure per month. This is because oxygen molecules in air "migrate" out tires. Nitrogen molecules migrate out of tires 300 to 400 percent more slowly than oxygen molecules. That makes your vehicle's handling significantly safer for a longer period of time. 🅰

USING THE RIGHT CLOTH FOR CAR AND HOME

MICROFIBER CLOTHS are one of the wonders of modern science. Because of their composition, they can clean and polish at the same time and purportedly hold seven times their weight in water.

Making microfiber cloth into a mitt makes it even more versatile. The filaments trap dirt and dust and keep them from just being pushed around or floating about in the air.

In the home, microfiber cloths and mitts are perfect for dusting and cleaning any surface, such as kitchen countertops and cabinets, wood furnishings, plants, glass tabletops, granite counters and windows. They are the perfect answer for wiping down window blinds. You can also use them to clean electronic gear, such as DVD players, computers, scanners, etc. Be sure the cloth is totally free of dust particles if you use it on CRT or LCD monitors. The mitts or cloths can also clean CDs and DVDs.

Microfiber cloths also come in handy when washing or detailing a car—use them for dusting inside the car, for low-lint, streak-free cleaning of windshields and mirrors, and for wiping down the exterior after washing.

To wash microfiber cloths or mitts, simply wash with soap or detergent and rinse well. Do not use fabric softeners, which can damage the absorbency. Then machine- or air-dry. ▲

CHAMOIS FOR THE PERFECT FINISH

CHAMOIS IS A FINE leather made from sheepskin that achieves its smooth quality through a special tanning process. It's so scratch-free and absorbent that it's used to clean and dry the finest camera lenses and observatory lenses. Use these steps to get the same results on your vehicle.

- To use chamois, wet it first, then wring it out.

- Pull the chamois across the surface, first in a sweeping motion and then, after most of the water is absorbed, in a smaller circular motion. Chamois is absorbent, so you don't need to press firmly.

- When finished, rinse the chamois in clean water, firmly wring it out and allow it to dry out of direct sunlight.

- Never store chamois wet.

Take these easy steps and your chamois will give you countless successful applications. ▲

● HELPFUL HOW TO'S

PROPER TIRE INFLATION CAN SAVE GAS

WITH GASOLINE PRICES severely affecting every budget, finding ways to improve a vehicle's gas mileage is imperative. Factors such as rapid acceleration, excessive idling and driving over the speed limit get lots of attention, but one issue is rarely addressed: tires.

Tires are a significant factor in vehicle fuel consumption, and people often fail to recognize that. A tire loses 1 pound of pressure per month. If you're not checking air pressure and adding air to get back to the proper pounds per square inch (psi), it affects rolling resistance. Rolling resistance is the force present from the instant the wheels begin to turn. It decreases with increased tire pressure, so an underinflated tire adversely affects fuel economy and accounts for one-fifth of all energy used by a vehicle. Stated another way, one tank of gas out of five is for the tires.

Underinflated tires can lower gas mileage by 0.2 percent for every 1 psi drop in pressure of all four tires. If all passenger-car tires were properly inflated, 2 percent of fuel would be saved. Considering the number of drivers on the road, that's a substantial savings of a valuable resource. ▲

For Your Health

HOW'S THIS FOR A PLAN to get in shape: Walk, jog and ride your bike across the country on historic Route 66?

Well, that might be a little dangerous, and actually impossible in some stretches. But you can do it virtually through AARP's Get Fit on Route 66 program. Here's how it works: You log in exercise minutes from any workout you do. One minute of activity equals one mile on the route. As you tally up the miles, your online vehicle will take you along the route, passing famous highlights along the way.

How long will it take to cover the 2,448 miles from Chicago to Santa Monica? That depends on how hard you're working. If you average 30 minutes a day you'll complete the route in about 12 weeks. Check out the program at *http://aarp.getfitonroute66.com.* △

Taking steps for a healthy RealAge

By Michael F. Roizen, M.D.

MOST OF US TEND TO have the same view about the way people age: As we grow older, we start losing things. We lose some hair, lose our minds, lose our balance, lose our eyesight, lose a little of this and a lot of that—until we eventually wither away into a hunched-over senior who takes 3-inch steps and eats dinner at 4 p.m.

But thinking that a life of frailty is an inevitable outcome of aging is a mistake. In fact, thinking that you have to age at the same rate as your neighbor is the first myth to forget. After all, you have the power to change your rate of aging by making smart choices about the way you live. Here are the main principles for living younger—and better (and happier and healthier and … aw, you get the point).

Aging fact 1: You can choose your age

Whether you look at clocks, calendars or hourglasses, time doesn't stop. It ticks and tocks at the same pace day after day, minute after minute, second after second.

Everyone ages at the same rate with birthdays every year—that's your calendar age. But you have the power to turn your clock faster or slower with the lifestyle choices you make regarding what you do with your body and what you put into it. For example, a 50-year-old who douses her lungs with nicotine and builds her food pyramid with chopped liver and sausage actually may have the body of a 65-year-old because of the destruction she's doing, while a 50-year-old who eats well, stays away from toxins and takes care of her body with moderate physical activity could have the body and health of a 36-year-old.

That is, the actual age of your body—your RealAge—can be many years older or younger than your calendar age. (You can determine your RealAge for free at *www.realage.com.*)

To show you the power you have, consider this: You control more than 70 percent of how well and how long you live. By the time you reach 50, your lifestyle dictates 80 percent of how you age; you largely get to control your genes (more on that later).

Of course, you can't stop aging. That's because your body is continually aged through oxidation or wear and tear or other internal processes. But you can control and slow a large portion of your aging process. From a purely scientific perspective, we don't really know everything that causes aging, but we do know an awful lot. So we can give you a month-by-month priority list.

While we want to show you how all of these systems work and what you can do to keep yourself young, we'll give you a few highlights. The important concept to remember is that the RealAge choices you make will help you slow your aging processes. How much they do so is the RealAge effect. It's almost like longevity currency.

Aging fact 2: Genes are not an excuse

We live in a society where making excuses is as easy as making a sandwich. Nowhere is that more apparent than when it comes to our health. The reason we're frazzled with stress? Blame the boss. The reason we're sick? Blame the sniffling kids. The reason our societal waistbands are stretching and snapping at an alarming rate? Blame auntie's Alfredo sauce or those alluring arches.

The top health excuse, however, revolves around the biggest four-letter word of them all: gene. Blame your genes.

The truth is that we blame our genes for just about everything—for baldness, for fatness, for sickness, for illness and for every other health-related problem we can think of. In our minds, that means Mom, Pop and the rest of the family tree are on the hook for the ultimate health question of them all: How long—and how well—will we live?

But that's exactly where most of us have it wrong. While we're certainly born with genes that help determine everything from our height to our risk for heart disease, we're making a monumental mistake by assuming that we can't influence our genes—especially when it comes to aging. Truth is, much of aging is actually in our control; we have the power to nudge our biological systems so that even our unwanted genes can work in our favor—as long as we know what to do and why we're doing it.

Aging fact 3: You can chip away

A lot of people believe that changing one's body completely requires a complete overhaul. But the truth is that you can take baby steps. Here are the

top 12 things you can do to slow your rate of aging. Adopt one each month, starting today. As the next month starts, add another. The maximum overall benefit adds up to about 15 years younger for somebody who is 55.

1 and 2. Walk 30 minutes a day (speed doesn't matter), and tell a friend you did it. Walking makes your heart and immune system healthier, and calling someone keeps you doing it (and provides support in times of trouble). Together, walking and talking can make you up to eight years younger. Bonus: Buy a pedometer and aim for 10,000 steps a day.

3. Eat six walnuts 30 minutes before lunch and dinner, or take a DHA supplement (from algae, 600 mg). That decreases your desire for food later. Less food equals smaller waist. Smaller waist equals longer life. Add a glass of water or wine and take a walk, and you've made your RealAge five years younger.

4. Eat 100 percent whole grains, which keeps your blood sugar low and pumps you up with fill-you-up fiber. Eating 35 grams of fiber a day if you're a woman or 25 grams if you're a man makes you up to 2.3 years younger.

5. Eat 10 tablespoons of tomato sauce a week to make yourself up to four years younger.

6. Eat curry dishes or foods with mustard once a day to decrease your risk of Alzheimer's disease.

7. If you're angry or annoyed at someone, try to harness your emotions into doing something with the opposite emotion. Instead of being hostile, try being empathetic (maybe that person who cut you off was trying to get his ultra-pregnant wife to the hospital).

8. Start a routine in which you build muscle, which is essential for keeping the fat around your belly at a minimum (it's called omental fat). That also helps keep inflammation in your arteries low. Doing 30 minutes of resistance exercise a week makes you 1.6 years younger.

9. Vitamin D helps to prevent cancer, incorporate calcium into your bones and slow the aging of arteries. Get 1,000 IU a day if you're younger than 60 or 1,200 IU a day if you're older.

10. Take two baby aspirin a day (162 mg). Aspirin decreases your risk of heart attack, stroke, impotence, wrinkles and some cancers. But check with your doc to make sure it's right for you, and take it with half a glass of warm water before and after to help prevent gastrointestinal side effects.

11. Get to know your blood pressure. It should be 115/75, and it's the second most important number you can know (after your spouse's birthday).

12. It's never easy to break an addiction, whether it's to cigarettes, alcohol or jelly doughnuts. Check out the addiction-breaking plan at *www.realage.com* or *www.oprah.com* and plan to set aside five minutes a day to get some quiet time for yourself. A great place to meditate: the bathroom, where you're less likely to be disturbed.

13. Bonus: On your next Costco trip, check out the books I've written with Mehmet Oz to help keep you young: *YOU: The Owner's Manual, YOU: On a Diet* and *YOU: Staying Young.* Take our advice to heart and you'll keep your heart much happier, healthier and younger. ◪

Dr. Roizen is chief wellness officer and chair designate at the Wellness Institute of the Cleveland Clinic in Cleveland, Ohio.

EXERCISING TO FEEL YOUNGER

You can't stop getting older, but you can stop or slow the aging process with a simple exercise plan. That is the premise of the book *The RealAge® Workout* by Dr. Michael F. Roizen and Tracy Hafen. *The RealAge Workout* proposes a four-phase plan.

Kneeling stretch: one of several stretching exercises for after a walking regimen

Dumbbell chest fly: Works the chest and front of the shoulder muscles

PHASE 1 (DAYS 1–30)
Walk 30 minutes every day—either all at once or 10 minutes or more at a time. Walking is the single best thing you can do for your health. Start slowly to warm up: For a 30-year-old, start with a one-minute warm-up; for a 40-year-old, two minutes. Add a minute of warm-up for each additional decade of age. Then, do a fast-walking regiment—just fast enough so you can't hold a conversation. End the session with stretching exercises for about two to three minutes.

Dumbbell squat: targets front and back of thighs, and buttocks

PHASE 2 (DAYS 31–60)
Increase your level of activity by adding seven to 10 minutes of strength training of your foundation muscles every other day to the half hour of walking. There are seven groups of foundation muscles:

- Central abdominal muscles
- Lateral abdominal and rotator muscles
- Lower back muscles
- Buttocks, quadriceps and hamstring muscles
- Upper back muscles
- External rotators
- Internal rotators

As with walking, it is essential to start with warming up, and the muscles should get 48 hours of rest in between workouts.

PHASE 3 (DAYS 61–90)
Increase your level of activity by adding eight to 10 minutes of strength training of your non-foundation muscles—chest, shoulders, biceps, triceps and forearms—every other day, alternating with foundation muscle training.

PHASE 4 (DAYS 91 ONWARD)
Increase your level of activity with 21 minutes of stamina or aerobic exercises three times a week (this is the minimal time for maximum benefit, according to data collected). These activities include jogging, stair climbing, biking and swimming. They train your heart, make arteries more flexible and bolster the immune system.

WARNING
You may feel stronger after 10 days of walking, but that doesn't mean you're ready for phase 2. Check with a health-care professional before moving from one phase to the next to be sure you are ready. Warm up, stretch, rest and eat properly.

For more information, read *The RealAge® Workout* and visit *www.realage.com*

Dumbbell side raise: exercises the front and top of the shoulder, as well as deltoid and shoulder girdle muscles

Sides-of-torso stretch

The sun and your skin

By Maritza I. Perez, M.D.

THE SUN GIVES OFF ENERGY in the form of light waves of different lengths and intensity. The sunlight we see is called visible light. Ultraviolet radiation (UVR) is located just above visible light. UVR is classified according to different energy levels. From shortest to longest wavelengths, they are UVC, UVB and UVA.

UVC: UVC rays have the shortest wavelength, the most energy and fortunately do not penetrate the atmosphere.

UVB: UVB rays are the most potent rays that reach the earth. UVB rays cause sunburn (think "B is for burning rays") and can also lead to the development of skin cancers. Sun protection factor (SPF) ratings measure a product's ability to block UVB rays.

UVA: UVA rays have less energy but penetrate deepest into the skin. These rays cause aging (think "A is for aging"). They are the least associated with skin cancer, but if delivered in high dosages can cause skin cancer, allergic and nonallergic sun-induced eruptions, darkening and pigmentation of the skin and acceleration of the aging process. After chronic long-term exposure to UVA rays, the skin may appear dry, scaly, spotted, wrinkled and leathery.

As a dermatologist, I recommend daily use of a broad-spectrum (UVA/UVB) SPF 15 or higher sunscreen for optimal sun protection. However, wearing sunscreen should not give you a false sense of security, regardless of the SPF rating. Even a sunscreen with an SPF rating of 40 still doesn't completely block the sun.

Also, SPF measurements don't strongly factor in all of the damaging UVA rays. That's why it's important to use a broad-spectrum product formulated to help block most UVA rays as well. Plus, the cumulative effect over a lifetime of UVB and UVA rays that still get through sunscreen is not negligible.

Application as frequently as needed is important (e.g., at least every two hours when sweating or swimming). Also, wearing protective clothing and taking shelter during midday, at high altitudes and from reflective surfaces can protect your skin from skin cancer and premature aging. ◳

DID YOU KNOW? **Water, snow and sand can reflect up to 85% of the sun's rays**

Maritza I. Perez, M.D., is director of cosmetic dermatology at St. Luke's–Roosevelt Hospital Center in New York.

A sun-smart checklist

WE NEED THE SUN TO LIVE, but we also know of the grave dangers of over-exposure. Follow these tips to protect yourself.

- Wear protective clothing, including a wide-brimmed hat, a long-sleeved shirt and long pants, during prolonged periods of sun exposure.
- When possible, avoid direct sunlight between 10 a.m. and 3 p.m.
- Wear sunglasses with UV protective lenses outdoors and while driving to protect your eyes. If you wear prescription glasses, these can be fitted with UV protective lenses as well.
- Avoid years of aging sun damage on your hands by wearing driving gloves in the car every day or using hand cream with UV protection.
- Use sunscreen with a sun protection factor (SPF) of 15 or higher once a day or more on all exposed skin. If you have short hair, don't forget the tops of your ears and the back of your neck.
- Make sure your sunscreen offers true broad-spectrum UVA and UVB protection (see illustration below). Apply enough and reapply often.
- If your skin is sensitive, use a sunblock containing titanium dioxide or zinc oxide with a minimum SPF of 30.
- Apply a lip balm with an SPF of 15 or higher, and reapply frequently.
- Be sure to apply sunscreen at least 30 minutes before exposure or going outdoors.
- Keep sun protection products close at hand—in the glove compartment of the car, in your bag, in your desk at work—everywhere you're likely to be, and not just in the bathroom.
- Cosmetic and skin-care products with SPF ratings won't provide all of the sun protection you need. For maximum protection, use both, layering one over the other.
- Visit your dermatologist yearly for a full-body skin examination, particularly if you got bad sunburns as a child or teen or have had close relatives with skin cancer. ▲

➤ THIS&THAT

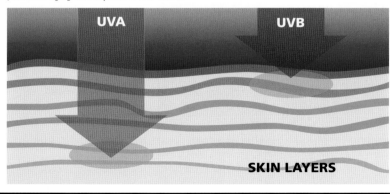

THERE ARE TWO TYPES OF UV RAYS

UVA rays are more penetrating, damaging collagen and elastin, which results in signs of premature aging and may lead to skin cancer.

UVB rays harm the skin's surface and are the primary cause of sunburn.

UVA   UVB

SKIN LAYERS

Making your skin look young again

WHEN YOU'RE YOUNG, skin cells continuously renew themselves, which keeps your skin looking smooth. As time passes, however, your skin's ability to renew itself gradually slows down. Skin loses its elasticity and wrinkles become more evident.

Is it possible to stimulate the skin's renewal process to keep it looking younger and healthier? Skin experts believe that Retinol, a pure form of vitamin A, is very effective in achieving this.

Vitamin A's importance to vision and bone growth has been well established for a long time. In its pure form, vitamin A can penetrate the outer layers of the skin and work to repair the lower layers. In doing so, it smoothes wrinkles and lines and increases moisture and elasticity in the skin.

Research has shown that taking certain steps can increase the effectiveness of Retinol. Here are some suggestions.

Start early. If possible, begin using a Retinol product in your late 20s to early 30s. Early use can actually help to combat fine lines and wrinkles before they become apparent, so your skin stays looking younger and healthier.

Start slowly. Using Retinol is like exercising. Begin by applying a small amount (a little goes a long way) every other day for about two weeks. After two weeks, you may begin applying Retinol more frequently until you find the best routine for your skin.

Stick with it. The benefits of Retinol are seen over time. It's important to be consistent with usage. If you happen to experience minor skin irritation, this may be temporary while your skin adjusts to the product.

Protect your skin. Whether you use a Retinol product during the night or day, always remember to wear a sunscreen of SPF 15 or higher during the day. ◢

➤ THIS&THAT

CLINICALLY PROVEN RESULTS

Before

After 12 weeks

Before

After 12 weeks

(Based on a clinical study of Retinol Correction® Night Cream)

The image to the left illustrates how RoC® Retinol works to stimulate the skin's renewal process and smooth wrinkles. Notice how the skin is renewed and looks smoother and tighter.

BENEFITS

This advanced formula is clinically proven to:

• Diminish the appearance of expression lines

• Visibly reduce even deep wrinkles

• Moisturize skin throughout

• Leave skin smoother and younger-looking

A look a month can save your life

YOUR BATH OFFERS a perfect opportunity to perform a very important task once a month: examining yourself for skin cancer. According to the American Cancer Society, skin cancer is one of the most common types of cancer and has been on the rise over the last few decades.

What you'll need:
- A bright light
- A full-length mirror
- A hand mirror
- A comb and a blow dryer

1. Examine your head and face, using one or both mirrors. Use the comb and the blow dryer to inspect your scalp.
2. Check your hands, including nails, plus elbows, arms, underarms, neck, chest, torso and under your breasts.
3. With your back to the mirror, use the hand mirror to inspect the back of your neck, shoulders, upper arms, back, buttocks and legs.
4. Sitting down, check your legs and feet, including soles, heels and under the toenails.

Notify your doctor if you notice any skin changes or new spots from the previous month.

To learn more about skin cancer prevention and early detection, visit the American Cancer Society's Web site at *www.cancer.org.*

THIS&THAT

SUN-SMART FACTS

DID YOU KNOW?

- Skin cancer and skin aging result from exposure to UVB and UVA rays that builds over the years. The sun damage to the dermal matrix is cumulative, which is why the pace of developing leathery skin, wrinkling and age spots seems to accelerate as one gets older.

- Everyone needs daily sun protection, because natural pigment does not provide surefire insurance against skin cancer. While darker skin appears to be more resistant to UV damage (in contrast to fairer skin, which burns more easily, is quicker to age and has higher rates of skin cancer), it is by no means immune.

- Beware of claims of a "safe" tanning bed or a "healthy" tan. When you use these machines, you may be adding years to your looks while increasing your skin's vulnerability to skin cancer. If you want a little color, salon spray tans or at-home self-tanners are the way to go.

The healing power of oats

By Star Lawrence

THE ANCIENT GREEKS, Romans and Egyptians knew a good plant when they applied it to their skin. *Avena sativa*, more commonly known as oats, softens skin, calms skin irritation and helps skin become a better barrier against the elements, which can mean less visible wrinkles, too.

Oats are a grass that has flat leaves. The seeds, as well as the straw, contain minerals such as iron, manganese and zinc. According to Jeffrey I. Ellis, M.D., director of dermatological surgery at North Shore–Long Island Jewish Hospital, ground-up oatmeal is 60 percent polysaccharides, which help the skin provide a barrier against ultraviolet rays and air pollution. Proteins in oats make the substance pH neutral, which prevents irritation.

Oatmeal also contains much-coveted antioxidants, which prevent rogue cells called free radicals from destroying other skin cells. Another ingredient of oatmeal—saponins—helps clean the skin gently and tease off dead cells. Finally, lipids, or fats, in oatmeal are an effective moisturizer.

Traditionally, oatmeal has been mixed in bathwater to coat the skin and calm inflammation. Since the 1930s, a number of scientific studies have found that oatmeal performs well on patients with skin disorders and even burns. An oatmeal bath is especially useful when one has eczema, chicken pox or poison ivy, but is also recommended by physicians for insect bites, winter itch (dry skin), ichthyosis, hives and sunburn, among other conditions. (If you try one, put the oats in a muslin bag to prevent them from clogging the drain).

Apart from soaks, colloidal oatmeal (finely ground and suspended in a fluid) is found in soaps, body washes and lotions, cleansers and makeup. Dr. Ellis recommends fragrance-free forms for anyone with allergies to scents. According to a recent study of children, almost no one is allergic to oatmeal itself and it can be used safely by almost anyone. The elderly and little children do need to exercise caution in an oatmeal bath because the tub can become treacherously slippery.

As for that "wild oats" reputation, this applies to internal use, which has been said to have an aphrodisiac quality. Used externally, oatmeal can create pretty, smooth skin, which could have a similar effect. ◭

Star Lawrence is a longtime health writer for WebMD and others. Her health humor site can be reached at http://healthsass.blogspot.com.

HELPFUL **HOW TO'S**

People who want to make their own colloidal oatmeal can buy an organically grown product and grind it in their coffee grinder or a blender.

To prepare your own moisturizing facial mask, add brown sugar, a great exfoliator, to the mix, dab into a paste, and massage into the skin, then rub off.

Steps to fight cellulite

ALMOST NINE OUT OF 10 WOMEN will show signs of cellulite at some point in their lifetime. Cellulite results from storage of excess fat in the deeper skin layers beneath the connective tissue. As a result, the skin becomes uneven, loses elasticity and develops dimples.

Though many women think nothing can be done about cellulite, there are steps you can take to keep your body looking as sleek and ripple-free as possible.

Get moving

Find time to incorporate cardio and strength training exercises into your daily routine. Just a half hour of activity each day can make a difference in your skin tone as well as your overall health.

If you don't have time for a 30-minute workout, dividing it into smaller 10-minute pieces can be just as effective. And don't forget to focus on cellulite problem areas with muscle-toning moves such as lunges, squats and crunches.

Hydrate, don't dehydrate

Drink plenty of water and avoid salt and caffeine. Salt contributes to water retention, which can leave you feeling bloated and puffy, and caffeine acts as a diuretic, depriving your muscles of the water they need to function properly.

Drinking at least eight glasses of water each day helps flush out impurities and can help increase your body's metabolism.

Massage away your worries

Massaging common problem areas—especially thighs, buttocks and stomach—can help to reduce the appearance of cellulite. Start at the lowest point, using moderate pressure in a circular motion, and slowly work your way upward.

Massaging every day with a smoothing anti-cellulite product that contains L-Carnitine will provide even better results. L-Carnitine is found naturally in the skin and supports the conversion of fat into energy. ◭

Skin care made simple

By Georgette Mosbacher

IT'S IMPORTANT FOR EVERY WOMAN at any age to take good care of her skin. Here's a simple system I've developed that's guaranteed to keep your face glowing, healthy and flawless. It incorporates just four simple steps, both morning and night.

1. Gently cleanse your face to remove makeup and impurities

A good cleanser will give you treatment benefits in addition to leaving moisture and pH at an optimum level. Instead of stripping or drying your skin, it should condition and soften skin as it cleans. Your face should feel smooth, not stretched taut when you finish.

Natural herbal/botanical ingredients help soothe and calm skin while helping to boost circulation. Look for:

• Hydrating humectants to plump, smooth and soften skin

• Emollient oils to replenish the lipid layer

• Hydrolyzed wheat protein to moisturize and enhance strength and elasticity. Always opt for a luxurious formula that can be splashed or tissued off. If you do choose to use water, make sure that it's tepid water: Hot water is very drying to the skin.

2. Treat your face to an age-defying serum

Serums are very special because they provide the ultimate in reparative treatment. Plus, they help forestall lines and wrinkles, as they help replenish the collagen matrix. A good serum will have a light, fluid texture that penetrates easily into the skin. And that's where its work begins, as it helps firm and tighten skin, restoring a youthful vibrancy. You'll notice a definite "glow" from the first application.

Serums should be formulated with natural and restorative ingredients to help fill in lines, even skin tone and provide a radiant look. These important ingredients include:

• Atelocollagen dehydrated filling spheres to plump, soften and smooth skin

• Silicone and vitamin C to absorb excess oil and provide a touchable texture

• Aloe to help heal dry, dull and damaged skin

• Mulberry extract to battle bacteria and balance skin

• Wheat bran extract to replenish and moisturize

• Willow extract to soothe and calm complexion imperfections

• Vitamin E to help fight free radicals, diminish daily damage and prevent premature aging

3. Use the right moisturizer at the right time

Follow the serum application with a moisturizer formulated to do what it should. The primary purpose of a day moisturizer is to protect skin, so be sure yours has an effective sun protection factor (a minimum of SPF 15 is recommended) to help defend your skin against the sun's harmful rays and environmental pollutants. It should also boost your skin, helping to rebuild from within.

The right day moisturizer will instantly soften, smooth and hydrate skin and help it defend itself with naturally energizing ingredients, such as:

- Yeast extract and hydrolyzed rice protein to boost collagen production
- Vitamin E acetate to fight free radicals, diminishing daily damage
- A balanced blend of ultraviolet B sunscreens to protect skin against harmful radiation
- Black currant fruit extract to provide anti-inflammatory protection
- Mineral salts and sea salts to gently exfoliate dulling surface cells, leaving skin soft and smooth

At night, your skin doesn't want to sleep, it wants to work: helping to repair and restore skin, stimulating blood circulation, renewing cellular production and detoxifying skin from within. It's critical to use a nighttime moisturizer formulated to work overnight, lifting, firming and smoothing away wrinkles while you sleep.

When choosing a night cream, look for essential, natural ingredients your skin will welcome, such as:

- Orange extract and vitamins C and B complex, vital skin energizers
- Rosemary leaf extract, a natural astringent, to stimulate and soothe
- Green tea extract, a powerful, protective antioxidant and anti-irritant

4. Give your eyes a touch of care

After you've applied your all-over moisturizer, take a good look at the skin around your eyes. This is the most fragile area of your face, and it needs special attention. A light, quickly absorbed eye cream will help rehydrate this area. It will also diminish dark circles, reduce fine lines and wrinkles, and restore smoothness and brightness.

Gentle, natural ingredients work to repair and revitalize the eyes. Look for:

- Yeast extract to help strengthen skin and enhance elasticity
- Hydrolyzed rice protein to moisturize and help rebuild skin from within
- Sweet almond seed extract to tone, tighten and soften fine lines and wrinkles
- Olive fruit extract to hydrate and refresh eyes
- Aloe to soothe and comfort

After this, your face will be ready to glow. It's never been easier to give your skin the care it needs. ▲

Georgette Mosbacher is president and CEO of Borghese.

Help your skin and hair weather the weather

JUST AS YOU NEED to dress differently for the different seasons, you need to address the needs of your skin and hair during the changing conditions throughout the year to keep them healthy and looking their best.

Spring and summer

This is the time of year to come out of hibernation, spend more time outdoors and rejuvenate yourself after the long winter. Get your skin and hair ready for the new season with these fresh and simple ideas.

Skin:

• Exfoliate. Use an exfoliating lotion regularly to free your body of rough, dry skin that may have accumulated in the cold weather.

• Before you get out in the sun for an invigorating jog or a walk in the park, prepare your skin. Use a mild, fragrance-free body bar to cleanse your face of any makeup prior to exercising. The idea is to keep any residue from clogging your pores when you start to break a sweat. This will ensure that your skin can breathe the way it needs to when you're working out.

• When you're finished running, biking, planting flowers or any other outdoor activity, be sure to cleanse again. Perspiration is a large contributor to acne and other skin issues. Also, dust and dirt particles that accumulate while you spend time outside can cause rashes or outbreaks. A deep-cleansing body wash or body bar will keep these problems at bay.

Hair: While this is a great opportunity to show off your spring 'do, be aware that sunny days, with additional humidity and UV rays, can wreak havoc on your hair.

• To control frizz, try anti-frizz shampoo and conditioner together with a mousse or serum. Be mindful that touching your hair often can break up the formulas that help to keep frizz under control.

Fall and winter

Your skin endures harsh treatment in the fall and winter months. The blustery cold outside and the artificial heat indoors can bring on rough spots and severe dryness. It's important to revamp your skin-care routine to combat dry, dull skin. Here are some tips to protect your skin during the winter, all day and all night.

Skin:

- Hot water dries the skin, stripping it of its protective layer of oil. When you're cleansing your face or bathing, switch to warm or tepid water.

- If you love to soak in a tub, add bath oils.

- Try a moisturizing body wash or bar to hydrate your skin when you shower. This is a good way to start reversing any damage.

- A gentle cleanser that doesn't rob skin of its natural oils may be a better choice to wash your face than soap.

- Pat your skin gently to dry it. Leave it somewhat moist to let follow-up skin treatments help seal in that moisture.

- Smooth on a moisturizing lotion that will hydrate and nourish your skin all day long.

- If you're going outside, even briefly, and the sun is shining, the rays are amplified by 80 percent on snow. Use sunscreen.

- The thin skin around the eyes is more vulnerable and more likely to dehydrate. A protective eye cream will rehydrate, restore smoothness and brightness, and help reduce fine lines and wrinkles.

- A restorative night cream helps to lift, firm and smooth away wrinkles while you sleep. As it aids in skin renewal, it helps to restore hydration, soothe your skin and allow you to awaken with a more radiant, more youthful look.

Hair: Dry and cold winters can be very damaging to your hair. As the cold weather hits, you probably notice that your hair starts to behave differently. Hair easily becomes dry during this time of year—from dry indoor heating and the dry cold weather outside—and becomes more difficult to manage. Proper steps need to be taken to ensure that your hair does not get damaged.

- Wear a scarf, hat or cap to protect your hair from the cold and wind, but make sure that it's not so tight that it will restrict circulation in your scalp.

- Use a conditioner daily.

- Once you have your hair moist, lock in the moisture by running your hair through cold water; this will also give your hair extra shine.

- Don't go outside with your hair wet: Your hair will freeze if it's cold enough outside and may break.

- Limit your use of "hot" items such as blow dryers and curling irons.

- If you need to use a "hot" item on your hair, use a leave-in conditioner first.

- Avoid taking hot showers or washing your hair in hot water; use warm or cool water instead. The heat can dry out and/or damage your hair.

- Hair products that have the word "replenish" on the label are made to moisturize hair.—*T. Foster Jones*

THIS&THAT

ALL ABOUT SKIN

DID YOU KNOW that skin is the body's largest organ? And, some might argue, it's the most fascinating, though often taken for granted.

Skin makes up between 15 and 20 percent of an adult's body weight. It is constantly being regenerated. In fact, 2 billion to 3 billion skin cells are shed daily in a month-long renewal.

In skin regeneration, cells are born in the lower layer of the skin, called the dermis. They migrate upward for about two weeks until they reach the bottom part of the epidermis, which is the outermost skin layer. The cells then spend another two weeks in the epidermis, where they continue to move toward the surface until they finally die and are shed.

Why this constant regeneration? The skin is the body's first line of defense against infection, injuries, dehydration and other problems. Like the liver, skin can break down harmful substances. And skin absorbs and uses nutrients.

Given such an important role, it only makes sense to know your skin—and take good care of it. 🄰

The perfect haircut at home

THANKS TO TODAY'S MODERN haircutting equipment and some very helpful how-to guides, you don't have to go to the barbershop to get a great cut. Here are some handy tips for the perfect haircut at home—a practice that can save you lots of money over the course of a lifetime of a head of hair!

- Inspect your clipper to make sure it is free of hair and dirt, is properly oiled and is running smoothly. Clean tools are the first step to success in any project.
- It's helpful to lay an old sheet on the floor to catch the clippings if you want to save cleanup time.
- Place a towel or cape around the neck of the person getting the haircut.
- Seat the person so that his or her head is at your eye level. This gives you greater visibility and control.
- Comb hair until it is tangle-free. Hold the clipper in a comfortable grip.
- For a medium to long cut, begin cutting only a small amount of hair until you become familiar with the length each attachment leaves the hair. Try the longest attachment on the clipper first. If you want a shorter cut, you can then use shorter combs.
- When cutting children's hair, use a specially designed, child-friendly blade. These blades safely cut children's hair without pulling or tearing and without sharp edges.
- When cutting bangs, make sure your "client" doesn't lift his or her eyebrows. The bangs will end up looking too short! △

DID YOU KNOW?

On average human hair grows about half an inch every month

A brief history of facial tissue

WHAT HAS BECOME a staple in our lives—facial tissue—started out about 85 years ago. On June 12, 1924, the very first facial tissue, Kleenex,® was introduced. The first ads introduced this new product as a "marvelous new way to remove cold cream."

In the 1930s, the Kleenex brand was swamped by letters from consumers advocating use of its tissues for colds. The company responded with a new description: "the handkerchiefs you can throw away." When one of the first daytime radio soap operas, *The Story of Mary Marlin*, was introduced consumers heard the very first radio ads for Kleenex facial tissue.

The early 1940s found much of the world at war, and Kleenex tissue was part of the effort. The material used to manufacture Kleenex tissue was also used by field doctors and nurses as a sterile dressing.

During those years Kleenex adopted the cartoon character Little Lulu from *The Saturday Evening Post*, where she reminded Americans to conserve to support the war effort. Little Lulu demonstrated the numerous uses of Kleenex tissue in advertising. By 1949 she was a brand icon and appeared on one of the largest billboards ever to grace Times Square.

In 1957, 50 cents and a Kleenex tissue box tear-out strip earned customers a Perry Como record album. There were 330,000 requests for the album, which retailed for $1.29.

In the 1960s, American habits, images and icons were changing quickly. Kleenex moved its advertising on CBS from evening to daytime programming to capitalize on the new popularity of daytime television. And entertainer testimonials, popular in the 1920s, reemerged as Harry James tried unsuccessfully to blow through a Kleenex tissue draped across the bell of his trumpet, proving that new Kleenex tissue was not only softer, but stronger too.

Of course, the product didn't stay the same over the years, nor does it today. New lines of Kleenex were introduced in bright, stylish colors and designs to coordinate with modern trends. Also released were scented tissues; tissues that provide comfort for people suffering from colds, allergies and the flu; and tissues in various pack sizes.

What's next? The future will certainly bring more innovations and comforts in a staple that has been around for more than eight decades. ▣

1924 ·········· 1930 ·········· 1940 ·········· 1949 ······▶

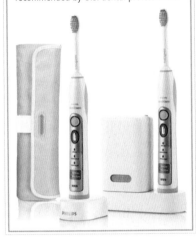
Your teeth and your overall health

DID YOU KNOW that good oral health contributes to good overall health? Think of your mouth as the gateway to your body.

It makes sense that you should be as mindful of how you care for it as you are of the nourishment you put in it. Recent studies published in the *Journal of Periodontology* and *Annals of Periodontology* show that, along with regular exercise, proper nutrition and plenty of rest, the way you care for your teeth plays an important role in your overall health and well-being.

DID YOU KNOW

Chewing sugarless gum after meals can help neutralize acid in the mouth

You are what you eat

A balanced diet can positively contribute to oral health. For instance, many foods, such as fruits and vegetables that supply vitamins and minerals to the entire body, are also good for teeth and gums. However, poor nutritional habits can hurt your oral health, and there is more to it than just keeping your hand out of the cookie jar. Overly starchy foods can cause additional plaque buildup, so it pays to be aware what foods you're eating and when.

Brushing after each meal will help remove plaque and leave your mouth feeling fresh and clean. If you're pressed for time, consider a power toothbrush.

Brushing for two

Moderate exercise and good nutrition during pregnancy are beneficial for both mom and baby. Extend these healthy habits to your oral-care routine and you may increase your chances for a full-term pregnancy. When severe gum disease is present, pregnant women may be more likely to deliver a preterm, low-birth-weight baby.

TIPS FOR GOOD ORAL CARE

1. Brush your teeth twice a day for two minutes. Put a clock in the bathroom or get a power toothbrush with a built-in timer.

2. Replace your toothbrush or toothbrush head every three months to keep bristles in optimal working condition.

3. Store your toothbrush in a clean, dry place or safeguard it with a UV sanitizer.

4. Drink a glass of water after snacks and meals if you're not able to brush. This will help dislodge food from in between your teeth.

5. Get to know your dentist. Schedule a checkup every six months.

A thorough oral-care routine, as recommended by a dental professional, can help pregnant women remove plaque and offset the risk of gum disease.

Gum disease as a risk indicator

Recent studies by the American Heart Association have revealed that people with periodontal disease very often have heart disease as well.

While periodontal disease doesn't necessarily cause heart disease, it nevertheless can be a good risk indicator. Excellent plaque control through good oral hygiene ultimately may help you enjoy better overall long-term health.

In addition, research published in the *Journal of Clinical Periodontology* has uncovered a bidirectional relationship between diabetes and gum disease, which means that good oral health care may improve quality of life for more than 500 million diabetics and prediabetics globally.

It's important to establish and maintain good oral-care habits through all stages of life. Brushing your teeth helps you take care of your body. ◭

TIPS & TRICKS

SPONSORED BY

SKIN-CARE ESSENTIALS

EVERY BATHROOM CABINET should include two skin essentials: a gentle cleanser and a moisturizing cream. Here's why.

• The cleanser is essential for daily makeup removal.

• It also can be part of a regimen to treat dryness caused by topical medications used in the treatment of acne, fine lines and wrinkles.

• Moisturizing cream is essential to rehydrate the skin on a regular basis. This rehydration helps keep skin healthy, in winter and summer. ◭

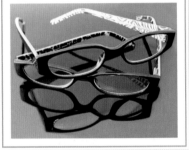
When to obtain reading glasses

AS WE AGE, OUR EYES' ability to focus at close distances tends to diminish. While many joke that their arms are growing shorter, it's a real medical condition and may necessitate a change in lifestyle.

The condition is known as presbyopia, which is caused by a loss of elasticity of the lens and becomes especially apparent in middle age. The result is an inability to focus sharply for near vision. This can make it difficult to read magazines, packaging labels and books, and can lead to headaches, eyestrain and a feeling of fatigue when performing close-up work, such as needlepoint, embroidery or craftwork. In other words, it's time for reading glasses.

The eye's lens stiffens with age, so it is less able to focus when you view something up close. The result is blurred near vision.

It's always best to have your eyes checked by an eye-care professional, such as those in Costco's Optical Department, but a general rule of thumb is that if you see well at a distance without glasses, you might only need over-the-counter reading glasses to overcome presbyopia.

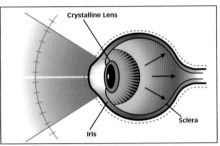

The eye undergoes natural changes as we age. One change is a loss of elasticity of the lens, shown here. The result: blurry vision.

These come in different powers from +1.25 to +2.75. One way to choose is to hold a newspaper or magazine at the distance at which you want to read. (Many reading-glasses displays, including the ones at Costco, offer testers that incorporate lenses and stationary text.) Choose the reading glasses that give you clear vision at the distance tested.

Weaker glasses (+1.25) allow you to read farther from your eyes, while stronger glasses (+2.75) allow clear vision when the reading material is closer to your eyes. Glasses are correct prescriptions only for the distance at which they allow clear vision.

The type chosen should depend on the task at hand—i.e., weaker for computer work or stronger for reading a newspaper or magazine. Eye-care professionals recommend that reading glasses be worn only for reading. Leaving them on full-time may blur distance vision over time. ⒶAI

CHOOSING THE BEST READING GLASSES

Many choices are available when it comes to choosing the best reading glasses for your particular needs. Here's a look.

TYPES OF FRAMES

Frame materials have been revolutionized with the advent of new plastics and various types of metals. Frames generally are fabricated from plastic or metal, but can be made from any workable material. People who suffer from skin allergies might need hypoallergenic materials, such as Monel or stainless steel, to avoid a skin condition known as contact dermatitis.

The most popular choices for modern reading glasses are:

• Aluminum frames, which are extremely lightweight, have a comfortable fit and are often made in brightly colored anodized finishes

• Stainless steel frames, a good choice for durability combined with a modern, minimal design aesthetic

• Handmade frames, which offer a unique combination of handmade quality, artful design and a rich patina

• Frames that use memory plastics, which are extremely lightweight and virtually unbreakable

• Monel frames, made of a special metal alloy that is highly resistant to corrosion and offers a high-luster finish. They are among the best quality available.

FACE SHAPE

According to the Vision Council of America, you should consider three main points when choosing an eyeglass frame for your face shape:

• The frame shape should contrast with your face shape.

• The frame size should be in scale with the size of your face.

• Eyewear should repeat your best personal feature, such as a blue frame to match blue eyes.

Consider the following frame suggestions for different face shapes.

• Base-down triangle. Try frames that are heavily accented with color and detailing on the top half, or cat-eye shapes.

• Oval. Look for frames that are as wide as the broadest part of the face.

• Square. Try narrow frame styles, frames that have more width than depth and narrow ovals.

• Oblong. Try frames that have top-to-bottom depth or a decorative or contrasting temple that adds width to the face.

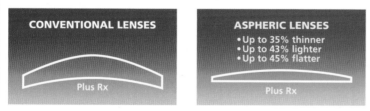

CONVENTIONAL LENSES
Plus Rx

ASPHERIC LENSES
• Up to 35% thinner
• Up to 43% lighter
• Up to 45% flatter
Plus Rx

LENS TYPES

The last consideration is lens type. Conventional lenses have a front surface that is spherical, like the surface of a ball. Aspheric lens designs reduce or eliminate distortions. Another benefit of aspheric lenses is that they are thinner and positioned closer to the face. This is a major benefit for anyone wearing a strong correction.

Strong lenses for farsightedness (plus Rx) have a tendency to enlarge the wearer's eyes, producing an unattractive magnified look. Positioning the lenses closer to the eyes lessens the effect.

TIPS&TRICKS

WHEN GIVING MEDICATION TO CHILDREN

• Use only the medicine that treats your child's specific symptoms.

• Do not use oral cough and cold medicines in children younger than 2 years old.

• Never use an over-the-counter medicine to sedate a child.

• Never give aspirin-containing products to children and adolescents for cold or flu symptoms unless told to do so by a doctor.

• Read and follow medicine labels carefully: Read the name of the active ingredient(s); read and follow the information in the "Uses," "Warnings" and "Directions" sections.

• Never give two medicines with any of the same active ingredients.

• Do not give a medicine intended only for adults to a child.

• Always use the correct measuring device.

• Never use for a longer time than the label instructs or at higher doses, unless your doctor specifically tells you to do so.

• Stop use and call your doctor if your child shows any side effects or reactions that concern you.

• Consult a doctor, pharmacist or other healthcare professional with any questions.

• Keep all medicines out of your child's reach and sight. △

Source: *www.otcsafety.org*

Eyes as a window to your health

PEOPLE KNOW THE importance of good eyesight, yet many don't take the necessary steps to protect it. It's not merely getting eyes checked in the occasional visit to an eye doctor, but taking steps to protect them between visits.

Regular, comprehensive eye exams can help correct vision and provide early detection of serious eye diseases such as glaucoma, cataracts and macular degeneration. They may even uncover serious health problems such as diabetes, high blood pressure and brain tumors.

While most people value their vision, many do not know that poor or wrongly corrected vision can negatively affect overall health by causing headaches, fatigue from eyestrain and visual discomfort. Diet and various medications can also have side effects on the eyes, and common conditions, such as diabetes, can greatly affect vision.

As bad as poor vision is for adults, it can be potentially more devastating for children. Vision problems in children can cause low self-esteem, poor literacy, debilitating headaches or squinting. Sometimes, they're wrongly viewed as "slow learners." For these reasons, quality eye care should begin early in life and continue throughout, as age affects even the healthiest of eyes.

Many factors affect eye health, but one very important one is the sun. Research sponsored by Transitions Optical reveals that only 9 percent of consumers know the sun can damage their eyes—while 82 percent realize it can damage their skin. This is alarming, considering UV radiation has been linked to serious eye diseases such as cataracts and macular degeneration.

Certain eyewear options, such as photochromic lenses, can help block UV rays and protect vision for a lifetime. Photochromic lenses are clear indoors but darken outdoors in proportion to UV light—shielding the eyes from harmful UV rays. The best photochromic technologies also offer availability in impact-resistant lens materials and anti-reflective coatings. ▲

DID YOU KNOW?
About 80% of a person's lifetime sun exposure occurs before the age of 18

Choosing the right diaper

FROM BIRTH TO toddlerhood, your baby will be wearing a diaper most of the time. So it makes perfect sense to pay attention to the finer points of diapers and diapering to make sure your little one is comfortable, protected and free to move about. Knowing the diaper basics will help you choose the right diaper and avoid diaper mishaps.

Shape and fit top the list when it comes to finding the right diaper for your baby. Start with the right size. Size can play a big role in finding the right fit. But how can you tell if your baby is wearing the right-size diaper? Leaks, red marks, gaps or a diaper that fits more like a bikini bottom are all signs of an improper fit.

Pay close attention to the weight chart on the package to help you choose the size that's best for your child's age and stage. If your baby is nearing the top of the weight range, it may be time to consider moving up a size for optimal diaper performance.

Stretch plays an important role in fit and leakage protection. That's why so many parents prefer diapers that provide all-around stretch. That means side to side with stretchy side tabs, as well as a stretchy waistband in the back. This all-around stretchy combo leads to a good fit and great leakage protection.

Also consider what will be touching your baby's tender skin. Opt for soft and comfy materials. It's little details like these that offer added reassurance that your baby will feel comfy and secure while wearing the diaper.

Once you're sure about size, make sure the diaper has been put on in a way that will help prevent leaks. If the diaper looks crooked or is riding up on your baby, it's probably not on right. After each change, make sure all of the right spots are covered, including the backside and hips. No coverage on these areas can mean leaks or an uncomfortable baby.

So check that the diaper is straight and symmetrical front and back, side to side. Make sure the waistband falls right at the waist—not too high in front or too low in back or vice versa.

The right size and fit will keep your baby comfortable. ▲

→ **THIS**&THAT

DIAPER USAGE RATES

STEP SIZE	WEIGHT RANGE	DIAPERS PER DAY	ESTIMATED USAGE PER CHILD
1–2	Up to 15 lbs.	7.1	921
3	16–28 lbs.	5.5	1,271
4	22–37 lbs.	4.9	1,401
5	Over 27 lbs.	4.5	716

Home is where the germs are

MANY PARENTS THINK THAT their children are usually exposed to cold- and flu-causing viruses and bacteria while they're in day care or playgroups. But in reality, it's at home where problems can be found. Many surfaces in the home can be contaminated with the flu virus during cold and flu season. Here are some tips to help you keep your kids and your home cold- and flu-free this year.

Eat a balanced diet

The right foods boost your immune system's illness-fighting power during cold and flu season. Encourage your child to maintain a healthy diet, packed with immunity-boosting foods, such as fish, citrus fruits and leafy vegetables, to keep his or her immune system strong and healthy.

Practice good hygiene habits

Hand washing: According to the Centers for Disease Control's "Ounce of Prevention" campaign, hand washing is the most effective way to help prevent the spread of illness-causing bacteria.

Elbow trap: Sneezing and coughing into your hand is a great way to spread germs. To help keep hands germ-free, teach your child to cough and sneeze into the crook of his or her elbow.

Bright smile: In addition to regular visits to the dentist, teach your child to brush at least twice a day for two minutes. Set a timer or find a song for your child to brush to.

Regularly disinfect surfaces

A recent study from the University of Virginia found that the flu virus can live on surfaces for days. Protect your family by cleaning surfaces with a disinfectant spray formulated to help kill cold- and flu-causing viruses and bacteria.

Playgroups: The home is one of the germiest places for families and a playgroup. Spray or wipe shared toys with a disinfectant, then rinse them in warm water and let air-dry. Encourage kids to wash hands before and after playtime.

Changing areas: Be sure to wash your hands before and after changing your child. Bring your own mat to place beneath your child or carry a travel-size disinfectant spray to clean the table before use. Wash or wipe your child's hands before you leave.

Playgrounds: Playground equipment and picnic tables harbor millions of germs. If you are heading to a park where soap and water are not available, pack alcohol-based wipes or hand gel. Have your child use them to disinfect his or her hands before and after play.

Prepare in advance

If you can't avoid flu symptoms, you can at least avoid last-minute trips to the pharmacy. Stock up on items such as tissues, vitamin C, fever-reducing medicine, hand sanitizer and portable disinfectant. Keep them in one handy place to make illness prevention even easier. ◭

• **TIPS**&TRICKS

HOW CAN YOU TELL IF IT IS A COLD OR THE FLU?

COLD AND FLU viruses are the leading causes of doctor visits and children missing school each year. In fact, 22 million school days are lost every year due to the common cold.

COMMON COLD (RHINOVIRUS)

Rhinovirus is among the most frequently acquired infections in young children. Primarily transmitted via contaminated hands, it causes an acute infection of the upper respiratory tract characterized by a runny nose, sneezing, weepy eyes, nasal passage congestion, chilliness, body aches and fatigue lasting two to seven days.

FLU (INFLUENZA)

In general, the flu is worse than the common cold, and symptoms such as fever, body aches, extreme tiredness and dry cough are more common and intense. The virus spreads in respiratory droplets produced by coughing and sneezing. Airborne person-to-person spreading predominates. However, a person may become infected by touching an object or surface with virus particles on it and then touching his or her eyes, nose or mouth. ◭

Coming to terms with germs

IN HIS BOOK *The Secret Lives of Germs* (Atria, 2004), author Philip M. Tierno Jr. says, "We're all infected with the psychic fear that at any moment, in any setting, invisible agents may as easily give us an incurable, lethal disease as they would a common cold." Tierno goes on to point out that, while germs are important to our existence, we are extremely vulnerable to harmful, deadly infections—despite vast advances in medicine and widespread information about prevention.

A recent study conducted by the Hygiene Council *(www.hygienecouncil. com)* shows that the average American household is home to millions, if not billions, of germs and bacteria. As a result, more than 65 percent of colds and 50 to 80 percent of food-borne illnesses are caught at home.

The kitchen and the bathroom are two areas where there can be large numbers of germs—and where there is a possibility that these germs could be spread to others. The best way to keep these germs at bay is to practice good personal hygiene and to minimize exposure to harmful germs and bacteria. In the bathroom, experts recommend minimizing the opportunity of spreading germs by not sharing cups. Here are some other tips.

Kitchen sponges and rags are ideal environments for bacteria to flourish. Wiping counters and dishes with a bacteria-rich sponge or rag spreads the offending culprits around the kitchen. To combat this scenario:
• Replace kitchen sponges and rags regularly.
• Allow them to dry out between uses, as most bacteria can survive only a few hours on dry surfaces.
• Make sure to remove all food particles from sponges or rags before leaving them to dry.
• Disinfect sponges regularly by putting them in the dishwasher. You can also sterilize sponges in the microwave. A dry sponge can be sterilized in the microwave in 30 seconds, a wet sponge in one minute.

Dishcloths should be washed in the washing machine and then dried on high heat.

Cutting boards are susceptible to cross contamination. If you use your cutting board for raw meat or fish, sanitize it thoroughly before chopping vegetables.
• Clean cutting boards first by hand-washing them with hot water and dish detergent to remove any food particles. Next, use a mixture of 1 teaspoon of chlorine bleach in 1 quart of water to sanitize boards, leaving them to air-dry, or clean them in the dishwasher.

Kitchen surfaces often harbor germs, especially if you've "cleaned" them with a dirty sponge or rag. Disinfect all surfaces using hot water and soap or a diluted bleach solution.

Faucets and faucet handles in kitchens and bathrooms should be cleaned in the same manner suggested for kitchen surfaces.

Sinks and drains are other environments in which bacteria thrive.
- Clean stains, grit and grime around drains with baking soda and an old toothbrush.
- Disinfect drains regularly with the diluted bleach solution.
- Reduce the germs your children are exposed to by keeping a ready supply of disposable drinking cups in the bathroom and kitchen.

Doorknobs and handles, including the refrigerator handle, are often repositories for bacteria. Anyone can transfer bacteria from their hand to a doorknob, and these bacteria can cause illness, especially if the person is sick, doesn't wash his or her hands after going to the bathroom or has touched raw food. When you touch a doorknob you may also pick up the bacteria, which can then enter your body if you touch your eyes, nose or mouth.
- Wash your hands frequently, even if they don't look dirty.
- Clean doorknobs and the refrigerator handle regularly with a clean cloth soaked in a diluted bleach solution. △

● MEMBER**TIP**

COURTESY OF
CAROL ZAREMBA
LOS ANGELES, CA

TO CLEAN dentures, soak them overnight in white vinegar, then brush away tartar with a toothbrush. △

Jack La Lanne's tips for life

"BILLY GRAHAM IS ALL about the hereafter. I am about the here and now," says 93-year-old legendary health and fitness pioneer Jack La Lanne. The fervor still resonates in La Lanne's voice after 71 years in the industry.

Considered a senior statesman of the modern health and fitness movement, La Lanne is associated by many with *The Jack La Lanne Show*, the first nationally syndicated exercise show on television, which ran from 1951 to 1984. Before that, however, he was a well-known bodybuilder. He's been honored with a host of fitness-related awards and a star on the Hollywood Boulevard Walk of Fame.

The *Household Almanac* asked our friend and legendary fitness guru for his top 10 health tips.

1. Think of yourself as a "walking billboard." Does your billboard say, "I over-eat. I don't care how I look and feel?" or does it say, "I exercise every day. I care how I look and feel." Take charge of your life!

2. Don't snack between meals. Ten seconds on the lips and a lifetime on the hips.

3. What you put in your mouth today you will wear tomorrow. Before you put something in your mouth, ask yourself, "What is this going to do for me?"

4. Whenever possible, eat vegetables in their natural state. Eat right and you can't go wrong.

5. Don't skip breakfast. It is the most important meal of the day. It helps bring your blood sugar level up for more energy during the day.

6. Don't salt your food before you taste it.

7. Stretch before you exercise and do some form of exercise daily and regularly.

8. Change your exercise program every three to four weeks, because when muscles get used to doing the same thing they don't respond as well.

9. Your waistline is your lifeline. Keep it in line by consistent daily exercise.

10. Always check with your health professional before starting an exercise program, then start with a goal in mind and move toward it slowly. ◬

Tips on Nutrition

THIS CHAPTER IS ALL ABOUT great things to feed your body for optimal health. But there's another "supplement" that's easy to take, readily available, as important as any vitamin—and free: sleep.

As part of its daily activities, the brain creates serotonin and dopamine, known as neurotransmitters because they carry impulses between nerve cells. When the body doesn't get the seven to eight hours of sleep it needs to rejuvenate, it looks for ways to compensate for neurons not secreting the normal amounts of these chemicals. It typically does this by craving sugary foods. So you grab a big doughnut or a candy bar—which doesn't adequately do the trick and also leads to weight gain.

Lack of sleep plays a bigger role as you get older. So take an adequate dose of sleep tonight—and don't call the doctor in the morning. ▲

Supplements for when our bodies need a little help

By Dr. Mehmet C. Oz

IN AN IDEAL SCENARIO, most of your meals would be peppered with such nutritional medicine as fruits and vegetables, lean sources of protein, 100 percent whole grains and all of the foods most fit to feed humans. Instead, the reality is that many of today's diets consist of the four modern foods groups: fast food, frozen pizzas, icing-laced anything and coffee drinks that contain more calories than a cafeteria refrigerator. As a result, now more than ever, our bodies need a little help (some, of course, more than others).

Even if your diet isn't quite that bad, the fact is that 99 percent of us don't get all the nutrient support we need in foods alone. So it only makes sense to supplement with supplements. That is, you can fortify all of your inner biological systems and help keep your body young and strong by simply popping a few pills (and you can do so at reasonable prices).

Trouble is, the supplement/vitamin/pill world can often be more confusing than trying to read Chinese road signs (unless you can read Chinese). The pill aisles at today's stores are packed with promises; I want to cut through the hype, as well as the mystery, to help you make sense—and make changes that can help you.

Below is a list of some of the important supplements that I believe you should take in order to slow down the aging process, followed by a comprehensive list of the ultimate supplement plan. (By the way, I recommend that you take these in a divided dose—half in the morning and half at night, so you can keep a constant vitamin level in your blood the entire day.)

Of all the changes you can make to improve your health and live younger, this is one of the easiest. Just open your mouth and fire down the hole. Here's a look at the essentials.

Omega-3 fatty acids/DHA

These have been shown to have anti-aging benefits to the heart, brain and immune system. One of the big reasons why: These fats help relax your arteries to improve blood flow (nasty fats like trans fats make your arteries spasm, and thus promote dangerous inflammation). You can get the good fats through fish and walnuts, as well as through fish oil supplements or the pure DHA form from algae. If you're going the supplement route, aim for 2 grams of general omega-3 fats or 600 mg of the pure DHA variety daily.

Vitamins B, C and D

If our diets were packed with leafy greens, lots of fruit and low-fat dairy (or if we spent 15 minutes bathing in the sun), we might not need as much supplementation, but most of us do, in fact, need a multivitamin. All of the types of vitamins have body benefits, but these are three of the powerhouses, working to do everything from building bones to protecting against cancer. Look for a multivitamin that includes the recommended doses (see below).

Aspirin

I know, I know. It's not a nutritional supplement, technically. But this little bugger is so strong that you should include it in your daily pill box (check with your doc first because of potential side effects). Research shows a 40 percent decrease in arterial aging, a major cause of memory loss, for instance, for those who take 162 milligrams a day (that's two baby aspirin). It may help by improving circulation and by clearing a gunky substance that can muck up your neurological wiring (that gunk is called beta-amyloid).

Coenzyme Q10

This supplement has been shown to have a beneficial effect in protecting against Parkinson's disease and may help prevent inflammatory damage to the brain, as well as to the heart. The ideal dose is 100 milligrams twice a day, but many of these supplements don't actually contain Q10, so it's important to check *www.consumerlab.com* to see if what's listed on the label is the real thing. ◩

Dr. Mehmet C. Oz is co-author with Dr. Michael Roizen of the highly successful *YOU* book series. He serves as vice chair of surgery and professor of cardiac surgery at Columbia University.

→ **THIS**&THAT

THE IDEAL DAILY VITAMIN DOSE

RIGHT NOW, THERE'S no one brand that perfectly matches the doses best supported by research. So you're a bit on your own when it comes to choosing a multi that matches your needs. These are our recommended doses, broken down by individual vitamins and minerals.

VITAMINS

A: 2,500 IU is all you need; more than 5,000 IU is too much

B_1 (thiamin): 25 mg

B_2 (riboflavin): 25 mg

B_3 (niacin): At least 30 mg

B_5 (pantothenic acid): 300 mg

B_6 (pyridoxine): 4 mg

B_9 (folic acid or folate): 400 mcg

B_{12} (cyanocobalamin): 800 mcg

Biotin: 300 mcg

C: 800 mg, or 50 mg twice a day if you're taking a statin drug

D: 1,000 IU if you're 59 or younger; 1,200 if 60 or older

E: 400 IU in the form of mixed tocopherols (100 IU from supplements if taking a statin)

K: You likely get enough from your diet

MINERALS

Calcium: 1,600 mg for women, 1,200 mg for men (including from dietary sources)

Magnesium: 400 mg

Selenium: 200 mcg

Zinc: 15 mg

Potassium: 4 servings of fruit should do it

TIPS&TRICKS

TRICKING YOUR SYSTEM

YOU CAN CUT down on the amount you eat at a meal if you trick your hormonal system by sending a signal to your brain that you're full.

If you eat a little fat about 20 minutes before your meal (70 calories in the form of six walnuts, 12 almonds or 20 peanuts, you'll stimulate production of cholecystokinin, or CCK. This will do two things: communicate with your brain and slow your stomach from emptying to keep you feeling full.

Another key is to eat slowly. This gives time for the hormones that signal that you are full to do their work. The average person is finished eating well before these "satiety signals" kick in.

One more tip: Use smaller serving plates. We commonly think that availability should dictate what we eat, rather than physical hunger. You can give yourself visual and psychological clues that you're full, rather than working to eat that whole large box of popcorn.—*Dr. Oz*

The many healthy benefits of fish oil

MORE THAN 20 YEARS AGO scientists in Sweden discovered that Greenland Eskimos had fewer heart conditions than the general population. Since Eskimo diets contained large amounts of fish, scientists began to study the link between fish oil and heart health.

According to the American Heart Association and the National Institutes of Health (NIH), there is strong evidence from multiple large-scale population studies that dietary fish oil supplements may help promote healthy cholesterol levels and maintain ideal heart function, promote vascular health and maintain normal blood pressure.

Today, studies continue to show the many healthy benefits of fish oil, including not only heart health but also mood and joint health.

Heart health

Eicosapentaenoic acid (EPA) and docosahexaenoic acid (DHA) are omega-3 fatty acids found in cold-water fish.

The American Heart Association says several studies show that regular consumption of fish oil or omega-3 supplements containing 850 to 1,800 mg of EPA and DHA improves cardiovascular function.

According to the NIH, other studies report help with maintaining ideal blood pressure with intake of omega-3 fatty acids. Benefits may be greater in those with less than ideal blood pressures. Effects appear to be dose responsive (higher doses have greater effects).

Mood support

In *The Journal of the American Medical Association*, *The American Journal of Psychiatry* and the *Journal of Affective Disorders*, researchers concluded that people who commonly experience low moods had significantly less omega-3 in their red blood cell membranes. Psychiatry department researchers at the University of Sheffield, along with many other research studies, found that fish oil supplements helped support positive moods and emotional well-being.

The underlying theory is that serotonin, a messenger chemical affecting mood, passes through cell membranes more easily when more omega-3 is present. The NIH agrees that there has been "promising initial evidence."

Joint health

According to the NIH, fish oils may help with joint mobility. Omega-3 fish oil fatty acids, particularly EPA, have a very positive effect on the body's inflammatory response.

Many studies report improvements in joint comfort and function with the regular intake of fish oil supplements for up to three months. Benefits have been reported when fish oil is used as a supplement to medications that contain ibuprofen and aspirin.

Introducing yourself to omega-3

Increasing omega-3 fatty acid intake through foods is preferable. The American Heart Association suggests that all adults eat fish at least two times per week. In particular, fatty fish—including mackerel, lake trout, herring, sardines, albacore tuna and salmon—are recommended.

However, those with concerns about their heart health may not be able to get enough omega-3 fatty acids by diet alone. Fish oil supplements make a convenient option for those who don't eat enough fish or do not like it. Supplements also could help people with maintaining ideal cholesterol levels.

A physician should be consulted prior to starting treatment with supplements.

THIS&THAT

READING FOOD LABELS

Serving sizes in familiar units such as cups or piece, followed by metric amount (for example, grams).

Calories are per serving, and tell you how much energy you get from that single serving.

Americans generally get enough fat, saturated fat, trans fat, cholesterol and sodium. You should limit your intake of these nutrients; eating too much of them may increase your risk of certain chronic diseases. In addition, eating too many calories is linked to overweight and obesity.

Your daily values may be higher or lower depending on your caloric needs.

Nutrition Facts

Serving Size 1 cup (228g)
Serving Per Container 2

Amount Per Serving

Calories 260 Calories from Fat 120

	% Daily Value*
Total Fat 13g	**20**%
Saturated Fat 5g	**25**%
Trans Fat 2g	
Cholesterol 30mg	**10**%
Sodium 660mg	**28**%
Total Carbohyrate 31g	**10**%
Dietary Fiber 0g	
Sugars 5g	
Protein 5g	

Vitamin A 4%	•	Vitamin C 2%
Calcium 15%	•	Iron 4%

*Percent Daily Values are based on a 2,000 calorie diet. Your Daily Values may be higher or lower depending on your calorie needs:

		Calories:	2,000	2,500
Total Fat	Less than		65g	80g
Sat Fat	Less than		20g	25g
Cholestrol	Less than		300g	300g
Sodium	Less than		2,400g	2,400g
Total Carbohydrate	Less than		300g	375g
Dietary Fiber	Less than		25g	30g

Calories per gram:
Fat 9 • Carbohydrate 4 • Protein 4

Serving sizes are based on amounts people typically eat. Allows you to compare to your usual portions.

Calories from fat tell you how many of the calories per serving are from fat.

Americans often don't get enough dietary fiber, vitamin A, vitamin C, calcium and iron in their diets. This part of the label is designed to help you understand which foods contain more of these nutrients.

The bottom part of the Nutrition Facts panel includes language that is the same on every package. It shows dietary advice for all Americans, and is not about the specific product. The information reflects nutrition experts' advice on the nutrients specified. For example, total sodium should be less than 2,400 milligrams per day on both a 2,000-calorie- and a 2,500-calorie-a-day diet.

Restoring your emotional balance

TRANSITIONS IN LIFE can affect your mood and emotional well-being. Whether it is a major life change or a stressful period of time, these situations can make you feel moody and overwhelmed. Supplements such as SAM-e (S-adenosyl-methionine) may help to restore a healthy emotional balance in your life.

Richard Brown, M.D., a practicing psychopharmacologist and an associate professor of clinical psychiatry at Columbia University, is a leading clinical expert on SAM-e and emotional well-being, and co-author of *Stop Depression Now*. In the following interview, he provides practical tips for improving mood and reviews the benefits of SAM-e.

Q: Doesn't everyone get in a bad mood every once in a while?

Dr. Brown: Sure they do. Getting down in the dumps every so often is an essential part of the normal range of human emotion. But for many people, the doldrums never seem to let up; it's not something they can just "snap out of" or "get over." If you're one of these people who find it difficult to feel happy on a consistent basis, there are things you can do to cope with setbacks.

Q: What can I do to restore a healthy mood?

Dr. Brown: By making minor changes to diet, exercise and social regimens, feelings of sadness and constant anxiety can be curbed and reduced, creating positive experiences that lead to a more positive, optimistic outlook on life.

Q: How can I alter my diet to help restore a healthy mood?

Dr. Brown: Many of us are out of balance. We eat too much of the wrong foods and not enough of the right ones. To maintain a more balanced mood, go for the "good" or complex carbohydrates such as fruits and vegetables, as well as whole-grain unrefined products such as multigrain breads and cereals. Stay away from the "bad" (or simple) carbohydrates found in refined flour, cakes, cookies, soda, chips and other foods with high sugar content.

Eating too many bad carbohydrates can result in a sugar crash, leaving you hungry, depleted and feeling down. Also, be sure to eat the right amounts of healthy proteins such as fish and poultry, as well as the right fats (unsaturated versus saturated). I also recommend taking a daily multivitamin that contains folate and important B vitamins such as B_6, B_{12} and thiamine.

Q: What if I already eat healthy, but am still feeling moody and overwhelmed?

Dr. Brown: If you still feel moody and feel like you need additional help, it is important to talk to your doctor. As a physician, I recommend the dietary supplement SAM-e, a naturally occurring compound found in all living organisms. It helps to maintain healthy emotions, but your SAM-e levels can run low due to various factors such as poor diet and aging.

By replenishing your natural levels with a daily supplement, you can help to restore emotional balance in your life. Still, it's important to first talk to your doctor about all the options, including regular counseling or therapy, trying a supplement and making other lifestyle changes, depending upon each individual case.

Q: How does SAM-e work?

Dr. Brown: SAM-e affects mood by helping to increase the availability of neurotransmitters, such as serotonin and dopamine (which are attributed to feelings of emotional well-being), as well as increasing the number of neurotransmitter receptors. These are vital chemicals that affect one's mood. Studies have shown that SAM-e often starts working in as little as seven to 14 days, or half the time that is needed for traditional products.

Q: What kind of side effects does use of SAM-e avoid?

Dr. Brown: SAM-e does not cause side effects like dry mouth, constipation, bladder problems, sexual problems, drowsiness and insomnia that can happen with other traditional products.

Q: What about exercise?

Dr. Brown: As always, exercise is an important part of feeling good. Just a 10-minute walk three times a day is enough to help regain energy. Yoga, which is helpful for relieving feelings of anxiety due to its breathing and meditative practices, is another excellent choice.

Q: How else can I lift my spirits?

Dr. Brown: By connecting with other people. Withdrawal is a classic symptom of the blues, so it's important to stay connected to other people. Socializing engages the mind and forces you to think constructively, helping to overcome feelings of loss and confusion. And if you have trouble socializing on your own, contact your doctor or local hospital to find a support group near you. You may also consider joining a religious organization or simply try nurturing someone or something else, such as a family pet. ◣

The benefits of bottled water

IT'S NO SECRET that water is an essential part of our diet. We suffer when we don't drink enough, and we do ourselves harm when we drink too many other fluids instead of water. In many situations, bottled water is the right solution for getting enough water into our bodies.

We're not drinking the right thing

Doctors say that Americans are facing a growing crisis of obesity and type 2 diabetes. A contributing factor of this crisis is believed to be increased consumption of sugary beverages.

Seventy percent of what Americans drink comes from packaged goods, and all too often it's in the form of a high-calorie soda. More than 20 percent of calories consumed by Americans over the age of 2 come from beverages, predominantly soft drinks and fruit drinks with added sugars. The calories from these sugary drinks account for half of the rise in caloric intake by Americans since the late 1970s.

Just how much sugar is in soda? Some varieties have about 12 teaspoons of sugar per 12-ounce can. In a 20-ounce can, there can be more than 20 teaspoons, or nearly half a cup of sugar.

And sugar isn't limited to soda. Some fruit juices, which often come in squeeze boxes, are just as sweet. An 8-ounce box of fruit juice can have about 10 teaspoons of sugar.

Weight-loss possibilities

Replacing high-calorie sodas with bottled water while on the go reduces the amount of empty calories. According to a recent study, dieters who substituted water for all sweetened drinks lost more weight in one year than those who did not (an average of 5 pounds or more). The same study also found that those who drank more than four cups of water a day lost an additional 2 pounds more than those who did not drink as much.

Here's another way of looking at it: Drinking bottled water instead of sugary drinks just three times a week for a year could save you more than 21,000 calories, or more than 6 pounds, in a year.

On-the-go lifestyle

An on-the-go lifestyle makes following any eating plan difficult. It's inevitable that you often eat and drink outside the home. It's often difficult to drink enough water while on the go because a water supply might not be available and you might be wary of the quality of the local water.

Bottled water solves these two problems. With bottled water, you can make sure that you have an adequate supply. And you can be assured that the water has been filtered to remove contaminants.

Environmental concerns

Concerns have been raised about the environmental impact of plastic containers. These concerns center on two issues: the cost of manufacturing bottled water and recycling the bottles.

In terms of manufacturing costs, every time you choose bottled water over a drink such as soda, water is saved. According to a 2006 survey, it takes 1.37 gallons of water to make 1 gallon of bottled water, 2 to 3 gallons of water to make 1 gallon of soda and 42 gallons of water to make 1 gallon of beer (including the water used to produce the barley, hops, etc.).

In terms of recycling, most bottled-water containers are now made from 100 percent recyclable PET. These containers can be re-recycled.

The bottom line is that water (tap or bottled) is a more healthful option than other drinks, and drinking bottled water is a safe, convenient method to increase water consumption for the whole family. It's important to provide family members with low-calorie or no-calorie, on-the-go beverage alternatives such as bottled water.

→ **THIS**&THAT

THE 411 ON H₂O

1. Most people tend to drink more water in the hot summer months, but cold weather can dehydrate too.

2. Blood is thicker than water, but not by much—79 percent of blood *is* water.

3. The elderly have proportionately less water in their bodies than the young.

4. Water is a nutrient for every cell in the body.

5. Stay one step ahead—drink water before you get thirsty and keep dehydration at bay.

6. Beat the heat—travel, hot weather and exercise all increase the body's need for water.

7. Our teeth contain 10 percent water!

8. Eighty-five percent of the brain is water!

9. Water acts as a shock absorber to help protect vital organs, such as the brain, spinal cord and interior of the eyes.

10. Small sips throughout the day are a smart way to keep well watered.

11. Did you know that kids lose proportionately more fluids through sweat than adults?

12. Studies show that a water loss amounting to a mere 2 percent of body weight can have an effect on a person's physical endurance.

13. Water has no fat, no calories and no cholesterol!

• **TIPS**&TRICKS

A SMART DRINKING PLAN

HOW MUCH WATER do you need? That depends on a variety of factors, including whether you're exercising. The general goal is to replace as much fluid as you burn up or release during a day.

Here's some sound advice from *www.mayo clinic.com.*

It's generally not a good idea to use thirst alone as a guide for when to drink. By the time one becomes thirsty, it is possible to already be slightly dehydrated.

Be aware that as you get older your body is less able to sense dehydration and send your brain signals of thirst. Excessive thirst and increased urination can be signs of a more serious medical condition. Talk to your doctor if you experience either.

To ward off dehydration and make sure your body has the fluids it needs, make water your beverage of choice. Nearly every healthy adult can consider the following:

- Drink a glass of water with each meal and between each meal.

- Hydrate before, during and after exercise.

- Substitute sparkling water for alcoholic drinks at social gatherings.

- If you drink water from a bottle, thoroughly clean or replace the bottle often. Refill only bottles that are designed for reuse.

ONE LAST POINT

Though uncommon, it is possible to drink too much water. When your kidneys are unable to excrete the excess water, the electrolyte (mineral) content of your blood is diluted, resulting in a condition called hyponatremia (low sodium levels in the blood). Endurance athletes— such as marathon runners—who drink large amounts of water are at higher risk.

Water and our lives

WE ALL HEAR how important water is for our health. But water may actually be even more significant than many of us know. For example:

- Research shows that mild dehydration can lead to lethargy in infants and significant impairment of cognitive function, leading to confusion and irritability in children and adults. In children, dehydration may even cause diminished mental capabilities.
- It takes about 2 liters of water (a little more than eight cups), along with your normal diet every day, to replace the fluids lost through breathing, perspiration, urine and bowel movements.
- Drinking more water can help prevent kidney stones by helping to flush away the substances that form stones.
- Drinking water can help prevent death from a heart attack. Studies show that women who drank more than five glasses of water a day were 41 percent less likely to die from a heart attack during the study period than those who drank fewer than two glasses.
- Water can help prevent kidney and liver problems by helping to flush toxins that burden these vital organs.
- Water is an important part of an exercise routine. Water makes up a portion of your body's fluids that help to cushion your joints through shock absorption. Drinking plenty of water before, during and after exercise can prevent dehydration and cramping.
- Increasing your water intake has been proven to aid in weight loss and in the battle against obesity.
- Substituting water for a regular soda (approximately 150 calories) every day, along with participating in moderate activity, could aid in weight loss of approximately 10 pounds in six months and 20 pounds in one year.
- Drinking water can satisfy the urge to nibble when you are trying to lose weight. Water has no calories and is the best bet overall when it comes to satisfying thirst and trying to cut the urge to snack. △

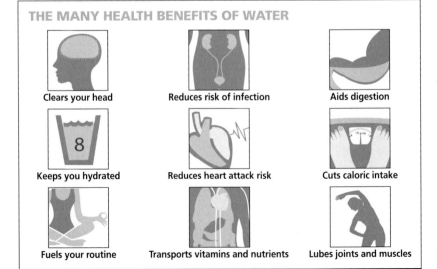

THE MANY HEALTH BENEFITS OF WATER

Clears your head	Reduces risk of infection	Aids digestion
Keeps you hydrated	Reduces heart attack risk	Cuts caloric intake
Fuels your routine	Transports vitamins and nutrients	Lubes joints and muscles

Rustproofing your immune system

IN THIS CORNER, free radicals. Free radicals—molecules that are the consequence of stress, exposure to environmental pollutants and even exercise—damage the body's systems through a process called cellular oxidation, which experts compare to rusting. Cellular oxidation damages the cell's vital genetic material—DNA and RNA. The result is cell mutation, cell degeneration and a weakened immune system. It's no wonder scientists associate free radicals with an increased risk of cancer, cardiovascular disease, loss of eyesight, acceleration of the aging process and innumerable other health problems.

In the opposite corner are antioxidants, the body's rustproofing agents. Antioxidants are a series of enzymes and essential nutrients within the body that can protect it from the destructive effects of free radicals in every cell. They work together like a fine mesh screen over a fireplace.

Over and over again, researchers' studies point to a strong correlation between the presence of antioxidants and good health.

The top three antioxidants are vitamins C and E and beta-carotene (the body converts beta-carotene into vitamin A). Bioflavonoids and minerals such as selenium and zinc, as well as choline, L-cysteine, superoxide dismutase and glutathione peroxidase, are also beneficial antioxidants. Tannins such as punicalagin, found in pomegranate juice, and xanthones, biologically active plant phenols found in a few select tropical plants, such as mangosteen, have been found to support and enhance the body's immune system.

So how do you fill up on antioxidants? You can eat an abundance of antioxidant-rich foods or take them in the form of vitamin and mineral supplements.

The challenge is that you need at least two portions of fruit and three portions of vegetables to supply a protective level of beta-carotene and vitamin C. And the best sources of vitamin E are fatty foods that many people are cutting back on, such as oils, nuts, wheat germ and egg yolks.

Therefore, the justification for supplemental antioxidants is considerable.

It's important to remember, however, that while antioxidants are extremely important, they are but one part of a healthy lifestyle. Exercise, good nutrition and sensible habits need to be observed as well.

Ranges in the recommended daily allowance for supplements can vary due to age, gender and other factors. As with any new medicine or supplement, you should consult your physician to choose a regimen that's best for you. A

→ **THIS**&THAT

MANGOSTEEN: FRUIT AND FLOWER

MANGOSTEEN, THE fruit of an evergreen that originated in Malaysia, the Philippines and Indonesia, has been cultivated for thousands of years, not only for its fruit, but also for its magnificent pink flowers. Its rind is very thick, tough and inedible. The delicate fruit inside makes up only one-quarter of the weight of the fruit. The white flesh is split into five to seven segments, similar in appearance to a mandarin, with very small edible seeds. The texture has been described as somewhere between a well-ripened plum and ice cream, with an incomparable delicious flavor.

—*The Food Encyclopedia* (Robert Rose, 2006)

Finding your way through the secrets of the garden of health

IF YOU'RE LIKE MOST people, your knowledge of herbs extends to which ones go well in certain recipes. However, as evidenced by the expanding selection in herb and supplement aisles, many herbs are gaining popularity among health-conscious people. There's been an increasing emphasis—which really began to pick up steam in the '90s—on the use of herbal supplements to help prevent illness or maintain good health.

With that explosion of choices, however, comes confusion, sending shoppers down the aisle with little idea of where many of these odd-sounding items are from or what they do.

Here's an (admittedly) noncomprehensive look at some of the herbs—as well as a couple of fruit- and vegetable-sourced supplements—available in the marketplace.

Black cohosh (*Actaea racemosa*)

A plant native to North America, black cohosh has a history of use for arthritis and muscle pain, but has been used more recently to treat symptoms that can occur during menopause. Although study results are mixed on its effectiveness, for many women it is an effective herbal alternative to estrogen hormone replacement therapy for hot flashes, night sweating, vaginal thinning and dryness, depressive moods and sleep disturbances. This may be because the root of the plant contains phytoestrogens, chemicals found in plants that are similar to the female hormone estrogen.

Possible side effects and cautions: Black cohosh can cause headaches and stomach discomfort. In clinical trials comparing the effects of the herb and those of estrogen, a low number of side effects were reported, such as headaches, gastric complaints, heaviness in the legs and weight problems. No interactions have been reported between black cohosh and prescription medicines. It is not clear if black cohosh is safe for women who have had breast cancer or for pregnant women.

Cranberry (*Vaccinium macrocarpon*)

Historically, cranberry fruits and leaves were used for a variety of problems, such as wounds, urinary disorders, diarrhea, diabetes, stomach ailments and liver problems.

Recently, cranberry products have been used in the hope of preventing or treating urinary tract infections.

Some studies testing cranberry products for their ability to prevent urinary tract infections have shown promise. Research shows that components found in cranberry may prevent bacteria, such as *E. coli*, from clinging to the cells along the walls of the urinary tract and causing infection.

Possible side effects and cautions: Eating cranberry products in food amounts appears to be safe, but drinking excessive amounts of juice could cause gastrointestinal upset or diarrhea. People who think they have a urinary tract infection should see a health-care provider for proper diagnosis and treatment.

Ginkgo (*Ginkgo biloba*)

Ginkgo is one of the oldest living tree species, and its leaves are among the most extensively studied botanicals in use today. In Europe and the United States, ginkgo supplements are among the bestselling herbal medications, and it consistently ranks as a top medicine prescribed in France and Germany.

For centuries it has been used throughout Asia as a tonic for the brain. European studies have shown that ginkgo increases blood flow to the brain and extremities, helping to improve memory and mental sharpness. Ginkgo may also be helpful for early stages of Alzheimer's disease, circulation problems, vertigo and tinnitus.

Possible side effects and cautions: Side effects of ginkgo may include headache, nausea, gastrointestinal upset, diarrhea, dizziness or allergic skin reactions. More severe allergic reactions have occasionally been reported. There are some data to suggest that ginkgo can increase bleeding risk, so people who take anticoagulant drugs, have bleeding disorders or have scheduled surgery or dental procedures should use caution and talk to a health-care provider if using ginkgo.

Grape seed (*Vitis vinifera*)

Grape seed extract is used for conditions related to the heart and blood vessels, such as atherosclerosis (hardening of the arteries), high blood pressure, high cholesterol and poor circulation.

Other reasons for the use of grape seed extract include complications related to diabetes, such as nerve and eye damage; vision problems, such as macular degeneration (which can cause blindness); and swelling after an injury or surgery.

Grape seed extract has more antioxidant activity than grape seed alone, and is one of the richest sources of proanthocyanidins, antioxidants that may limit damage by free radicals and help to keep artery walls flexible, an important part of circulatory system well-being.

Possible side effects and cautions: Side effects that have been reported most often include headache, a dry itchy scalp, dizziness and nausea. The interactions between grape seed extract and medicines or other supplements have not been carefully studied. Check with your physician.

From top to bottom: black cohosh, ginkgo, milk thistle and saw palmetto.

THIS & THAT •············

LUTEIN AND ZEAXANTHIN

LUTEIN AND ZEAXANTHIN are carotenoids found in vegetables and fruits. They act as antioxidants, protecting cells against the damaging effects of free radicals, and help support healthy eyes and vision.

Lutein and zeaxanthin occur naturally in the macula of the eye. They are the key components for fighting age-related macular degeneration (ARMD), a condition that can lead to impairment and/or loss of vision. If you use a computer, work or shop under fluorescent lights you have been exposed to damaging blue light, a leading cause of ARMD.

As we age, our bodies cannot restore lutein and zeaxanthin in the macula, therefore daily supplementation is necessary.

Lutein can be found in carrots and yellow potatoes. Lutein and zeaxanthin are abundant in a number of yellow/orange fruits and vegetables such as mangoes, papayas, peaches, prunes, acorn squash, winter squash and oranges. Egg yolks are the richest source and also contain a large amount of zeaxanthin.

Individuals who consumed between 6 mg and 12 mg of lutein per day in their diets are less likely to develop cataracts, macular degeneration and colon cancer. Lutein, in supplemental form, should be taken with fat-containing food to improve absorption.

Most people consume lutein as part of a normal diet containing fruits and vegetables, but elderly and ill people can gain from taking a lutein supplement, because their digestive systems may not be functioning at an optimal level.

Green tea (*Camellia sinensis*)

Green tea and green tea extracts have been used to prevent and treat a variety of cancers, including breast, stomach and skin cancers.

Green tea and green tea extracts have also been used for improving mental alertness, aiding in weight loss, lowering cholesterol levels and protecting skin from sun damage.

Laboratory studies suggest that green tea may help protect against or slow the growth of certain cancers, but studies in people have shown mixed results.

Some evidence suggests that the use of green tea preparations improves mental alertness, most likely because of its caffeine content.

Possible side effects and cautions: Green tea is safe for most adults when used in moderate amounts. Green tea and green tea extracts contain caffeine. Caffeine can cause insomnia, anxiety, irritability, upset stomach, nausea, diarrhea or frequent urination in some people. Caffeine can also raise blood pressure, and in very high doses it can cause seizures, delirium or irregular heart rhythms. Green tea contains small amounts of vitamin K, which can make anticoagulant drugs, such as warfarin, less effective.

Milk thistle (*Silybum marianum*)

Several scientific studies suggest that active substances in milk thistle (notably silymarin) protect the liver from damage caused by viruses, toxins, alcohol and certain drugs.

A comprehensive review by the U.S. Agency for Healthcare Research and Quality recently identified 16 scientific studies on the use of milk thistle for the treatment of various forms of liver disease. Preliminary laboratory studies also suggest that active substances in milk thistle may have anti-cancer effects.

Silymarin has strong antioxidant properties and has been shown to inhibit the growth of human prostate, breast and cervical cancer cells in test tubes. Further studies are needed to determine whether milk thistle is safe or effective for people with these forms of cancer.

Treatment claims also include lowering cholesterol levels and reducing insulin resistance in people with type 2 diabetes who also have cirrhosis.

Possible side effects and cautions: In clinical trials, milk thistle generally has few side effects. Occasionally, people report a laxative effect, upset stomach, diarrhea and bloating. Milk thistle can produce allergic reactions, which tend to be more common among people who are allergic to plants in the same family (for example, ragweed, chrysanthemum, marigold and daisy).

DID YOU KNOW? Milk thistle has been used since Greco-Roman times as an herbal remedy for a variety of ailments, particularly liver problems

Saw palmetto (*Serenoa repens*)

Looking much like a miniature palm tree, saw palmetto produces berries that contain a prostate-friendly compound. Studies have demonstrated the effectiveness of saw palmetto in reducing symptoms associated with benign prostate enlargement, such as nighttime urination, urinary flow and overall quality of life.

Saw palmetto is used popularly in Europe for symptoms associated with benign prostate enlargement. Although not considered standard care in the United States, it is the most popular herbal treatment for this condition.

Possible side effects and cautions: There are no known drug interactions with saw palmetto. Saw palmetto may cause mild side effects, including stomach discomfort. Some men using saw palmetto have reported side effects such as tender breasts and a decline in sexual desire.

Pomegranate (*Malum punicum*)

Pomegranates are traditional sources of potent heart-healthy antioxidants that help protect against free-radical damage.

Pomegranate fruit has been revered through the ages for its medicinal properties. Pomegranate fruit and its extract are widely used in several traditional medicinal systems for the treatment of inflammation and pain in arthritis and other diseases. The edible part of pomegranate fruit is rich in anthocyanins, a group of polyphenolic compounds that stimulate antioxidant and anti-inflammatory activities.

Possible side effects and cautions: Tightness in the throat or chest, chest pain, skin hives, rash or itchy or swollen skin. Some people who are allergic to fruits, pollen or nuts are also allergic to pomegranate.

Talk to your doctor if you are taking medicine or are allergic to any medicine (prescription or over-the-counter or dietary supplement); are pregnant or plan to become pregnant while using this supplement; are breastfeeding; or have other health problems, such as high blood pressure or heart or blood vessel disease. Pomegranate fruit should not be taken if you have diarrhea.

Noni

Noni has a history of use as a topical preparation for joint pain and skin conditions.

Today, people drink noni fruit juice as a general health tonic, as well as for cancer and chronic conditions such as cardiovascular disease and diabetes.

In laboratory research, noni has shown antioxidant, immune-stimulating and tumor-fighting properties. These results suggest that noni may warrant further study for conditions such as cancer and cardiovascular disease.

Possible side effects and cautions: Noni is high in potassium. People who are on potassium-restricted diets because of kidney problems should avoid using noni. There have been reports of liver damage from using noni. It should be avoided if you have liver disease because it contains compounds that may make your disease worse.—*T. Foster Jones*

Sources: Health Canada; University of Maryland Medical Center; National Center for Complementary and Alternative Medicine; Cancer Research UK; Agency for Healthcare Research and Quality; MedlinePlus; NetDoctor.co.uk; American Academy of Family Physicians; Botanical.com.

• **THIS** &THAT

LUTEIN AND ZEAXANTHIN

Zeaxanthin is one of the most common carotenoid alcohols found in nature, and is the pigment that gives saffron, corn and other yellow plants their characteristic color.

More important, zeaxanthin is one of the two carotenoids contained in the retina (the other being lutein).

Experiments have shown that low levels of zeaxanthin can have a detrimental effect on the eye, in the same way that a lack of lutein can. For that reason, some studies support the view that supplemental lutein and/or zeaxanthin helps protect against ARMD.

There's also a fair bit of evidence that increasing your intake of lutein and zeaxanthin will lower your risk of developing cataracts. ◢

Taking care of your joints

JOINTS ARE AN INTEGRAL PART of your everyday life. Joints and cartilage absorb shock as well as provide the mobility function for you to move around. In normal, healthy joints, a smooth layer of cartilage protects the bones and acts as a cushion when you move.

Joints can be injured and over a lifetime can become worn, causing inflammation and discomfort. More than 66 million Americans suffer from some form of joint discomfort. It can occur at any time and affects people of every age. Often caused by repetitive or strenuous activities, it can limit your range of motion and make everyday tasks more difficult.

While there's no single cause for achy joints, there's a lot you can do to help ease joint discomfort and other problems in the future. Looking at your everyday lifestyle and making small changes now can make a big difference later.

The supplement approach

Supplements can help out where typical modern diets fail in terms of providing essential nutrition to the body. Here are the basics when it comes to joint health.

Glucosamine: Glucosamine naturally supplements the nutrition of joints. It is one of the major building materials for the production of molecules called glycosaminoglycans. These molecules are necessary for proper cartilage formation, adequate joint lubrication and healthy connective tissue.

Glucosamine has been clinically studied to find if it helps lessen joint stiffness associated with normal aging and improved joint flexibility.

Like bone, cartilage is constantly rebuilding itself. The study found that glucosamine helps support normal, healthy rebuilding of cartilage, maintaining healthy joint structure. Glucosamine stands out among nutrients for helping to maintain cartilage as people age.

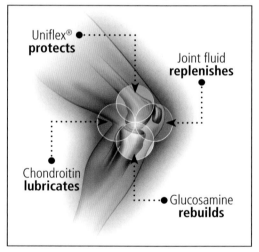

Uniflex® **protects**

Joint fluid **replenishes**

Chondroitin **lubricates**

Glucosamine **rebuilds**

While glucosamine is not significantly present in most foods, supplemental over-the-counter sources are plentiful. The clinical dosage recommendation is 1,500 mg a day. Noticeable improvements in flexibility, less stiffness and greater range of motion should be expected after taking this supplement as directed for about six weeks.

Chondroitin sulfate: Chondroitin sulfate is a structural component of cartilage, connective tissue and compounds that assist in the movement of nutrients to cells. Chondroitin provides the necessary element for essential nutrients to move through cartilage. It is especially critical as a transporter because there is no blood supply to cartilage.

Chondroitin provides proper nutrition to joint tissue, which in turn helps support maximum flexibility, range of motion and joint lubrication. It protects existing cartilage and serves as a building block for healthy new cartilage.

Glucosamine and chondroitin combination: The combined effect of these two ingredients has been clinically proven effective in a landmark 2005 study supported by the U.S. National Institutes of Health.

Supplements by themselves aren't enough. Taking proper care of your joints requires some other lifestyle steps.

Shed those pounds

Every extra pound you gain puts four times more stress on your knees. All that extra stress puts unnecessary strain on your joints, which can increase the likelihood of difficulties later on in life. Losing as little as 11 pounds may cut your risk of knee problems by 50 percent.

Straighten up

Good posture—standing and sitting up straight—can benefit your joints. It helps protect the joints in your neck, back, hips and knees.

Exercise regularly

Exercise is one of the most effective treatments to support healthy joints. Not only does exercise increase flexibility, strengthen muscles and improve the overall function of the affected joints, it may also help minimize soreness. The three most beneficial types of exercise are:

- Range-of-motion exercises, also known as flexibility exercises, such as tai chi and yoga
- Aerobic conditioning, which includes activities that increase the heart rate for 20 minutes or more, such as brisk walking or jogging
- Targeted muscle-strengthening exercises, such as weight training

Lose the high heels

While they may look good, high-heeled shoes are hardly good for you. According to experts, a 3-inch heel stresses your foot seven times more than a half-inch heel. That extra height also increases the stress on your knees. And all the extra strain you put on your feet and knees now may increase your risk of developing problems later. △

HOW TO KNOW IF YOU HAVE OSTEOARTHRITIS

MORE THAN 20 MILLION people in the United States probably have osteoarthritis. Both men and women can be affected by the disease. Before age 45, more men have it; after age 45, it's more common in women. Young people may be at risk due to injuries.

Here are some of the warning signs:

- Steady or intermittent pain in a joint
- Stiffness after getting out of bed
- Swelling or tenderness in one or more joints
- A crunching feeling or the sound of bone rubbing on bone

Check with your doctor if you think you might be at risk. Not everyone with osteoarthritis experiences pain in association with the disease. In fact, only a third of people with osteoarthritis in their X-rays report pain or other symptoms. Early diagnosis and treatment are the keys to controlling osteoarthritis. For more information, go to www.arthritis.org. △

(From the Federal Citizen Information Center, www.pueblo.gsa.gov)

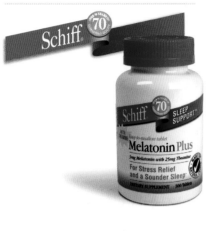

Melatonin: myth or magic bullet?

IT MAY EASE INSOMNIA, combat jet lag, protect cells from free-radical damage, boost the immune system, prevent cancer and extend life. According to some, it can even reverse aging and improve your sex life.

Melatonin: Is it a magic bullet or myth? An established sleep aid, melatonin has attracted attention for other uses. The majority of these claims have yet to be proven, but there are elements of substantiated truth.

At the center of the issue is a pea-size gland in the brain known as the pineal gland, which sets your body's biological clock and initiates sleep. Darkness stimulates the pineal gland so that it secretes the hormone melatonin during the night, keeping you in sync with the rhythms of the days and seasons. Daylight stops your body's production of melatonin.

Over time, the pineal gland's ability to produce melatonin diminishes. As melatonin production slows, the body stops receiving the messages that help regulate hormonal systems and begins to fall out of rhythm.

It would make sense, then, that taking melatonin supplements would bring your body back into rhythm.

"Even the harshest critics will admit that melatonin is an effective sleep hypnotic," says Dr. Ray Sahelian, a Los Angeles physician who has been treating insomnia sufferers for years. He says that people who take melatonin often experience sounder sleep, more energy the next day and better moods, and sometimes need fewer hours of sleep: "It's useful to prevent jet lag, helps people readjust their sleep patterns and has aided those with poor sleep patterns."

"It certainly has proven beneficial in those areas related to sleep," agrees Russel Reiter, professor of neuroendocrinology at the University of Texas Health Science Center, who has been researching melatonin since 1964.

Does melatonin do more than that? Melatonin is a powerful antioxidant that penetrates water- and fat-soluble areas of every cell, protecting cells from damage. Some believe that it is an age-reversing, disease-fighting and sex-enhancing hormone.

Reiter discounts the claims. "We've seen no evidence in terms of a direct effect on sexuality," says Reiter. "And nothing can reverse aging."

Ultimately, all researchers urge caution before anyone begins blithely consuming melatonin as a cure-all. It's always prudent to check with your physician and research any major change you make in your diet.—*T. Foster Jones*

→ **THIS**&THAT

TIPS TO AGE WELL

✔ Healthy diet (USDA guidelines)
- Emphasizes fruits, vegetables, whole grains, fat-free or low-fat milk and milk products
- Includes lean meats, poultry, fish, beans, eggs and nuts
- Is low in saturated fats, trans fats, cholesterol, salt (sodium) and added sugars

✔ Regular exercise
✔ Stress-management techniques
✔ No smoking
✔ Protecting skin from sun exposure
✔ Positive thinking
✔ Supplement program

A look at coenzyme Q10

MANY PEOPLE WHO ARE interested in supplements to improve their well-being have heard of one compound that is gaining attention for potential health benefits: coenzyme Q10 (CoQ10). What exactly is CoQ10, and what role does it play in maintaining good health?

Coenzyme Q10 is an important compound that is present throughout the body. It is specifically located in the cells' energy-producing machinery known as mitochondria. CoQ10 has two major physiological functions. Its primary function is to participate in electron transfer and production of energy, called oxidative phosphorylation, in the mitochondria. It also functions as a fat-soluble antioxidant to help prevent cellular damage by free radicals.

Because CoQ10 is a critical component in energy production, it is found in highest concentrations in those cells, tissues and organs that have high energy requirements—e.g., muscle and cardiac tissue.

Potential heart-health benefits

Lecturers at the Fourth Conference of the International Coenzyme Q10 Association in Los Angeles in 2005 advocated the use of higher amounts of CoQ10 in future clinical research for heart health, Parkinson's disease and other brain and nerve disorders.

In particular, experts believe CoQ10 should be further explored for its benefits in protecting heart health. For example, clinical studies show that 75 to 120 mg of CoQ10 a day increases cardiac function, decreases overall need for medication and hospitalization, and prolongs survival in people with various forms of cardiovascular disease. And a double-blind placebo-controlled study showed that 120 mg of CoQ10 a day for 12 weeks reduced blood pressure in people with high blood pressure.

Use with statins

Statin drugs are widely prescribed to lower high blood cholesterol and thus reduce the risk for heart disease. These drugs block cholesterol production in the body by inhibiting certain enzymes, including CoQ10. Therefore, anyone taking a statin drug may want to discuss CoQ10 supplementation with their health-care professional.

Other potential benefits

Experts are also researching potential benefits of CoQ10 for nerve health and maintaining proper blood sugar levels. It shows promise in decreasing symptoms in people with Parkinson's disease and in decreasing migraines. In addition to these health benefits, CoQ10 research in other areas of health, including eyes, the skin and the immune system, is emerging.

TIPS&TRICKS

DO NOT READ THIS WHILE DRIVING

ACCORDING TO *The Best Book of Useless Information Ever,* by Noel Botham and The Useless Information Society (Perigee, 2008), approximately 55 percent of people yawn within five minutes of seeing someone else yawn. Reading about yawning makes most people yawn.

Did it work?

FOOD FOR THOUGHT

SCIENTISTS BELIEVE THAT food that's harmful to your heart is also harmful to your brain. Likewise, heart-healthy foods are good for your noggin. These are the best foods for your brain:

- Nuts
- Fish (especially wild salmon, whitefish, tilapia, catfish, flounder and mahi-mahi)
- Soybeans
- Tomato juice and spaghetti sauce
- Olive oil, nut oils, fish oils, flaxseed, avocados
- Real (cocoa-based) chocolate

Source: From *YOU: The Owner's Manual: An Insider's Guide to the Body That Will Make You Healthier and Younger,* (HarperResource, 2005) by Michael F. Roizen and Mehmet C. Oz.

→ **THIS**&THAT

TYPICAL COQ10 DAILY DOSAGES

General health/antioxidant benefit: 60 to 120 mg
Family history of heart problems: 100 to 150 mg
Taking statin drugs: 200 to 300 mg

Congestive heart problems: 300 to 350 mg
Parkinson's disease: 1,200 mg

What's in your water? A case for filtering

WATER IS THE MOST PLENTIFUL, and useful, liquid on the planet. And yet, we take it for granted. Many people don't hesitate to turn on the tap when needed. This seems acceptable because most communities have filtration systems. Unfortunately, municipal water systems can't or don't always filter out everything, they often add other things that should be filtered out before drinking and there may still be risks if there is a breach in the system.

Here are some of the substances that additional filtration can remove, and the associated risks or problems.

Chlorine. Used widely by water utilities for water disinfection; may produce undesirable taste and odor in drinking water.

Copper. Widely used in household plumbing materials. Exposure to high levels of copper can cause stomach and intestinal distress, liver and kidney damage and anemia.

Cryptosporidium and giardia. Protozoan pathogens that contain parasites. If ingested, they can cause disease with symptoms of severe abdominal cramping and diarrhea.

Lead. Sometimes used in household plumbing materials or water service lines. Exposure to high levels can cause interference with red blood cell chemistry; delays in physical and mental development in babies and young children; slight deficits in attention spans, hearing and learning abilities of children; and slight increases in the blood pressure of some adults. Long-term exposure can cause stroke, kidney disease and cancer.

Mercury. Exposure to high levels can cause kidney damage.

Turbidity. An indicator of fine particulate matter that makes water appear cloudy. Increased turbidity decreases the effectiveness of chlorination and other types of disinfection.

To be safe, use a water filtration system in your home or office.

➤ **THIS**&THAT

RESOURCES

- To find out what's in your local water supply, consult the U.S. Environmental Protection Agency. A 1996 amendment to the Safe Drinking Water Act requires public water suppliers to provide a consumer confidence report. You may find one for your area at *www.epa.gov/safewater/dwinfo/index.html* or call your local water supplier.

- For more information on current national drinking water standards, go to *www.epa.gov/safewater/contaminants/index.html*.

- For more information on water quality and filtration products, visit the Water Quality Association's Web site, *www.wqa.org*.

Super foods for super health

NUTRITION ACTION, a publication of the Center for Science in the Public Interest (CSPI) has identified these "super foods."

Sweet potatoes. A nutritional all-star, sweet potatoes are one of the best vegetables you can eat. They're loaded with carotenoids, vitamin C, potassium and fiber. Bake and then mix in some unsweetened applesauce or crushed pineapple for extra moisture and sweetness.

Grape tomatoes. They're sweeter and firmer than other tomatoes, and their bite-size shape makes them perfect for snacking, dipping or salads. They're packed with vitamin C and vitamin A, and you also get some fiber, some phytochemicals and (finally) some flavor.

Fat-free (skim) or 1 percent milk (but not 2 percent). Fat-free milk is an excellent source of calcium, vitamins and protein with little or no artery-clogging fat and cholesterol. Likewise for low-fat yogurt. Soy milk can have just as many nutrients—if they're added.

Broccoli. Lots of vitamin C, carotenoids and folic acid make broccoli a natural winner. Steam it briefly and add a sprinkle of red pepper flakes and a spritz of lemon juice.

Wild salmon. The omega-3 fats in fatty fish such as salmon can help reduce the risk of sudden-death heart attacks. And salmon that is caught wild is likely to have fewer PCB contaminants than farmed salmon.

Crisp breads. Whole-grain rye crackers, such as Wasa, RyKrisp and Ryvita—usually called crispbreads—are loaded with fiber and often fat-free.

Microwaveable or "10-minute" brown rice. Enriched white rice is nutritionally weak. When the grain is refined, the fiber, magnesium, vitamins E and B_6, copper, zinc and phytochemicals that are in the whole grain are lost. Try quick-cooking or regular brown rice instead.

Citrus fruit. Citrus fruit is great-tasting and rich in vitamin C, folic acid and fiber. Perfect for a snack or dessert. Try different varieties: juicy Minneola oranges, snack-size clementines or tart grapefruit.

Diced butternut squash. Look for peeled, diced butternut squash that's ready to go into the oven, a stir-fry or a soup. Every half cup has 5 grams of fiber and payloads of vitamins A and C.

Spinach or kale. These standout vegetables are jam-packed with vitamins A, C and K, plus folate, potassium, magnesium, iron, lutein and phytochemicals.

For CSPI's list of foods you should never eat, go to *www.cspinet. org/nah/10foods_bad.html.* A

MEMBER**TIPS** ←

KAREN CONNOLLY
TIGARD, OR

MY TIP IS TO sprinkle coarsely ground black pepper on the carpet where you have a trouble spot from your cat or dog. After sprinkling black pepper in an area where our pet loved to relieve herself, we've never had any problems since. It's a lot cheaper than pet store chemicals and works better. 🄰

COURTESY OF
ANDREA FINK
EVERETT, WA

HERE'S MY "GREEN" IDEA: Costco apple containers make excellent germination kits. The see-through tops can open up to allow sunshine and watering or come down to keep seedlings warm and dry. 🄰

COURTESY OF
PAM BREWER
SAN DIEGO, CA

ANOTHER USE FOR that "spongy" shelf liner: I use it to line the deli and vegetable drawer in the fridge. It protects the fruits and vegetables, keeps the drawer clean and helps keep moisture down so the food lasts longer. 🄰

COURTESY OF
CHRISTINA C. PHILLIPS
CASTAIC, CA

DOGS HATE THE SMELL of coffee in the garden and will stop digging it up, so pour leftover coffee and grounds in the garden every day. It's great for the plants, too, especially roses. 🄰

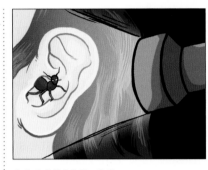

COURTESY OF
VINAYAK SING
FORT WORTH, TX

IF YOU (OR ONE OF THE KIDS) have a bug stuck in the ear (ant, etc., while being outdoors), try this:

Go to a dark room. Now take a small flashlight, point it in your ear (get a friend or parent to do it for you) and watch how the bug/ant finds its way out.

It works! 🄰

COURTESY OF
JAMES SANDSMARK
NEWCASTLE, WA

WE ALL WONDER what to do with the Styrofoam packing material that is used to protect electronics and other products. (Garbage recyclers will not accept it.) My wife and I break it into small pieces and use it as filler for planter boxes. Fill the planter half to three-quarters full of the Styrofoam, then several layers of newspaper, then the rest of the way with potting soil. This saves a lot of potting soil, and the planter weighs a fraction of one with soil only. 🄰

COURTESY OF
KYUNG-HWA RAFFERTY
PRATTVILLE, AL

USING A COLORFUL STRING, hang unusable or unwanted CDs from fruit trees around gardens and in orchards. Birds like to eat cherries, plums and other fruits, and the shiny surface keeps birds away by reflecting sunlight and moonlight as it spins in the wind. 🄰

COURTESY OF
ROBERT DEMARTINI
IONIA, MI

"REROOFING" YOUR wooden steps is easy and safe. Just take some flat shingles, cut off the tabs and staple them to the treads of the stairs. Then when it snows or rains, you will be much safer and secure with your steps, and they last for years to come. I've had them on my deck steps for about 15 years and they are like new. 🄰

COURTESY OF
DEIDRA BIGHAM
SAN DIEGO, CA

TO DEEP-CLEAN your dry-erase board, spray Lysol Disinfectant Spray on a paper towel and wipe down the board. 🄰

COURTESY OF
RONA HACKETT
ROHNERT PARK, CA

TO PREVENT LOST SOCKS, safety-pin the toes of a pair together before washing.

USE THE SCENTED perfume ads in magazines to line clothes drawers. 🄰

COURTESY OF
COURTNEY LEVASSEUR
ANCHORAGE, AK

MANY PEOPLE HAVE told me they would never shop with their children for a full two weeks' worth of groceries at Costco. We do it every week with our four children, 5 years and younger, stay sane and love it. Consider it family time, education and just pure fun "family dates," as our kids phrase it!

Here's how we do it.

As a family, choose your menus for the two weeks so everyone has a say.

Determine the ingredients you lack and create a shopping list.

Explain "public rules" to the children before entering the warehouse. Talk about products and price comparison while shopping. Keep them focused, and that will "entertain" them! Children love feeling needed, and Costco is the perfect place to assist with that.

Each child has a job. For us, the oldest reads aloud the list (already marked in basic categories) and crosses off items as we put them in the cart. The second enters the price into the calculator. The third helps hunt down an item called out by the first child. The fourth is either entertained by her siblings or we have a snack available for her, or there is an item she can hold and look at, or scrunch for noise.

Don't forget to take turns with who gets to hand the receipt at the exit, and watch the smiles that happen every time. ◭

COURTESY OF
JANET MCCOID
SOUTH PLAINFIELD, NJ

COLORED GEL PENS have so many uses.

Have each family member choose a gel pen color to keep your household calendar organized; you can see at a glance who has lessons, appointments, etc.

In the classroom, have students choose a color when working with partners or in groups; the teacher can see at a glance if each child is participating in the lesson.

These are also great for correcting papers and writing comments to students, as the colors stand out and get noticed! ◭

COURTESY OF
MARY LAUFER
FOREST GROVE, OR

FOR THE PRICE OF two bottles of water at the airport, you can buy a whole case of Costco bottled water. Empty a bottle before you go and fill it at a drinking fountain once you're past security. ◭

Supplier Listing

● Supplier Listing

Photography and Illustration Credits

Front of Book
Front cover: Radius Images
ii: Photodisc
iii: Comstock
iv–v: Photodisc
vii: Courtesy of Peter Walsh
viii–x: Vito Panini
xi: liquidlibrary

Sight and Sound
1: Digital Vision
2–5: Nikon
6: France Freeman
8: Olympus (camera), Stockbyte (beach)
9: Olympus
10–11: Old Town
12–13: Canon
14: PhotoAlto
15: Photodisc (family), Canon (printer)
16: Photodisc (Europe),
    Digital Vision (Las Vegas)
17: Panasonic (product),
    David Masuda (triathlon)
18: Blend Images Photography (birthday)
    Alloy Photography (bike)
    Digital Vision (dogs)
    Image Source (dolphin)
    Stockbyte (wedding)
19: Alloy Photography
20: Canon
21: Belkin (product)
    Photodisc (illustration)
22–23: iHome
24–25: Motorola
26: Uniden
27: VTech (product), Photodisc (phone)
28: Panasonic (product)
    Lisa Fossen (illustration)

Guide to Computing
29: Digital Vision
30: Stock Illustration
32, 34–35: Intel
32: Lisa Fossen
37: ViewSonic
38: Sony (product)
    Ken Broman (illustration)
39: Ken Broman
40: Western Digital

The HDTV Guide
41: Corbis
42: Sharp (product)
    David M. Wall (illustration)
    Comstock (baseball game on screen)
43: Philips (product)
    Photodisc (image on screen)
44: Samsung (product)
    Brenda Tradii (Adam on screen)
    David M. Wall (illustrations)
    Photodisc (Seattle on screens)
45: Panasonic
46: Vizio
47: David M. Wall
48: DIRECTV (product)
    David M. Wall (illustration)
49: Simplicity
50: Tripp Lite (product)
    David M. Wall (illustration)
51: Peerless (product)
    David M. Wall (illustration)
52: WireLogic (product)
52–53: David M. Wall

Office Basics
55: Corbis
56–59: True Designs
59: Lisa Fossen
60: uni-ball (product)
    Chris Rusnak (illustration)
61: Harland-Clarke
62: Lorex
63: Pentel
64–65: Fellowes
66: Smead (top product)
    Pendaflex (bottom product)
67: Photodisc
68: Avery Dennison (products)
    BananaStock (mail slot)
69: Comstock
70: Dust-Off (product)
    Photodisc (keyboard)
    InsideOutPix (dishes, books)
71: Design Pics (piano)
    Stockbyte (wood shavings)
    Tetra Images (dashboard)
    Polka Dot Images (office supplies)
72: Lisa Fossen

Home Project Primer
73: Fancy Veer
74–75: Punch! Software
76–77: Graber
78: Harmonics
80: Shaw
81: Ken Broman
82: Agio
83: Wagner Spray Tech
84: WaterRidge (product)
    Ken Broman (illustration)
85: WaterRidge
86: Photos.com (pool)
    Lisa Fossen (illustration)
88: Bayside Furnishing (product)
    Ken Broman (illustrations)

Home Essentials
89: Photodisc
90–91: First Alert
92: Ken Broman
93: First Alert
94–94: Hunter
96–97: Lights of America
98: Therapure (product)
    Ken Broman (illustration)
99: Corbis (leather chair)
    Lisa Fossen (illustration)
100–103: Lifetime Products
102: PhotoAlto (boy)
104: Duracell
106–107: Lisa Fossen
108: Brenda Tradii

Bed, Bath and Laundry
109: Photodisc
110–111: Space Bag
112–114: Universal Furniture
113: Lisa Fossen
115: Comstock
116: Divatex
117: Ken Broman
118: BananaStock (pillow fight)
    Thinkstock Images (man sleeping)
    Hollander (pillows)
    Rubberball (insomniac woman)
    Comstock (stressed man)
    Brand X Pictures (wild sleeper)

Photography and Illustration Credits

120–123: Pacific Coast Feather
124–125: Sleep Innovations
126: Mohawk Home (catalog)
  Brand X Pictures (faucet)
  Digital Vision (storage)
  Comstock (candles)
127: Clorox (product)
  Lisa Fossen (illustration)
128: France Freeman

Travel and Recreation
129: EyeWire
130: Photodisc (atlas)
  Courtesy of Rick Steves (image)
131: Photodisc (passport, suitcase)
  Courtesy of Rick Steves (images)
132: Lisa Fossen
134: Magellan GPS
136–138: Titleist
139: Verizon (product)
  Goodshoot (bottom photo)
140–141: Schwinn
142: Pactiv (product)
  Lisa Fossen (illustration)
143: Photodisc (photos)
  Lisa Fossen (illustration)
144: Invicta

Auto and Garage
145: Artville
149: David M. Wall
150: Chevron (product)
  David M. Wall (illustration)
152: Stockbyte
154: Whalen Storage
155: Michael Rhodig
156: Courtesy of David Woodworth
  (black-and-white image)
  Jake Early (color images)
157: Michelin
158: Lisa Fossen (illustration)
  Stockbyte (photo)

For Your Health
159: Photodisc
160: Chris Crisman (Dr. Roizen)
  Lisa Fossen (illustration)
161: Artville (tomato, onion, broccoli)
  Photodisc (strawberries, wine, apple)
162: France Freeman (yoga)
  Comstock (aspirin, walker, weights)
  Image Source (walnuts)
163: Greg Gillis
164: Olay (product)
  Stockbyte (woman in sun hat)
165: Neutrogena
166: RoC
167: Neutrogena (product)
  Image Source (woman and mirror)
168: Aveeno
169: Nivea (product)
  Photodisc (weight, water)
  Inspirestock (massage)
170–171: Borghese
172: Dove
173: Digital Vision
174: France Freeman (product)
  Comstock (haircut)
175: Kleenex
176–177: Sonicare
177: Brand X Pictures (smiley face)
178: Design Optics (photos)
  Varilux (illustration)
179: Ken Broman
180: Transitions Optics
182: Lysol (products, woman spraying)
  Corbis (boys and trains)
183: BananaStock (hand-washing)
  Corbis (medicine girl)
  PhotoAlto (baby changing)
  liquidlibrary (playground)
184: Dixie (product)
  Lisa Fossen (illustration)
  Digital Vision (cutting board)
185: Digital Vision (couple)
  Photodisc (fruit, kitchen)
  Comstock (water faucet)
186: Lyndsay Michaels Photography Inc.
  (Jack La Lanne in blue jumpsuit)
  Other photos courtesy of
  Befit Enterprises

Tips on Nutrition
187: Photodisc
188: Chris Crisman (Dr. Oz)
  Lisa Fossen (illustration)
189: Lisa Fossen
190: Nature Made
191: Iridio
192: Nature Made (product)
  Image Source (face)
  Photodisc (bagels, fruit)
  Brand X Pictures (card game)
  Comstock (yoga)
  Tetra Images (woman and cat)
194: Arrowhead (product)
  Comstock (woman)
195: Arrowhead
196: PUR
197: AgroLabs
198–199: Sam Trout
199: Karen Bergeron/altnature.com
201: Sam Trout
202: Schiff
203: Digital Vision
204: Schiff
206: Brita
207: Photodisc

Member Tips and More
208: images.com (roses illustration)
  Ken Broman (illustration)
209: liquidlibrary
Inside back cover: Digital Vision
Back cover: Radius Images (fence)
  Photodisc (ladybugs)

Index

Index

● Index

And in the end, it's not
the years in your life that count.
It's the life in your years.
Abraham Lincoln